Landscape Operations
management, methods, and materials

Leroy G. Hannebaum

Reston Publishing Company, Inc.
A Prentice-Hall Company
Reston, Virginia

Library of Congress Cataloging in Publication Data
Hannebaum, Leroy G
    Landscape operations.

    Bibliography: p.
    Includes index.
    1. Landscaping industry—Management. 2. Nurser-
ies (Horticulture)—Management. 3. Landscape
nurseries—Management. 4. Landscape gardening.
I. Title.
SB472.5.H36   635.9'068   80-13984
ISBN 0-8359-3937-5

10   9   8   7   6   5   4   3   2

Printed in the United States of America

CONTENTS

For my wife, Linda, and my children, Tyrone, Tanya, and Tara

Preface

My interest in the operation of a landscape nursery began during my junior year in college. I was enrolled in an ornamental horiculture curriculum at Kansas State University, with every intention of becoming a golf course superintendent.

Because of a dire need for funds and a feeling that the experience would somehow be of benefit, I began working part time at a landscape nursery. My initial experience in the landscape nursery business was hardly joyful. I spent the first afternoon breaking up a concrete slab with a sledge hammer and loading the broken pieces onto a trailer. The work continued to be very demanding physically, and although I had grown up on a farm and was accustomed to hard work, I soon developed a myriad of blisters and sore muscles. In spite of that, I began to enjoy the work, and I sensed that opportunities existed within the field for making a good living doing interesting work. My career objectives changed accordingly, and I began preparing for a career in the nursery business—my special interest being landscaping.

Technical training was easy to come by. I took the usual courses in botany, plant materials, soils, genetics, chemistry, plant pathology, arboriculture and turf management, among others. Still, my work experience was teaching me that technical knowledge by itself would not totally prepare me to become a good nursery manager. I was learning rapidly that a landscape nurseryman must also be a proficient businessman, part-time lawyer, public relations man, salesman, personnel manager, and sometimes accountant, in order to be successful. So, I also took courses in business management, accounting, business law, and journalism, all of which helped me prepare for participation in the business world.

This training, along with the practical experience I was receiving, proved to be of paramount importance to me after graduation, when I entered the business on a full-time basis. I was fortunate to work with Darrell Westervelt, the past president of the Kansas Association of Nurserymen, who is an excellent nurseryman and businessman. Given that background, along with 12 years experience, I believe that I know the landscape nursery business well.

I've always thought this learning process would have been much faster, and more thorough, had there been a text or reference book available to tie together all of the facets of landscape nursery operation. To my knowledge, there have been none, until now.

That dearth of material, and my own long training period, led me to write this book. Conversations with young persons entering the field and with those who have invested their entire careers in the landscape nursery business leave me no doubts that such a book is needed. It is my hope that the information on these pages will aid those students who desire to enter the landscaping field, encourage others to enter the business, and provide some new insights to those already in the business.

Few books contain hard and fast truths. This book is no exception. While everything presented here is tried and tested, it is intended mostly to help others form their own rules by which to operate. I hope it will develop and strengthen the management skills of all who read it.

LEROY G. HANNEBAUM

Acknowledgements

No book can be conceived entirely of one's own notions or be based exclusively on one's own experiences. I wish to thank Darrell and Dorothy Westervelt for their valuable contributions to my own knowledge and experiences. I also want to thank the rest of the staff at Blueville Nursery, Inc., in Manhattan, Kansas, for their help and cooperation during my years with that firm and during the subsequent writing of this book.

Dr. S.M. Still, Professor of Horticulture at Ohio State University, was immensely helpful in evaluating the material in this book, as was Dr. Gus A. Van der Hoeven, Extension Specialist in Landscape and Environmental Horticulture at Kansas State University. Dr. Charles Long, an Extension Horticulturalist at Kansas State University, also reviewed the material and made suggestions. All of these men provided much encouragement to me.

My thanks again to Darrell Westervelt of Blueville Nursery, Inc. and to Carl J. Meyer of Horticultural Services and Tom Hittle of Nature's Way Landscape Co., all of Manhattan, Kansas, for allowing me to photograph their crews and their work. Thanks also to Thomas B. Shackelford, Superintendent of Grounds at Kansas State University, for allowing me to photograph equipment.

Last, but not least, my thanks to my family, whose understanding and cooperation was vital to the successful completion of this book.

L.G.H.

CHAPTER 1
THE NURSERY BUSINESS

Brief History

The nursery business came to the United States with the pilgrims. In Europe plants and grasses had been cultured for many years, and the foundation was well laid for our forefathers to propagate and nurture many of the beautiful plants that we value so highly today. Perhaps even the Native Americans might have delved into nursery operations somewhat. We know, of course, that they were quite adept in other fields of horticulture because many of them were expert vegetable gardeners.

The value of the nursery industry in Europe to the growth of the nursery industry in this country is immeasurable. Many of the varieties of trees and shrubs that we treasure were brought to this country from foreign ports. True, many of the undesirable varieties arrived here in that fashion also, as did many of the dread diseases that affect our plant life. On balance though, the plants we have today and our techniques for handling them owe much to our European heritage.

Although the modern nursery industry in the United States still relies on many of the old techniques, many changes have taken place since World War II. The landscape and garden store industries flourished with the housing boom in the post-war years, along with all of the other nursery industries. Whereas a nurseryman used to be considered a jack-of-all-trades, now he is frequently a specialist, concentrating primarily on one facet of the nursery business. Specialization has occurred in the nursery industry, as in other industries, because of a need for a higher degree of competency in order to remain competitive. To become a competent nurseryman it is not enough to be a well-qualified horticulturalist. In today's nursery industries, one must also be thoroughly indoctrinated in business management, special studies, personnel management, and accounting. Many excellent horticulturalists have not succeeded in the nursery business simply because they did not recognize the need for training in these other areas.

Businesses within the Nursery Industry

There are four distinct divisions of the nursery industry, with further breakdowns within some of these divisions:

- Nursery stock growing operations
- Greenhouse operations
- Garden store operations
- Landscaping operations

Although there are overlaps between the divisions and often an enterprise will operate within several of the divisions simultaneously, each is distinct: each is an industry within itself. This is best related by discussing each division separately.

Nursery Stock Growing Operations

Many of our leading wholesale nurseries are well over 100 years old. Trees, shrubs, roses, groundcovers, and other plants are grown by these nurseries strictly for the purpose of being sold wholesale to other nurseries, who make retail sales of those plants to their customers. The wholesalers combine to grow the largest volume of plant material in the United States. Also included in the growing operations are mail-order nurseries, sod-growing operations, specialty growers, and retail nurseries, who grow some or all of their own stock.

The growing of nursery stock requires a strong horticultural background. The propagation of different species, by both sexual and asexual means, must be clearly understood, along with the cultural measures required for successful growth of each species and the proper harvesting and storage procedures. Additionally, the grower must be expert in promotion, sales, and shipping of the products grown. Like the wheat or corn farmer, the grower of nursery stock must understand both the soil features of the land and the requirements for the growth of his or her particular crops. Both the farmer and the grower are dependent, to a large extent, on the weather conditions for a good crop. Both must be properly equipped to harvest and store their produce. The farmer, however, does not exert much influence on the market for his products. He sells his products at a market for the current price, but, generally, he knows that the market exists. The nursery owner must market his products, but he does have more control over prices. The wholesale nursery owner must cultivate a regular clientele among retailers. He does so by producing high quality plants, which please both the retailer and his customers, at a price competitive with other wholesalers and by giving the retailer prompt and courteous service. The wholesaler must always be conscious of the general demand for nursery products at retail levels, because, ultimately, his success depends upon the retailer's success. To this end, wholesalers have created the Nursery Marketing Council, into which the wholesale nurseries put their money, which is used to promote the sale of nursery stock to the general public. The success of this fledgling enterprise will be a boon to all nursery-related businesses.

Wholesale growers of nursery stock are further specialized according to the types of material grown, the conditions in which material is grown, and the type of marketing approach used. The location of a wholesale nursery will certainly influence the types of plants produced, although many wholesale nurseries have several locations, each for the purpose of growing certain types of stock. A single nursery might have land in the Midwest for growing fruit trees and shrubs, land in California or Texas for growing roses, and land in the Pacific Northwest for growing shade trees. Growing plants in special locations enables the growers to produce higher quality nursery stock at a faster pace.

Specialization of growing continues at a rapid pace, which is possibly best exemplified by the container-growing industry. Many growing operations now grow their stock exclusively in containers. These growers are able to utilize land not suitable for growing plants, since the plants are grown in their own soil medium within the container, and are able to grow much higher populations per acre. They are also able to more

Figure 1-1. Container growing has become increasingly popular.

easily control the environmental influences on their crops by applying water, fertilizer, and other chemicals as they wish. Container growing is quite successful, considering the portability of the plants, minimal transplanting shock, and pleasing appearance of the entire package, but all plants cannot be successfully grown in containers.

Other specialists exist in the wholesale nursery industry. Some grow-ers cultivate only roses, others specialize exclusively in young stock to be planted out in nursery fields, which are often called "liners." The propagation and growth of such lining-out stock is an industry unto itself. Sod growers are normally specialists, since the expertise is unique, as is the equipment required. Sod growers tend to specialize in particular varieties, which are often dictated by the climate of the sod farm area. Some sod farmers have many locations in order to produce many different types of sod.

Some nurserymen specialize in growing larger, speciman-type mate-rial. In or near the large cities particularly, these growers cater to a need for large plant material. Others specialize according to harvesting method, by growing primarily material that can be sold in a bare-root or a balled and burlapped condition. Still others grow and sell only groundcovers.

The mail-order nursery industry combines the wholesale and retail operations by sending out catalogs or otherwise advertising the plants they sell and shipping plant material directly to their customers. This is a large, vibrant industry, dealing primarily in bare-root stock.

Many retailers grow at least some of their own stock for various rea-sons. The retailer may have entered the nursery business because of a desire to grow plants and may realize great enjoyment from this activity. Or he or she may be unable to obtain certain types of material satisfac-torily from wholesale sources. Quality control might also be a motivation for growing certain plant materials, or, in a few cases, the retailer might be able to grow some plants less expensively than he or she can buy them from others. The retailer might also consider it important to adver-tise plants that are "locally grown."

Greenhouse Operations

The growing of plants in a greenhouse is really a divergent field of its own. The field encompasses almost every type of plant material from bedding plants to propagation of trees, shrubs and roses, to the growing of tropical plants. The growing of vegetable crops, such as tomatoes, which cannot be properly considered within the ornamental nursery industry, should also be mentioned as a facet of the greenhouse growing operations, as should the floral industry.

Figure 1-2. Interior view of a greenhouse. This one is being used for early forcing of potted roses.

Growing plants indoors is quite different from growing them out-doors. In a greenhouse, the grower creates the desired climate instead of depending on the weather to provide growing conditions, as the outdoor grower must. Although there are many obvious advantages to this type of control, some disadvantages do exist. Artificial heating and cooling devices must be monitored continuously, as must the moisture controls. Failure of these devices, even for a brief period, can result in total crop failure. Greenhouse operation is an around-the-clock proposition.

Although the grower creates artificial climatic conditions within the house, the operation of a greenhouse depends on the weather in many regards. Not only do external temperatures and moisture conditions dictate the degree of adjustment necessary to produce the proper climate within the greenhouse, but wind, hail, and heavy snow can endanger the structure of the house as well.

Most wholesale growers have greenhouses for propagation purposes and also for winter protection of semihardy species. Some retailers have greenhouses to store bedding plants, tropical plants, and to protect plants that might not survive a winter outdoors.

Greenhouse specialization is complicated by the fact that the cultivation of a species within a greenhouse involves certain factors that need not concern the outdoor grower of that same species. Moisture and temperature conditions must be carefully monitored, and plants must be protected against diseases that they are not ordinarily susceptible to when planted outdoors.

Garden Store Operations

Garden store operations are wide-spread: feed stores, discount operations, and gardening departments within hardware and grocery stores all deal in plants and gardening merchandise. There are also many garden stores that deal exclusively in gardening products.

The garden store industry is a vital part of the entire nursery business field because of the large volume of nursery products sold through these outlets. Indeed, many of these operators grow at least a portion of their own stock. Often, garden store operations are combined with successful landscaping and/or greenhouse operations.

Figure 1-3. The lath shade sales area at a garden store.

The range of products offered by garden stores is wide, and the variety is highly imaginative. These outlets have nearly always offered plant materials of varying types, tools, seeds, fertilizers, and soil amendments. Now, in order to create higher traffic volume and lengthen their sales seasons, many have ventured into the areas of pet supplies, crafts, and rental equipment. Dealers look for these new product areas, knowing that the cost of their buildings, land, and many other assets can be returned to them more quickly if they make more sales from these facilities. Also, better use can be made of personnel if the seasons are extended or new sales seasons are created. Of course, additional training is required to take on any new line, as well as additional inventory and possibly increased expenses. Still, assuming that all sales can be made on a profitable basis, garden store operators continue to expand their horizons.

Many a garden store operation that is combined with a landscaping service was started as an office where business telephoning, accounting, and other management duties were performed. As the clientele grew, so did the demand for cash-and-carry products, resulting in the creation of a garden store to meet that demand. Similarly, many landscaping operations have resulted from customer requests for such services from a garden store.

Landscaping Operations

While the majority of garden store sales are cash-and-carry, or at least most of the products are installed by the customer, the landscaping industry depends on both the sale of products and the installation or maintenance of those products. Landscaping firms, like those within other divisions of the nursery industry, are quite variable. For further study, landscaping firms can be broken down into three areas of concern.

- Maintenance and spraying companies
- Design-build firms
- Landscape contractors

There is an ever-increasing trend for businesses to engage in strictly landscape maintenance operations, particularly in larger cities. More than that, many companies are specialized for fertilizing and spraying lawns only, tree spraying only, tree surgery, lawn mowing, trimming, and other care associated with lawns. Large chain operations are growing quite vigorously at this date in the chemical lawn treatment area; some by selling franchises and some by internal company growth. Each

Figure 1-4. Commercial lawn mowing is a large part of many maintenance operations.

type of maintenance operation requires an expertise of its own, not to mention specialized equipment and operational measures.

Design-build firms specialize in creating their own business, usually by contracting to design and then install a landscape. The range of services offered by these businesses is quite variable, from those that restrict their operations to the sale and installation of plant material to those that extend their services to include all types of landscape construction and the installation of sprinkler systems. Often, though a design-build firm may restrict its own operations to planting, subcontractors may be used to enable those firms to offer a wide range of construction services. Most design-build firms employ their own designers, although some contract these services from a landscape architectural business.

Landscape contractors present bids for landscaping jobs designed by others. Highway landscaping contractors, among others, fall into this group of nursery operators, who must follow the specifications written by the designer. Since these specifications are quite variable, these contractors often do not maintain a regular inventory of plants, choosing

Figure 1-5. Members of a landscaping crew put the finishing touches on a group of plantings.

instead to order their plants following the awarding of a successful bid. These contractors are usually quite mobile, since the jobs on which they bid are often far apart.

Even though the three areas of concern just mentioned do require considerably different equipment, personnel, and expertise, they are often combined in one landscape operation, especially in the smaller cities. In the larger cities, specialization usually occurs to a greater degree.

Opportunities in the Nursery Industry

The description of each division within the nursery industry has been very brief and was intended to point out that nursery operations are a vigorous and rapidly expanding enterprise. Employment opportunities are increasingly available as the industry continues to grow and prosper. All of the nursery businesses require people with high degrees of specialized training. It is an industry that invites those interested to learn, experience, and enjoy its benefits.

A general horticultural education is not enough to highly qualify an individual in any one of these divisions of the nursery industry. Although one must have a basic understanding of plants and the way they grow, much necessary information can only be mastered through experience. Anyone desiring to enter any one of the nursery industries should strive to achieve some practical experience from those recognized as leaders in that industry, while acquiring a strong educational background at the same time. Even so, those new to a business cannot expect to "start at the top." Although experience is the best teacher, it is not the fastest teacher.

Specialized studies can aid students in their preparation to enter any business field. Exposure to the principles of accounting, business management, business law, and other related areas can speed one on to management responsibility more quickly. Voracious reading of related material can also speed the learning process, augmenting the practical experience of working on the job.

Trade magazines for each of the nursery industries just discussed are full of help-wanted ads. Opportunities abound for those with the proper training and experience, or a willingness to become properly trained and experienced. Franchises are readily available, particularly in the chemical lawn treatment area, to anyone who desires to start his or her own business, but who also wants the backing of a large company. Opportunities exist almost anywhere for a person with the proper training, background, and financing to start his or her own business in the other nursery areas. Additionally, many owners nearing retirement age are selling existing businesses that are already established on a sound basis. Those with foresight often bring in a younger person for training prior to the time they wish to sell, insuring a better chance for the success of that younger person.

One opportunity that anyone aspiring to a career in one of the nursery industries should be sure to avail themselves of is the chance to visit with those already in the field, particularly those who have been in a business for many years. This can be an invaluable experience for an aspiring horticulturist and one that can also teach him or her something about the life styles of those in the nursery business—a life style that often is dictated, at least in part, by their work.

The nursery business is large, wide spreading, and exciting. The remainder of this book will be concerned with one facet of the entire field: the landscaping industry. Several references are listed in Appendix B for those wishing to learn more about the other the other fields within the industry.

SUMMARY

The nursery industry is as old as this country. Many of our plants, techniques, and procedures originated in Europe.

Today's nursery operations require not only horticultural training but familiarity with business management, accounting, personnel management, and communication skills.

Nursery stock growing operations, greenhouse operations, garden store operations, and landscaping operations are the four divisions of the nursery industry.

Nursery stock growing operations include wholesale nurseries, mail-order nurseries, sod-growing operations, specialty growers, and retail nursery owners who grow at least part of their stock.

Greenhouse growers encounter a totally different set of problems than do the outdoor growers, and, therefore, their training and experiences are much different.

Garden stores are highly variable, ranging from feed and seed stores to discount houses, to pet and garden stores, hardware stores with garden departments, and full-line garden stores. The majority of the sales made by a garden store are usually cash-and-carry, with the customer doing his or her own installation. Garden stores have increased their scope of products recently in order to produce a higher sales volume and to extend their sales season.

The landscape industry is broken into three areas of concern: maintenance and spraying, design-build landscapers, and landscaping contractors. The range of services offered by different businesses is highly valuable, and often these services overlap into the other areas of concern.

Opportunities abound for those willing to achieve the proper education and work for the necessary experience. Education should be, if possible, geared to a particular nursery industry.

SUMMARY QUESTIONS

1. The nursery stock grower must have a good understanding of what four areas?
2. Why must the wholesaler be concerned with helping retailers advertise?
3. What are three advantages of container growing?
4. Why do some growers specialize?
5. What is a mail-order nursery?
6. How does greenhouse growing differ from outdoor growing?
7. What is the basic difference in the ways a design-build landscaping firm and a landscape contractor obtain their jobs?

8. In which landscaping industry is one most likely to obtain a franchise?

9. What is required of anyone wishing to enter one of the nursery fields?

CHAPTER 2
The Mechanics of Lawn Establishment

The lawn is a very noticeable and important feature of any landscape. An elaborate, well-designed landscape will suffer appreciably if the lawn is poorly installed or poorly cared for. The establishment of a fine lawn is, therefore, essential to landscape development. After selecting the proper grass for a particular geographical area, it is important to consider which method of lawn establishment is most suitable; that is, seeding, sodding, sprigging, or plugging. This chapter will focus on the practical aspects of grading, planting grass, and caring for a new lawn.

Planting the Proper Grass

Selection of the right variety of grass is a prerequisite to establishing a good lawn. Many types of grass are grown in this country, but they are not all suitable for all areas. Many fine textbooks are available that discuss the culture of individual grasses. In addition, each area normally has information available through agricultural extension bulletins that guide the property owner in the selection of the proper grass.

There are two basic types of grass: warm-season grasses and cool-season grasses. The warm-season grasses are grown primarily in the South and along the seacoasts in the southern half of the country. Grasses included in the warm-season group are zoysia, Bermuda, St. Augustine, and centipedegrass. Each of these grasses grows well in hot weather but will not survive the cold winters of northern climates.

Cool-season grasses include the bluegrasses, tall fescue, creeping red fescue, chewings fescue, and the ryegrasses. Bentgrasses are cool-season also, but they are intensely cultured grasses, more suitable for golf courses than lawns. Cool-season grasses can be grown over a larger part of the country than can the warm-season grasses, but only with intense management practices. These types of grass are more difficult to maintain in hot weather than are the warm-season grasses and, generally, are more susceptible to the ravages of diseases and insects. Since the cool-season grasses have a much longer growing season than warm-season grasses, they are used often in the warmer climates for areas where green grass is necessary, even in the winter.

The uses for a new lawn area will play a large role in the decision of which grass to select. Warm-season grasses are considered stronger because most of them spread by stolons or rhizomes, or both. They are able to fill in holes that develop in the lawn by this means. Some of the cool-season grasses, such as the bluegrasses and bentgrasses, also have the capability of spreading, but they are much slower. Most of the cool-season grasses prosper only under fairly high mowing, while most of the warm-season grasses respond to very short mowing. This low mowing is more conducive to play activities in the lawn area. Much research has been done, and is ongoing, to develop more grass varieties, particularly in the bluegrasses and ryegrasses, which will withstand lower mowing heights, warmer weather, and heavier traffic; the gap between the adaptability of the cool-season and warm-season grasses is narrowing.

While most of the cool-season grasses are propagated sexually, by seed, most of the warm-season grasses are propagated asexually, by means of sprigging, sodding, or plugging. *Sprigging* is a process by which the grass sod is separated into lengths of specialized stems called stolons or rhizomes, which are then spread over the prepared grass area, covered by soil, and watered. The grass roots at nodes on the rhizomes or stolons and develops into a sod. *Sodding* is a process in which the

Figure 2-1. A play area in a well-established lawn.

grass is lifted as an intact unit, usually in strips 12″ to 18″ wide and 6′ to 9′ long, then transplanted to another area, which has been previously prepared, where, given proper care, it begins to root immediately. *Plugging* is a process that, like sodding, involves the transplanting of pieces of sod intact. Normally these pieces are small, ¼″ to 3″ in diameter, either round or square, and are planted from 6″ to 18″ apart. As they root and begin to grow, these plugs spread toward one another by means of stolons or rhizomes. Planting by each of these methods will be discussed in more detail later in this chapter.

Each of the propagation methods requires a certain establishment time before a solid turf is evident. This establishment time must be considered so that the turf can be ready for its intended use at the proper time. Sodding, for example, requires very little time for establishment, since the grass must only root sufficiently. The top portions (leaves and stems) on sod are already mature when the sod is transplanted. Seeded grass must develop not only a sound root system but mature leaves and stems as well, before it is ready for heavy activity. Such development normally requires more than one growing season, as compared to less than a month for sodded grass. Sprigging and plugging both require more time than sodding also, but sprigging can be faster than seed, given proper care and climatic conditions suitable for growth. Of the propagation methods discussed, plugging is the slowest, often taking up to three years to completely cover a lawn area.

The cost of establishing a lawn area also must be considered when determining the type of grass to plant. Each type of grass and each method of propagation carries its own cost factors. Seeding can generally be considered the least expensive method of propagation for cool-season grasses, although if the area to be grassed is sloping severely, the possibility of erosion might make the additional cost of sodding more feasible. Plugging warm-season grasses is usually more expensive than sprigging, depending on the equipment available, but the maintenance cost of a sprigged area is higher, because more watering is necessary. Sodding is more expensive than either sprigging or plugging. Since, in most cases, some type of budget must guide the decisions, these cost factors become important in the determination of the type of grass to plant in an area.

Climatic conditions of the specific site, as well as the climatic zone, are also important considerations. A tree-laden site will not grow warm-season grasses, which require a great deal of sunlight. A south- or west-facing slope will be a difficult place to grow a cool-season grass, particularly in an area from the middle of the country on south, because of the intensity of the sun and wind on such a slope. Similarly, warm-season grasses are not likely to do as well on a north- or east-facing slope as they will in an area where the sunlight is more direct.

Other landscaping of an area will also affect the selection of a grass type. Intensely landscaped areas, with many free-formed flower beds, will be much more difficult to maintain if Bermuda or other aggressive spreading grasses are used. Unless a strong and secure edging, which extends below the ground to control rhizomes and above ground to control stolons, is used, it is a constant battle to control spreading grasses in flower or shrub beds. The texture required of the grass will also be dictated, in part, by the landscaping of the area. Large, sweeping beds of flowers and shrubs, which leave a small, central area of grass in the middle, require a lawn of finer texture than a large open area. Generally, the smaller the lawn area is, the finer the texture of the grass should be.

Although all of the above considerations for grass variety are important, it should be reemphasized that the most important factors are climatic. If the grass will not grow well in the climate in which it is planted, all other considerations are irrelevant.

Soil Preparation

Regardless of the variety of grass planted or the method of propagation used to establish that grass, some soil preparation is necessary prior to planting. Essentially the same preparation is needed for each type of planting, with minor differences. Soil preparation consists of cultivation, grading, firming for consistency, and texturizing.

Cultivation

Cultivation is necessary to loosen the soil, thereby relieving compaction, to remove weed growth or other vegetation present on the surface and to prepare the area so the other soil preparation activities can take place. Although cultivation is normally recommended to a certain depth, it is my belief that each soil requires a different treatment. If the soil is uniform in makeup and compaction to a depth of six inches or more, the cultivation is better done as shallow as possible. Repacking to a consistent firmness can then be accomplished with more ease. On the other hand, if there is a hardpan layer within the top six inches, the cultivation should be deep enough to loosen the hardpan, so adequate subsurface drainage can be established. Similarly, if there are layers of different types of soils within the top six inches, cultivation should be thorough enough to homogenize the soil by mixing the two types together. Although it might be advantageous to cultivate deeper than six inches in certain cases, generally such tillage is not practical, because the available equipment does not work to those depths.

Cultivation may be done with any kind of equipment that will loosen, pulverize, and remove vegetation from the soil. Commonly used are plows, discs, rototillers, and rotary-tooth tillage implements. Some advantage might be gained by using either discs or the rotary-tooth implements because they do not turn the soil over. The soil on top at the beginning of the cultivation process remains on the top, whereas a plow or a rototiller will move the top soil to a lower level.

Wet soil should never be cultivated. The soil must be allowed to dry out before being cultivated, or tight, compacted clods will result. This compaction will contribute to poor drainage and will impede the root development. Those who have tried to grade and texturize soil that was cultivated wet know that severe problems result because of the difficulty encountered in trying to break up these clods.

Grading

Grading is a process by which the area is smoothed, firmed, and arranged in the proper sequence of levels for the adequate drainage of surface water. Lawn grasses will not grow in an area that is consistently

Figure 2-2. This type of cultivation implement loosens and pulverizes the soil without changing soil particle levels in the soil stratum.

waterlogged. Thus, preparation of the soil must provide for the controlled run off of excess surface water. Good drainage on a grassy surface requires a slope of at least 2%, or 2' of decline in each 100' length. Slow drainage can be accomplished with less slope, but the lower the degree of slope, the less margin for error exists, and "puddles," of standing water are likely to occur. During periods of frequent rain or heavy watering, the grass in these puddles might decline or even die, because the saturated soil in the root zone does not allow oxygen to the roots.

Many times, it is advisable to check the drainage of an area to be grassed in advance of cultivation procedures. If major grading must be done to allow proper surface drainage, such grading might need to be done with a bulldozer. Cultivation done prior to grading by a bulldozer is time and money wasted, since the area will need to be recultivated anyway. An area of ground can best be checked for drainage by means of a building level, a transit, or a sight level, plus a target rod. The builder's level, transit, and sight level are all telescopic devices that allow a level sighting in all directions. By focusing on the target rod, which is a stick graded in feet, different area levels can be determined. It is not always possible to determine the relative levels of a plot of ground

Figure 2-3. A landscaper sighting through a builder's level at a target rod to determine the proper grading measures for adequate drainage.

without the aid of a level-sighting device. The higher the reading on the target rod, the lower the level of the ground. By sighting levels periodically, the degree and direction of slope can be determined, and simple calculations reveal the necessary cut or fill required for proper drainage. A *cut* is the removal of a prescribed depth of soil from an area, and a *fill* is the addition of a prescribed depth of soil in an area.

Normally, a few sightings will reveal the necessity of grading for drainage purposes. On most lawn areas surrounding new houses, rough grading has already been accomplished by the builder, so the landscaper need only check to see that the drainage patterns are properly set and that proper slope away from the house on all sides exists. To solve more complex drainage problems, it may be necessary to do a full-scale survey of the property. Such a survey is discussed in more detail in Chapter 3.

Smoothing and firming. A lawn area needs to be smooth to produce a good stand of grass and facilitate mowing and play activities. This smoothing process is a function of the grading process, second only to the drainage requirements in importance. Equal firming of the grade is important because if soft spots exist, settling will occur in those spots, resulting in depressions. In that regard, the smoothing and firming functions of grading are one and the same, because the failure to accomplish either one will result in a rough, uneven lawn. Some of the implements available for grading with tractors are the Roseman tiller-rake, various box-graders, and York rakes, as well as various blades.

Tractor grading. Lawns can be graded by hand or by tractor. But the only areas ordinarily graded by hand are those next to a structure or otherwise inaccessible by a tractor-drawn implement. Tractor-drawn implements are not only much faster, but are also more accurate in the establishment of a grade and equal firmness. The implements used for tractor grading generally pull a ridge of loose soil in front of a blade or rake, allowing some of the soil to filter into low spots as the implement passes over them, cutting the excess off of the high spots at the same time. Because of the width of the implement, some 5' to 6' compared to the 18" to 24" width of a hand rake, the leveling effect achieved is much better with the tractor implements. Soil firming is better accomplished also, since the tractor implement weighs much more.

Tractor grading is best accomplished by establishing the drainage patterns first. If large amounts of soil must be cut from one area and filled in another, this should be the first task. Only when the basic grades for drainage have been established and checked should the smoothing and firming processes begin. The tractor operator, upon arrival, should first evaluate the grading necessary, then proceed step by

Figure 2-4. A tractor-drawn grading implement, with teeth to loosen soil and a leveler bar to smooth and firm the surface. *(Courtesy of Roseman Tractor Equipment Co.)*

step to completion of the tasks. An orderly and carefully planned procedure ensures that no step will have to be repeated later. The objective should always be to accomplish the grading in the shortest possible length of time.

Tractor grading is usually accomplished in several passes over the entire yard, after the initial adjustments to the drainage patterns. The operator should plan ahead and set goals for each one of the passes. It might require only two passes to complete the grading, instead of three, if the operator is very conscientious and attentive to his goals for each pass.

A skilled tractor operator can work very close to the house or other structures and can ensure that the proper amount of soil is left next to those areas. This saves a lot of the time normally required for hand grading and is very helpful to the hand operator who will not have to move massive amounts of soil unaided. Of course, the tractor operator must not only be highly skilled, he must also be extremely cautious, so he doesn't hit the house with the implement or otherwise make damaging mistakes that negate the value of the time saved.

Finally, the graded lawn area should be tailored to the type of operation that follows. If the lawn is to be seeded with a culti-packer–type seeder, which has heavy rollers, the seedbed is best left in a slightly cloddy condition, so the culti-packer will adequately cover the seed by crushing the small clods. On the other hand, an area that is to be sodded should be relatively clod-free, so the sod will lie flat, tight against the soil surface.

Safety. It would be wise to consider a couple of safety considerations before completing a discussion of tractor grading. Many new lawns are planted in areas highly populated by children. A tractor operator must be constantly aware of the danger of small children darting in the path of his machine. No one except the operator should ever be allowed to ride on the tractor while in operation. There is only one safe seat on a tractor, and the operator must occupy it. The operator must know the degree of slope on which his tractor will operate safely and never drive on a slope that exceeds that safe limit. Occasionally, it is necessary to leave a tractor and implement on the work site overnight. When this is done, the operator should make sure the implement is set firmly on the ground, not suspended in air by the three-point hitch. He should also make sure he removes the keys, so the tractor cannot be started by anyone else. Unless absolutely necessary, equipment should not be left on the jobsite, particularly implements with sharp edges or points (like a disc) that may easily cut or puncture anyone falling against them.

Hand grading. Hand grading might seem less sophisticated than tractor grading, but in reality, it might be both more difficult and more involved. The tools available are certainly less sophisticated, and the successful use of these tools depends entirely on the skill and diligence of the handler, who must provide both the power source and the direction for these tools. Primarily, the tools for hand grading consist of shovels, rakes, and a wheelbarrow. The quality of these tools does matter, because high-quality tools not only last longer, they are easier to work with and to sharpen. A high quality bow rake will be a little heavier than one of low quality, for example, and the heavier rake will move quantities of soil, including clods, much more easily than will a lighter rake. A shovel of the highest quality is made of stronger metal, which sharpens better, and a sharp shovel is a good shovel.

Although hand grading is usually restricted to the areas around a foundation, near curbs and walks, and around trees or other obstructions, the requirements for such grading are no less stringent than those for tractor grading. The success or failure of a seeded lawn, for example, is related closely to the grading of that lawn, and if the tractor grading is up to par, but the hand grading is poorly done, a sharp distinction will always appear between the two areas. Hand-graded areas must provide

Figure 2-5. Preparing a seedbed by hand raking with a bow rake. Note the short grip on the handle, enabling the worker to move large quantities of soil with good control.

for proper surface drainage, smoothness, firmness, and a texture conducive to the type of lawn establishment operation to follow. Firmness is harder to establish evenly, because of the equipment's narrow width and its light weight. The lighter weight must be compensated for by more passes over each spot. Since part of the hand grading is done next to a foundation, where loose fill has been installed to a depth of possibly several feet, offering a greater potential for settling, the grade must be magnified in those areas. If soil is not banked higher next to the foundation, subsequent settling will leave a depression in those areas.

There are right and wrong ways to use hand tools. Most people grasp a bow rake on the upper portion of the handle and manipulate the rake in a back and forth action, both pushing and pulling soil. However, much more can be accomplished by grasping the rake lower on the handle, bending slightly at the waist to do so, and pulling the rake toward oneself in short, chopping strokes, keeping a small portion of soil in front of the rake at all times. The shorter grasp allows more control over the rake, so a level can be maintained. It also allows more soil to be moved with less effort, because the further the grip is from the load being moved, the more the leverage effect of that load. Clods are more easily separated from the finer soil by this method also, since they are constantly moved toward the handler, instead of being spread back over the prepared area, as in a back and forth motion.

The area immediately next to a foundation warrants special attention during the hand grading. Since this area is most susceptible to settling, clods that have lodged next to the foundation need to be removed or chopped finely with a shovel. When the seed or sod is rolled, the area adjacent to a foundation receives less packing than other areas, so it is important to firm it as much as possible during the the grading process.

Areas adjacent to curbs and sidewalks or drives must be hand graded to fit the lawn operation to follow. Grass looks best and is most easily maintained if the level of the soil next to curbs and flat concrete is nearly level with the concrete. If a seeding operation is to follow the grading, the soil should be graded off smooth, level with the top of the concrete. If sodding is to follow, the soil level must be left lower than the concrete by the approximate thickness of the soil on the sod. To neglect this part of hand grading is to duplicate efforts, since these grades will need to be established later, when the seeding or sodding is done.

Hand-graded areas must usually be graded to a finer texture than adjacent tractor-graded areas, again, because the rollers used in these areas will be lighter in weight and will not break clods as easily.

Methods of Lawn Seeding

Mechanical, tractor-operated seeders, hand-operated mechanical seeders, and broadcasting by hand are the three basic methods of seeding a lawn. Each of these methods can be very successful if the rules for seeding are followed.

Three rules exist for the proper placement of seed, regardless of the method used.

1. The seed must be evenly applied in the proper amount.
2. The seed must be adequately covered by soil to the correct depth.
3. The soil must be packed tightly against the seed, so soil and seed are in close contact on all sides.

Mechanical seeders do offer advantages, particularly those types that put the seed into the ground, instead of on top of it, covering and packing the seed at the same time. The stand of grass resulting from the use of these seeders tends to be more uniform and even, because all seeds are covered to an even depth, with uniform firmness. Hand-operated mechanical seeders might also be of a type that sow the seed into the ground, but more often they broadcast the seed over the top of the soil, then the seed must be raked in by hand or covered by a harrow on a tractor. Hand broadcasting is the least controllable of the three methods for seed placement, because, unlike the other methods, no gauge exists to control the amount of seed spread or the evenness with which it is spread, and the seed must still be covered by hand, resulting in an uneven planting depth.

Figure 2-6. A tractor-drawn, culti-packer-type seeder.

Figure 2-7. A tractor-drawn, disc-type seeder. *(Courtesy of Jacobsen Division of Textron, Inc.)*

Grass seed should normally be planted at a shallow depth, between ¼″ deep and ½″ deep, which makes for quicker germination and establishment. Exceptions to this rule occur in highway seeding, which is done with a drill, or in areas that will not be watered regularly. In such cases the seed is planted deeper to take advantage of the moisture at lower depths and to prevent its drying out before germination. In areas with plentiful quantities of water available, the shallower seeding produces a faster, thicker, more even stand of grass. Even in areas such as highway right of ways, where no watering will ever be done after the

Figure 2-8. One type of self-propelled, walk-behind, grass seeder.

grass is planted, the seed can be placed at a shallow depth by hydroseeding. Seed is mixed into a slurry of moisture-retaining mulch by a hydroseeder, and the slurry is then sprayed onto the top of the prepared seedbed. The mulch material becomes the covering for the seed. It has the capacity to retain moisture long enough to germinate the seed and start the grass plant on the road to maturity.

Mechanical, tractor-operated seeders insert the seed into the ground by means of either a disc or a culti-packer. The disc-type seeder has a series of discs at a spacing of 2″ to 4″, which cut grooves in the ground. The discs are mounted below a seedbox containing the seed, and connecting tubes allow the seeds to be dropped into the grooves. Packing wheels, rollers, or drag chains follow the discs and the drop-tubes to close the groove and pack the seed in place. In some cases, the discs are operated simply by traction as the seeder is pulled over the ground. In other cases, the discs are driven by the power takeoff from the tractor. A power takeoff allows the discs to be turned at a higher speed, while the groundspeed remains slow, thereby allowing a cleaner groove to be created. A culti-packer is a machine with two large rollers beneath the seedbox, which are ridged or ridged with knobs on them. The front roller firms the seedbed, crushing clods, and leaving a series of depressions in rows, normally 2″ apart, into which the seeds are dropped from the seedbox above. The back roller then breaks down the depressions

Figure 2-9. One type of hand-operated mechanical seeder. Often used to spread fertilizer as well.

and ridges left by the front roller, thereby covering the seed, and packs the seed firmly into the ground, pulverizing more clods as it does. The culti-packer requires a prepared seedbed, while the disc-type seeder does not always. The discs have the capability of penetrating unprepared ground, while the culti-packer will not. Both seeders serve the purpose of installing seed quite well, and each type has a series of agitators and seed openings inside of the seedbox, which allows the seed to be distributed in the proper amount.

Mechanical, hand-operated spreaders are basically of the drill or broadcast types. Included here are the self-propelled drill seeders, which are considered hand operated because they are not connected to a tractor. These operate in the same fashion as the disc-type tractor-operated seeder just described, except on a smaller scale. The power is supplied by an engine mounted on the top of the machine. Since these machines are much slower than their tractor-operated counterparts, their use is normally restricted to areas not accesssible by tractors.

Mechanical, hand-operated seeders that operate with no power source other than the operator are either broadcast or drop types. The broadcast, often called a Cyclone (a brand name), spreads seed, fertilizer, or other materials in a wider area than that covered by the spreader itself; it utilizes a whirling fan located below the seedbox. The seed is allowed to descend from the box onto the surface of the fan by means of a controlled opening. The seed is constantly stirred by an agitator located in the bottom of the seedbox. This ensures a constant flow of seed through the calibrated opening. The fan is driven by gears that are connected to the wheels of the spreader. The wheels turn as the seeder is pushed over the ground, causing the fan to spin and throwing the seed out to the front and sides of the spreader. Heavier seed is thrown further from the seeder than is light seed.

The drop seeder covers only an area equal to its own width, since the material in the seedbox is dropped straight down to the ground. An agitator, usually a roller type, is located in the bottom of the seedbox, which is driven by the wheels of the spreader. Seed is agitated through a series of openings in the bottom of the seedbox.

When seed placement is accomplished by hand-operated means, the coverage of that seed must also be done by hand. Commonly, rakes are used for this purpose. The objective should be to cover the seed uniformly while also covering the highest possible percentage of seeds. Both of these objectives can be more easily met if the seedbed is properly prepared. The final preparation of the seedbed should be done in a way that will leave a pattern of shallow grooves on the surface. This can be accomplished with rakes or with a harrow, mounted on a tractor. The seed from the spreader can then fall into these grooves, to be covered by soil, thereby simulating the actions of a tractor-operated, culti-packer–type seeder. The resulting stand of grass will be both thicker and more even in germination and growth. Light raking pulls the soil over the top of the seed. Care should be exercised, for a heavy raking might disturb the distribution of the seed as well as the depth of coverage. Any seeds left on the top of the ground will germinate only under conditions of extremely frequent watering or rain.

Tractor-operated seeders do an excellent job of packing the seedbed, so the seeds will lie in close contact on all sides with the soil. Hand-seeded areas must be packed by means of a hand roller, a flat board with weight placed upon it, or other such means. The hand roller is most commonly used. This device consists of a round drum, smooth on the outside, with a handle attached to it. A plug fits into a hole in the drum. This allows the drum to be filled with water, greatly increasing the roller's weight. This roller is simply rolled across the seeded area, its weight packing the soil beneath it. Although the hand roller is quite successful as a means of compacting a seedbed, it will not break clods readily, so an area to be hand rolled should be prepared by leaving only small clods.

Watering and maintaining newly seeded areas. The first waterings given to a newly seeded area can contribute to the packing of the seedbed. Thorough watering, applied heavily, will further firm the seedbed, resulting in a better stand of grass. Light, misty waterings can be applied thereafter, but the first waterings should consist of heavy droplets to ensure tight contact between seed and soil. Care must be exercised to prevent erosion during a heavy watering.

Even after all of the seedbed preparation, seed placement, covering, and packing have been properly done, the success or failure of the newly seeded area is very much in doubt. In order for a good stand of healthy grass to result, the seedbed must receive the proper amount of moisture at the right time. Once a seed absorbs water, the germination process begins. But if the seed embryo dries out and the germination process is interrupted, the seed will die. Water, in sufficient quantities and frequency, must be received by the seed, either naturally or artificially, during the entire germination process.

As a rule of thumb, for a shallow seedbed in which the seeds are planted in the upper ½″, the seeds should be watered whenever the surface of the soil becomes dry enough to walk on. It is not possible to water the seedbed too often, unless puddling or washing result, and the more moist the seed is kept, the quicker and better the germination will be.

Figure 2-10. A newly seeded area develops quickly after germination.

Watering of a new seedbed can be done either by hand-held hose or by sprinkler. The use of a sprinkler is better for two reasons: the water is applied more uniformly over the entire area; and a sufficient quantity of water is assured. Many types of sprinklers are available. The selection of sprinklers should depend upon the area to be covered, wind conditions, and the type of coverage afforded by the type of sprinkler. Some sprinklers water more heavily in one portion of their pattern than in other portions. This tendency can result in either overwatering to the point of washing out in one part of the sprinkler pattern or an insufficient quantity of water in another part of the pattern. The amount of wind encountered also will affect sprinkler selection. Sprinklers that apply water in fairly coarse droplets will not be affected by wind to the degree that those applying a fine mist will. The watering of an area can be facilitated by matching the sprinkling equipment to the size and shape of the area. Long, narrow strips beside houses might best be watered with a sprinkler hose. This is a flat hose with pinholes in it, from which a long, narrow pattern of fine mist sprays. Large, open areas might best be watered by large, pulsating sprinklers operating in a full circle. Because the water is applied to a larger area, the sprinkler will not have to be moved with as much frequency as one with smaller area coverage.

Many theories exist about the maintenance of a newly seeded area, but for the most part, the requirements of a new lawn are very much the same as those for a mature lawn of the same variety. Mowing should be started when the grass exceeds the recommended mowing height for that variety by 1″. Allowing the grass to grow much taller before the first mowing only serves to shock the grass when it is finally mowed, thereby slowing its development. Watering should be done when the grass needs it, as best demonstrated by the first sign of wilting, a bluish green cast to the leaves in spots, and a slight shriveling of the leaves in the same areas. Fertilizing is usually done at the same time as the seeding. Several weeks later, however, the new grass may demonstrate a yellowing that indicates a nitrogen deficiency in spots. Nitrogen moves through the soil, so all of the watering necessary on a newly seeded area contributes to the leaching of that element out of the root zone. New areas, freshly backfilled and graded, are often not uniform in soil type and structure and, therefore, not uniform in fertility, another factor resulting in the appearance of yellow spots. Unless the weather is hot and dry, a supplementary application of nitrogen as those spots appear will boost the grass toward quicker maturity.

Weeds often appear in a new lawn, especially one that is planted in the spring. The presence of these weeds sometimes initiates frantic efforts to eliminate them, when, in fact, they might be better left alone. Many of the weeds that accompany grass germination in the spring are annuals, whose seed is constantly present in the soil. If they naturally grow tall, the constant mowing of the grass will be sufficient measure for their removal, but if they are low growing varieties, such as crabgrass, they will likely stay in the lawn until fall, at which time their life cycle ends. Although they do provide competition for the grass, normally the grass plants will coexist with these weeds, and the following spring their germination can be chemically prevented. Spraying weeds in new grass with chemicals is risky, since immature grass is susceptible to chemical damage. If chemicals need be applied, as in the case of dandelions or other low-growing perennials, maximum care should be taken to follow the manufacturer's directions to the letter.

Sodding

Sod is a living, growing mass of plant material, which is highly perishable. The conditions under which it is installed can greatly affect its rooting and establishment abilities. Under adverse conditions the sod has little chance of survival. Transplanting shock is considerable, even under the best of conditions, but much can be done to ease that shock if the soil preparation, sod handling, and maintenance after transplanting are properly handled.

Figure 2-11. Worker carefully tucking in edges of sod tightly against adjacent edges, to be sure there is no overlapping or gaps.

Soil preparation is done in similar fashion to that of a seedbed, with cultivation, grading, and firming all necessary prerequisites to actually laying the sod. A sodbed must be of finer texture than a seedbed, however, because large clods prevent close contact between the sod and the ground below. Air spaces created by such a gap cause the root tips in that area to dry out, and this prevents the roots from growing into the soil below. As mentioned earlier in this chapter, the edges of areas that are bordered by concrete must be graded so the sod will butt tightly against the concrete; the soil level on the sod should be even with the concrete surface. Along other edges, the soil level needs to be lowered so that when the sod is placed there is soil solidly packed against the edge of that sod. Otherwise, some of the grass along the edge will dry out and die.

The sod will suffer less shock if the length of time between harvesting and installation is very short. Of course, sometimes the sod must be transported long distances before it can be installed. When this is the case, the condition of the sod when cut will dictate much about its survival and growth. If plentiful moisture is available at the time of harvesting, the grass tissues will all be filled with water, so the period between cutting and the permanent wilting point will be longer. Rolling the sod or stacking it in layers protects the sod on the inside of the rolls or stacks and allows moisture to be conserved for longer periods of time. But even then sod has a maximum life of only a few days, particularly in hot weather; tissue deterioration starts on the leaves and stems, and this reduces the livability of the sod.

Sod is laid in strips, usually of equal length. To facilitate the knitting of the sod, it is important to make sure that all portions of the soil on the sod are touching the ground beneath. Also, adjacent pieces of sod must not overlap. The sod in the overlap will most likely die back, because the root zone has become too dry. The end of the piece being overlapped is likely to die also, because the leaves will be unable to get enough light. The ends of adjacent pieces of sod should be staggered. This adds stability to the sodded area until it can become solidly rooted.

Occasionally, a corner will tear off of a piece of sod. The installers need to fill in these holes with pieces of sod that correspond in size, or the lawn area will be rough. The edges of the sod around exposed holes also stand a chance of drying out, producing die-back.

Once sod is layed, it must be rolled into close contact with the soil. This prevents air from drying the root tips and also facilitates the penetration of the roots into the ground beneath the sod. If the sod shows signs of wilting when it is layed, it should be watered lightly before rolling. The pressure of a heavy roller on wilted grass leaves will cause damage to the tissues and will inhibit the establishment of the sod. Light watering allows the grass to become turgid, a much healthier condition in which it will withstand the pressure of the roller. This watering, if needed, should be light, so the soft ground does not become muddy. If it does, rolling will result in deep ruts and footprints, instead of the desirable smooth, firm surface.

After rolling, the initial watering, which is very important, can be completed. The entire thickness of the sod must be thoroughly saturated during this watering, and the ground below should be moist. If the root zones remain dry, the sod will wilt and finally die.

Subsequent waterings on a newly sodded area must be frequent to allow the roots to penetrate into the soil below. During sod harvesting, many roots are lost. Evaporation and transpiration rates continue, affected only by the weather, but the grass no longer has the capacity to pull water up at the same rate. Water, applied frequently to the leaves, can be evaporated by the sun and wind in place of transpiration water from within the plants. If sod transplanting is properly done, the roots never cease growing, so within a few days the new sod is capable of utilizing, to some extent, the moisture-retaining capacity of the soil below, which is greater than the sod itself. Mowing the sod lower prior to harvesting would seem an answer to balancing the root loss, but in fact, such a practice results in a shock to the plants, which has a far greater negative effect.

Newly sodded areas should be mowed when the grass exceeds the recommended mowing height by one inch, just as with newly germinated grass. Care should be exercised not to mow the sod when the grass is wilted, nor when the lawn is soggy.

If the prepared sodbed is extremely dry and loose at the time the sod is layed, it might require a second rolling after receiving water frequently for a few days. The settling and packing effect of the waterings will prepare the loose and dry soil for further rolling, resulting in a more firm and even lawn.

Sprigging

Sprigging also involves basically the same soil preparation as for seeding and sodding. Sprigging involves the removal of individual sections of rhizomes or stolons from sod. These sections must contain at least one or two nodes from which new roots and stems can grow. Both rhizomes and stolons are modified stems; stolons grow on the surface of the ground and rhizomes grow under the surface. Both produce new roots and stems when properly transplanted and maintained.

Sprigging is commonly accomplished by drawing a series of shallow trenches in the prepared ground into which the sprigs are placed. Then the sprigs are covered over by soil and packed. These trenches can be spaced as desired, the spacing dictating both the cost of the operation and the speed with which coverage can be completed. Sprigs can also be broadcasted over the area, then disced partially into the ground. Or after broadcasting, the covering soil can be top dressed over the sprigs. Discing results in poorer coverage of the sprigs than trenching, and top dressing costs more. All methods require rolling to secure the soil tightly against the sprigs.

Initially, sprigs require very frequent watering because they are small in size and thus dry out very quickly, and also because they possess no roots, until they generate them. The moisture level of a sprigged area must approximate that of a seeded area; that is, watering is required whenever the ground is dry enough to walk on.

Since sprigging leaves much bare ground between the sprigs, it is best to apply a preemergent weed and grass control agent to limit the competition for water and nutrients. Fertilizing, although it can be done at the time the sprigs are planted, is best delayed until the sprigs root and begin to grow. Only at that time can the sprigs make use of the nutrients.

Plugging

Plugging is similar to sprigging in that the objective is to make the grass spread by means of rhizomes or stolons. It is basically a propagation method for warm-season grasses. Plugs are pieces of sod that are transplanted so they may spread laterally in all directions, ultimately growing together to form a sod.

Plugs can be made by cutting pieces of sod into squares or circles or by using a plug-making tool, which takes round plugs from existing grass areas. Commonly, plugs are made in 2″ diameter circles or in 2″ × 2″ squares. A 2″ plug is considered to be large enough to hold moisture for a substantial amount of time, and yet small enough to make efficient use of the sod from which plugs are taken. The important measurement is the surface exposure around the edge of the plug, since it will grow outward in all directions. Although plugs are often cut in long strips, there is no advantage to this method, unless the strips are being used to prevent erosion. Such "stripping," requires much more sod, but the surface area exposed on the edges is not much greater, so coverage does not occur any more quickly.

Plugs are commonly set in rows and spaced 6″ to 18″ apart. Naturally, the further apart the plugs are set, the longer will be the length of time

Figure 2-12. A grass plugger. Note the plug beside it.

required for complete coverage. Doubling the spacing between each plug has the effect of quadrupling the amount of area that each plug must cover. For example, if plugs are set in an area at a spacing of 6″, or .5′ apart, they must each cover an area of .25 square feet (.5′ × .5′ = .25 sq. ft.), but if plugs are set in that same area at a spacing of 1′, each will have to cover 1 square foot (1′ × 1′ = 1.0 sq. ft.), an area four times that required by the 6″ spacing. The same feature exists for the sod requirement, however. If one square yard of sod (3′ × 3′) is cut into 2″ square plugs, it will produce 324 plugs, which, at a 1′ spacing, will cover 324 square feet. That same 324 plugs will only cover 81 square feet at a 6″ spacing, one-fourth as much as the coverage at a 1′ spacing. The size of the plugs made affects the required sod similarly, for although 2″ square plugs number 324 per square yard of sod, 3″ square plugs number only 144 per square yard of sod.

Grading practices are the same for an area to be plugged as for a seedbed or sodbed. Trenches are drawn across a prepared area, the plugs are set at the prescribed intervals, and soil is backfilled around the plugs and packed securely. Then the entire area is rolled with a heavy, smooth roller. The plugs should be set slightly lower than the grade around them, so the backfill can just overlap their edges. This prevents the plugs from "floating" out of the ground as they are watered. When plugging is done on a bare area, it is best to apply a preemergent weed and grass control agent to limit competition, thus allowing the plugs to spread faster.

In some cases, plugging can be done in an existing stand of grass without tearing out that existing stand. For example, zoysia may be introduced into a bluegrass lawn in order to convert the lawn entirely to zoysia. The bluegrass might be left to prevent erosion or to preserve the appearance of a complete lawn during the conversion process. This type of operation is usually accomplished by the use of a plugger, which is a tool with a round blade and cylinder at the bottom of a handle. The blade cuts into the ground, forcing a plug of sod into the cylinder. As the handle is lifted the sod is removed. The plug, which is normally 2″ in diameter and about 3″ deep, can then be ejected from the plugger into a basket or tub. Similarly, plugs are removed from the existing lawn, and the plugs of new grass are then placed into the holes. Normally, some loose soil should be sprinkled around the top edges of the new plug. This seals the edges and prevents air from getting to the root system of the plugs. The period of time required for coverage will be longer by leaving the existing lawn intact, because of the competition for water and nutrients. When a warm-season grass is plugged into a cool-season lawn, this period of time can be shortened by mowing short and fertilizing at the times conducive to the growth of the warm-season grass.

Because of a tendency for new plugs to "float," as mentioned earlier, it is wise to roll or otherwise pack a newly plugged area a week or two after the plugging operation, so if any floating has occurred, the plugs can be pushed back down before they become securely rooted. In a newly plugged area, washouts occasionally should be filled with soil. Then, as the grass covers, the lawn will be smooth and even.

Overseeding

The requirements for introducing seed into an established lawn and successfully making it germinate are often misunderstood, even though they are basically the same as those for a newly seeded lawn. Much grass seed has been literally "thrown away," because it was casually broadcast into an existing stand of grass without any soil preparation. Although a few of those seeds may fall into cracks in the soil and germinate, most of them will serve only as birdseed. For successful germination, grass seed must always be covered by soil. Also, the seed must be packed into close contact with the soil.

Some of the mechanical seeders, which place the seed into the ground by means of discs, are excellent for overseeding. The discs slice grooves in a lawn area into which the seeds fall. A tandem disc can be used for this purpose, but when the discs are set to run straight, they are usually more cupped than those on a drill, so more disturbance of the lawn will occur.

Power rakes can be used quite successfully on a lawn area prior to overseeding if the machine has solid blades. Those types that use a flexible flange-type blade to beat thatch out of turf (instead of a solid blade to cut through the turf) will not disturb the soil enough to achieve proper coverage, unless preceded by aeration or some other operation that brings soil to the surface.

Spoon-type aerators punch holes in the turf, depositing the resulting plugs on the surface. The use of such an aerator, followed by a power rake that breaks the plugs, will provide adequate soil for seed coverage. This also allows seed to fall into the aerator holes where it can easily germinate.

Figure 2-13. A spoon-type aerator. A very useful tool for overseeding. *(Courtesy of OMC-Lincoln, Ryan Turf Care Products.)*

Spikers, which aerate without removing a core of soil, also provide excellent slots into which the seed can fall. The slots usually swell back shut with subsequent watering.

The old practice of broadcasting seed onto snow cover in the winter is an excellent means of feeding birds, but it does little to thicken a stand of grass; the seed simply has little opportunity to get into the ground.

SUMMARY

The lawn is the most conspicuous and, therefore, the most important feature of a landscape. The variety of grass selected dictates, in large part, the quality of a lawn. Selection criteria include: climate suitability, exposure of lawn area, type of propagation necessary, cost of planting, degree of slope in the area to be planted, and other landscaping of the lawn areas. The two general classes of lawn grasses are warm season, which are usually propagated asexually by sodding, sprigging, or plugging, and cool season, which are usually propagated by either seeding or sodding.

Soil preparation consists of cultivation, grading, packing for consistent firmness, and texturizing.

Grading allows for the proper drainage of surface water, which requires at least a 2% slope for a grassy surface, smoothness, and equal firmness. A survey might be necessary to properly check the degree of slope in all areas.

Grading is accomplished by either tractor-drawn implements or hand-manipulated tools. Tractor grading is the most successful, if properly done, because of the additional weight and width of coverage. Properly planned, tractor grading can facilitate easier hand grading in areas the tractor cannot reach and can be tailored to the type of lawn establishment operation to follow. The grading should be planned step by step to avoid any duplication of effort. Safety should always be emphasized during tractor operations.

Successful hand grading depends upon the quality of tools and the proper handling methods. More settling usually occurs in areas that are hand graded. Thus, special care is warranted when filling and packing these areas.

For successful germination, the seed must be applied evenly in the proper amount, the seed must be adequately covered by soil to the correct depth, and the soil must be packed tightly against the seed.

Seeding can be accomplished by tractor-operated seeders, hand-operated mechanical seeders, or hand broadcasting. Mechanical seeders that actually place the seed into the ground offer advantages because of their ability to produce a more even stand of grass.

Hydroseeding is a method that does not require seed coverage by soil because the mulch that is mixed with the seed serves the same purpose.

Newly seeded areas must be kept moist from the time they first receive water until germination is complete. The more moist a seedbed is kept, short of washing out areas, the quicker and better will be the germination.

Sodding involves the movement of a living section of grass from one area to another where it is rerooted. The root structure of the sod needs to be packed firmly into contact with the soil for successful penetration. Since sod is highly perishable, its condition at the time of cutting, its handling, and its first waterings after transplant are of paramount importance. If properly handled, the sod never ceases to grow.

Individual sections of either rhizomes or stolons, both of which are modified stems, are planted in a sprigging operation. Sprigs must contain at least one node from which new roots and stems can be generated. The sprigs are covered with soil by placing them in trenches, topdressing, or discing in, then packed securely. Since sprigging requires aggressive stolons or rhizomes, it is primarily a method of propagating warm-season grasses.

Plugging, similar to sprigging, requires spreading by means of stolons or rhizomes. Small pieces of sod are transplanted and then allowed to grow together to form a turf. Plugs can be installed in an existing lawn, eventually spreading throughout the lawn and changing the variety of grass.

Overseeding is successful only when the seed can be sufficiently covered by soil. Discing to provide slots or aeration to provide holes, followed by power raking, can provide an adequate seedbed.

SUMMARY QUESTIONS

1. What is the distinction between a warm-season grass and a cool-season grass?
2. Which classification of grasses is most conducive to activities requiring a closely cropped lawn?
3. Which propagation method results in the fastest lawn establishment?
4. Which lawn propagation methods are considered to be asexual?
5. Why should cultivation be done to a deeper depth if two types of soil are present in the top six inches?
6. On a grassy area, how much slope is required to drain an area 140' in length?
7. Why should hand-graded areas be more finely texturized than tractor-graded areas?
8. Why should grass seed be planted fairly shallow when water is available?
9. Why is it necessary to pack seed into the ground with a roller?
10. Why should the first watering of a new seedbed be fairly heavy?
11. Why is it better to water a new seedbed with a sprinkler than by hand?
12. Why does a nitrogen deficiency often show up quickly in a newly seeded lawn?

13. Why is it necessary to achieve close contact between the root mass of sod and the ground beneath it?

14. Why is frequent watering necessary to a newly sodded area?

15. What is a stolon?

16. What is a rhizome?

17. How many plugs can be obtained from a square yard of sod, if the plugs are 4″ square?

18. Why is broadcasting seed onto a snow-covered lawn area not usually a successful overseeding practice?

CHAPTER 3
Landscaping Construction

Landscaping operations often offer a wide range of services, including some construction work. Landscape construction is the erection of any structure that enhances the usefulness and beauty of a landscaped area. The development of a landscape may include the construction of patios, retaining walls, fences, decks, or other features that are an integral part of an outdoor living scheme. In this chapter, we will discuss the design and construction of such structures. Landscapers often subcontract such light construction work, but in some cases it might be necessary for the landscaper to do the work himself in order to achieve the quality or type of construction desired. Although some landscapers would prefer not to do this type of work, others find it a good way to stretch their seasons beyond the limitations of planting.

Retaining Walls

Retaining walls are structures that eliminate or minimize the slope in an area and provide for the proper direction of water drainage. Properly planned, retaining walls can create a series of relatively flat places where a slope formerly existed. The usefulness and beauty of an area can be greatly enhanced by the careful design and construction of retaining walls.

Surveys and Surveying Instruments

The design of retaining walls is dictated by the terrain. Normally, a survey of some type is required. A survey is a system that allows the plotting of the relative elevations in a given area of land. Surveying instruments, which allow level sighting by the surveyor, are used to sight a target rod with gradations written on it. As the target rod is moved from one location to another, different numbers will appear through the sighting device; that is, the target is changing elevations while the sighting device remains on a level sightline.

The *builder's level* is the most commonly used sighting device for simple elevation surveys. This device consists of a telescope, mounted on a tripod, that can be leveled by adjusting leveling bubbles mounted on the base of the telescope. Adjustment screws allow minute adjustments to be made until the instrument is level constantly as it is rotated 360° on the tripod. When the instrument is level in all directions, the sightings through the builder's level will always be on a level line, no matter how far away the sighting might be. A target rod accompanies the builder's level, which is graded in standard units of measurement, normally feet, that are further broken down into either inches or tenths of feet. Some of these target rods are graded on the metric system. As sightings are made through the builder's level, they are recorded on the target rod. At least two persons are required to make a survey of elevations, one to make the sightings through the builder's level, and one to maneuver the target rod to various locations. A builder's level and a target rod are shown in Figure 3–1.

A *transit* is a more sophisticated sighting device and can be used for a variety of purposes. For example, it can be used to measure angles when establishing rooflines and to indicate a level sighting in an elevation survey.

A *hand level* is a telescopic device, small enough to fit in a pocket, that can also be used for elevation surveys. Inside this device there is a

Figure 3-1. Surveying tools. The builder's level, mounted on its tripod, and the target rod are used together.

bubble that indicates a level sighting. The surveyor simply adjusts the device up or down until the bubble he is looking through indicates that his sighting is level. This instrument is less accurate than either a builder's level or a transit because it is hand held, which allows it to move up and down more, and because its magnification is not as great. An example of the hand level is shown in Figure 3–2.

To conduct an elevation survey, the area must first be plotted on a grid system. The grids might be 10' apart, 20' apart, or any dimension decided upon, as long as the grids are consistent and the locations of the sightings can be easily relocated at a later time. In a backyard, for example, sightings might be taken on a 10' square grid over the entire backyard, with at least one row of sightings extending straight back from

Figure 3-2. A landscaper using a sight level. A bubble inside tells him when he is sighting level.

one corner of the house. Later, those sightings can easily be relocated by again measuring a grid from the same corner of the house. To make such a survey, the sighting instrument must be set up and leveled in a location that will allow the unimpeded sighting of any spot in the backyard. The survey crew then places the target rod in a vertical position on each of the spots where the predetermined grid lines intersect. Then they sight the elevation through the instrument and record each reading. The higher the number recorded, the lower the elevation of that particular spot because, again, all sightings are level. Conversely, the lower the elevation of the ground, the higher the sighting on the target rod.

Each grid intersection is sighted and recorded in the area to be surveyed by the same method, without moving the sighting instrument. Then a benchmark is selected, sighted, and recorded.

A *bench mark* is a point of permanent elevation, such as a patio, sidewalk, or curb. The establishment of such a bench mark allows a permanent reference to be made back to that point. All other elevations in the yard can then be compared to that point. The sighting taken at the bench mark is referred to as the *height of instrument.* The height of instrument is a figure used in the conversion of sightings to *sea level elevations.* (Sea level elevations indicate the relative height of a particular spot in relation to the nearest ocean.) As mentioned earlier, sightings made on a target rod will result in readings that are higher for lower elevations. Most surveys, however, are converted to sea level elevations, which are lower as the elevations decrease, and higher as the elevations increase. Such recorded elevations are called *topographical maps.*

A *topographical map* shows the relative contours of a plot of ground. *Contours* are points of the same elevation connected by continuing lines.

To complete a simple survey of a backyard for the design of retaining walls, it is not necessary to know the actual sea level elevation of that yard, but it is best to convert all sightings to relative elevations. This can be accomplished by assigning an arbitrary elevation to the spot selected as the bench mark. For example, if a backyard is being surveyed, a step down to a patio might serve as the bench mark if the tread of that step is of consistent elevation. Arbitrarily, the surveyor might assign an elevation of 100' to that spot. All other sightings made in that backyard will relate to that spot, by being either higher in elevation or lower in elevation. Then all sightings taken must be converted to relative elevations.

The calculation of relative elevations involves the subtraction of each sighting from the height of instrument sighting defined earlier, with the

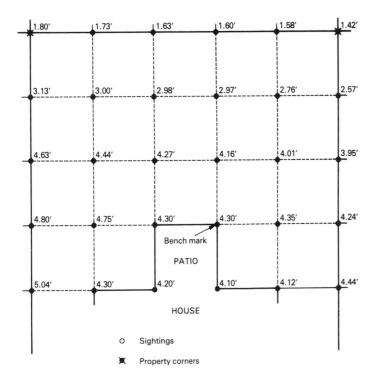

Figure 3-3. Raw sightings from a backyard survey.

result being added to the elevation of the bench mark. For example, the bench mark is sighted through a builder's level at 5.10′ and assigned the arbitrary elevation of 100′ above sea level. Another sighting in the yard is sighted at 7.10′ sighting on the target rod. The following calculation would convert the 7.10′ sighting to an elevation that will relate to the bench mark.

$$5.10' \text{ (height of instrument)} - 7.10' \text{ (sighting)} = -2'$$

$$100' \text{ (relative elevation—bench mark)} + - 2' = 98'$$

(relative elevation of the sighting)

Similar calculations are made for each sighting taken on a grid system for the entire backyard to convert the raw sightings into relative elevations. (Higher elevations will be reflected by a higher number, and lower elevations by a lower number.) Contour lines can now be established by connecting points of the same elevation in a continuous line. Examples of one backyard survey are shown in Figures 3–3 and 3–4. From such a survey, the design of retaining walls can be completed.

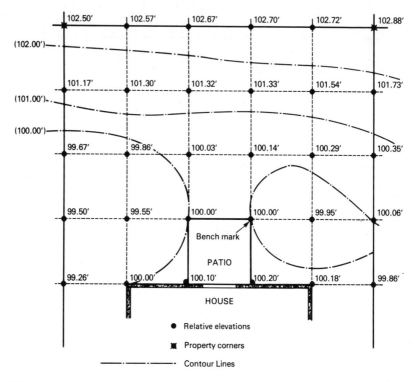

Figure 3-4. Converted relative elevations—from raw sightings in Figure 3-3.

In the survey shown there is a difference of 2.88′ in elevation from the patio—which is the bench mark—to the highest point in the backyard—which is in the upper right-hand corner. The survey also shows a slight degree of slope from the right-hand side of the lot but a greater slope from top to bottom. Figures 3–3 and 3–4 also indicate that there is slope from the patio to the sides of the yard.

The height of instrument is 4.30′, since that was the raw sighting taken on the bench mark. An elevation of 100′ was arbitrarily given to the bench mark.

Design Criteria for Retaining Walls

In this case, one retaining wall, approximately 3′ high, will be sufficient to change the backyard into two relatively level areas, in place of the slope now present. Three criteria must be considered as the wall is designed:

- The shape and substance of the wall
- Positioning of the wall for minimum soil movement
- Drainage of surface water, both above and below the wall

The shape and substance of the wall are partially dictated by the other two factors. The wall must follow a certain shape fairly closely, in order to prevent hauling in or hauling out large quantities of soil. The pattern of water drainage above the wall will dictate the shape to a certain extent also. The substance of the wall will primarily depend on the materials available and the aesthetic value of each. The shape of the wall will dictate the materials used somewhat, because certain materials conform more readily to some shapes than others. For example, it is difficult to build a curving wall out of railroad ties laid flat.

In all cases, surface drainage water should be routed to a point behind the wall where it can be released. If surface drainage is allowed to run over the top of a wall, it will soon erode the soil immediately behind the wall, and water pressure will build up. When that happens, the water will either be released through the wall, washing away soil, or if the wall is solid, the built-up pressure might force the wall forward, eventually causing its collapse.

The ideal positioning of a wall will allow the amount of soil taken out from in front for the base of the wall to be placed up above the wall for backfill. The movement of soil either into or out of an area is very expensive and time consuming. In our example, the average high elevations are about 102.70′, and the point at the bench mark is 100′, with a fairly even slope between the two. Thus, the wall should be placed at all points across the yard with an elevation of about a 101.35′, in order to remove the amount of soil needed at the bottom of the wall and place it at the top of the wall. Minor adjustments are usually made in the placement of the wall for cosmetic purposes, but still, the amount of soil removed at the base may be used at the top.

Adequate movement of surface water requires at least a 2% slope on a grassy surface. Since the lot in our example is 50′ wide, (10′ between sightings), it would require a total of 1′ of drop to make the surface water flow from one side of the lot to the other. Looking at the topographical map in Figure 3–4, we see that this would be possible, because from a high point of 102.88′ in the upper right-hand corner to 101.17′ in the second reading from the top on the left-hand side is a drop of 1.71′. However, other considerations must be made. If the surface drainage is run totally to one side of the lot, the levelness of the upper area will be minimized. Also, a retaining wall looks much better if its top is level or drops periodically into level stages, instead of gently sloping. It is more difficult to make the wall level on the top if the entire drainage above it goes in one direction. There must be a sizeable drainage ditch behind the wall in such a case.

One solution is to divide the drainage of the upper level, sending half of it in one direction and the remaining half in the other direction. Wherever possible, this gives a much nicer look to the yard and elimi-

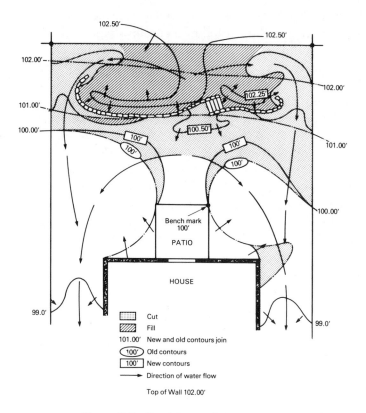

Figure 3-5. Retaining wall design.

nates much of the erosion danger, because only half as much water is
running down each side of the property. The same possibilities exist for
surface drainage below the retaining wall. In Figure 3–4 splitting the
drainage is the natural way of things anyway, since the elevations are
lower on each side of the patio.

Figure 3–5 shows a practical design for a retaining wall from the
survey completed earlier, along with the corresponding new contour
lines showing the newly graded areas.

The retaining wall design is simple yet effective. The surface drainage
will split in the middle of the upper level as well as the lower level, and
the amount of soil removed at the base of the wall will be utilized above
the wall, most of it being placed immediately behind the wall. The small
hooks at each end of the wall help keep the top of the wall level. A set of
steps is included in the middle of the wall for access to the top level.

Retaining walls can be built from any number of materials, but rock,
posts, railroad ties, and wood are used most frequently by landscapers.
The differences in construction merit attention.

Rock Retaining Walls

Two basic methods are used to construct rock retaining walls. *Mortared rock walls* are solid, with mortar sealing all of the joints between the rocks. *Dry walls* are built by stacking the rocks without the benefit of any sealing substance.

Mortared walls require a concrete footing, extending below the frost line, which is solid enough to prevent settling and any heaving caused by freezing and thawing. (Heaving action will cause a solid wall to crack.) Footings should be wider than the wall on top of them and should be reinforced with steel.

To further strengthen solid, mortared walls, small sections of footing and wall are usually run perpendicular to the wall, back into the grade. These are called *deadmen*, and their purpose is to provide a counter-balance to the pressure of the backfill against the wall, preventing the wall from leaning forward. Figure 3–6 is a schematic end view of a mortared wall, including the footing and the deadman.

For additional structural support, small holes are normally left or drilled at the bottom of the wall. These holes, called *weepholes*, allow water that might build up behind the wall to drain out, thereby preventing any pressure buildup. They should always be included in any kind of a solid wall.

The use of mortar in a rock wall permits greater freedom of design

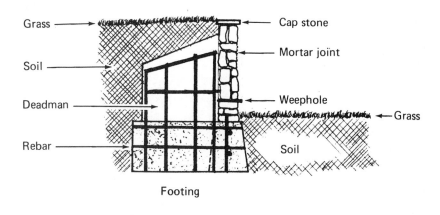

END VIEW

Figure 3-6. Mortared rock wall.

than does a dry wall, because more different types of rock may be used in the construction. Walls may be of formal design, using a cut stone of even sizes, or informal, using uneven fieldstone or cut rubble stone. Figures 3–7, 3–8, and 3–9 show just three of the many styles of mortared rock walls. The laying of the stone is a practiced art, with styles determining the method of construction. Whereas cut stone must be layed in level layers, and each layer must be tied together by alternating the vertical mortar joints, fieldstone must be layed more by rock selection to fit a given area in the wall.

The mortar mix used for rock walls should be about three parts fine clean sand to one part masonry cement. Masonry can be mixed either by hand or by mixer, but the consistency is very important. If large rock is being used, the mix must be fairly stiff to support the weight of the rock. As the rock is being placed, mortar in generous portions is spread on all surfaces as well as on the surfaces of rocks with which it will come into contact. This is known as "buttering" the stone. As the stone is settled into the proper position, the excess mortar will be squeezed out of the mortar joint and can be cleaned off and reused in the placement of other stones. Later, after the mortar in the joint has partially hardened, the joint can be cleaned up and troweled evenly.

Brick walls can be built in the same manner. In all cases the wall must be constructed plumb (straight up and down), and courses must be run in a straight line. The straight line is most easily held by setting string

Figure 3-7. A mortared rock wall built in even layers with equal size rocks.

lines to follow with the face of the rock or brick, while the plumb of the wall is checked periodically with a carpenter's level.

Figure 3-8. A mortared rock wall built in even layers but with unequal size rocks.

Figure 3-9. A mortared rock wall with uneven layers and different sizes of rocks.

Dry Rock Walls

As mentioned earlier, dry rock walls are constructed without benefit of any cementing substance. Consequently, the structure must be quite different to provide strength to the wall. The secret to the construction of a sound dry wall is building the face of the wall at such an angle that the soil behind will support the weight of the wall, while the weight of the rock will keep the soil in its proper place. The angle on the front of the wall is known as the *batter*. The minimum batter of a dry rock wall is 2″ of lean for each 1′ in height. For each 1′ in height, the face of the wall must move back toward the soil being retained by at least 2″.

Since there is no cementing agent between the rocks, there is no danger of a dry wall cracking. The rocks are free to move, independent of each other. For this reason, there is no need for any footing under the wall. A firm, solid base, between 6″ and 1′ below the surface of the soil will suffice for this type of wall. It is *extremely* important that the base of the wall be wide enough to accommodate the amount of batter on the front of the wall and still be at least perpendicular with the back of the wall at the top. The bottom of the trench dug for the base of a dry wall should be lined with at least 2″ of sand or fine gravel to allow for slight settling as the wall is built.

Since no cement agent is used, small "chalk" rocks are required to level and solidify the rocks as they are placed. Chalk rocks are normally most suitable if they are thinner at one end than the other and if they can be driven solidly into place. As the wall is built, it is vital that each rock be made solid before other rocks are placed on top. Soil is sometimes packed between rocks, but freezing and thawing will tend to make that soil "sluff,"(fall out) over a period of time. Placing soil between layers of rock also encourages the growth of weeds and grass out of the wall.

In Figure 3–10, notice that behind the wall the soil is rolled up slightly, so water drainage does not run over the top of the wall. This is imperative for a dry wall because water running through the wall can loosen it and cause its subsequent collapse.

The "courses," or layers of rock in a dry wall, must be tied together for strength. Each rock placed should provide weight to at least two rocks in the layer below. Notice in Figure 3–11 how each layer of rock is tied to the layer below and above it.

Rock walls are strong, beautiful, and functional, particularly since they can be built to conform to almost any lines of design. Under normal circumstances, dry walls are less expensive to build than mortared walls.

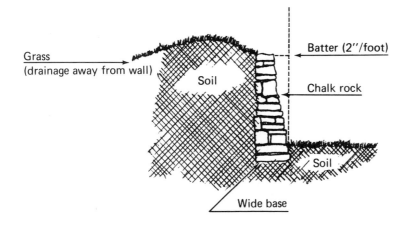

Grass
(drainage away from wall)

Batter (2''/foot)

Soil

Chalk rock

Soil

Wide base

END VIEW

Figure 3-10. Dry rock wall.

Figure 3-11. Dry limestone retaining walls.

Post Walls

Post walls present a very unique appearance and have become quite popular. Many variations exist because of the different sizes and types of posts available. Generally this type of wall should be limited to 4′ in height or less, although taller walls can be built out of large diameter poles.

In a post wall, the wall and the footing are a continuous unit. A trench is dug, into which the bottom of the posts are placed. The posts are then plumbed in each direction, and the trench is filled with concrete. The posts can be held in the proper place by nailing a strap along the back edge, then periodically securing the posts as a unit with diagonal braces fore and aft. It is helpful to make the trench a little deeper than necessary and the poles correspondingly longer than the concrete depth needs to be. Then some soil can be tamped around the bottom of the posts, which will help hold them in place until the concrete sets. The backfill should not be placed behind the wall until the concrete has had time to thoroughly cure. An end view, showing the construction features of a typical post wall, is shown in Figure 3–12.

For the necessary strength, the amount of post beneath the soil's surface should approximate the amount of post above the surface. A 3′ tall wall should have at least 2½′ of post below the ground, with a 2′ deep collar of concrete around it. The collar should also be of equal thickness on each side of the wall and must be at least 6″ wide (or wider for tall walls) on each side.

The size of the posts will be dictated by the height and length of the wall. Generally, the shorter the wall, the smaller the diameter of the

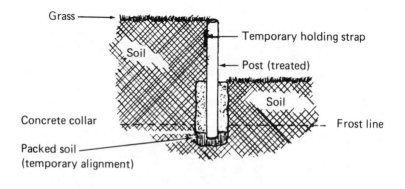

END VIEW

Figure 3-12. Post wall.

posts, but no posts should have less than a 3″ diameter for proper strength.

Because of the unevenness of the posts, there is no need to drill weepholes in a post wall. Small cracks will occur between the posts that will serve this purpose.

Posts, like any other wood surface that is to be placed into contact with the soil, must be treated chemically to prevent damage by termites, rot organisms, or other sources of deterioriation. Even redwood, which resists these pests, will last much longer if properly treated.

Creosote, which is the sticky black substance usually present in quantity in used railroad ties, is an excellent preservative, though difficult to work with because of its tarlike qualities. Creosote contains approximately 15% coal tar neutral oil, 35% petroleum asphalt, and 50% petroleum oil. When creosote is cool, it becomes very thick and cannot be readily absorbed. It should be heated to a temperature of at least 90°F in order to be properly absorbed into wood. By placing a can of creosote, with the lid removed, in a larger can of heated water, the creosote can be heated safely.

Penta-treatments, which contain between 4% and 5% pentachloro-

Figure 3-13. A vertical post wall.

phenol as the active ingredient, can also be used for wood treatment and are probably easier to work with than creosote. These treatments are more easily absorbed at low temperatures than creosote, but still work better at a temperature of 50°F or higher.

While both types of wood preservatives are somewhat effective when brushed on wood, they provide more protection if allowed to thoroughly soak into the wood. The wood should be placed into a bath of the wood preservative for 12 to 48 hours for thorough penetration. A good way to treat posts, for example, is to cap a length of PVC or other type of pipe, placing the capped end on the floor. Then the bottom portion of the pipe can be filled with the preservative, and the posts soaked inside of the pipe for the prescribed length of time. Other similar types of baths can be constructed for different purposes.

Railroad Tie Walls

Railroad ties, though difficult to cut and handle, make excellent retaining walls, particularly where a rustic effect is desired. Most ties used for this purpose are several years old, having been removed from abandoned tracks or sidings. New ties, though they can be used, are generally more expensive and have such liberal coatings of creosote that they present a constant hazard to clothing and carpets.

Horizontal railroad tie walls are built in similar fashion to dry rock walls; that is, they are built in layers, with each course being tied to the

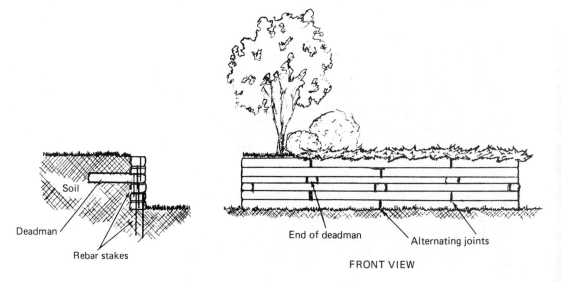

FRONT VIEW

Figure 3-14. Horizontal railroad tie wall.

ones below and above it. Ties are usually anchored together by long spikes or pieces of steel reinforcing rods, often called *rebars*. These rebars are traditionally used to strengthen concrete. Holes can be drilled partially through the top tie to facilitate driving the spikes or lengths of rebar. It is often advisable, particularly in a tall wall, to extend a part of a tie back into the grade periodically, perpendicular to the wall, to serve as a deadman. Typical construction of a horizontal railroad tie wall is shown in Figure 3–14.

Each tie should be anchored to those below it in at least two, and preferably three, places. If a rebar is used, it is possible to drive it completely through the tie below and on into the next one.

In lieu of a deadman anchoring system, tie walls can be built using batter as in dry rock walls. The face of each tie is moved back one or two inches behind the one below it. Backfilling should be done as the wall is built, and the soil should be very firmly packed.

Figure 3-15. A horizontal railroad tie wall.

Figure 3-16. A vertical railroad tie retaining wall. Notice that the tops were cut unevenly, at angles, for interest.

Railroad ties can also be used for vertical walls, in which case the construction is the same as that used for post walls. The tops of such walls can be varied to present an interesting design by cutting the end square, slanting the cuts, or making the tops uneven.

Railroad ties are extremely difficult to cut because they contain bits of gravel and often metal. Cutting them is hard on any saw. Chainsaws, large circular saws, or large crosscut saws are the types most commonly used. When designing a railroad tie wall, try to minimize the number of cuts that will be needed.

Wooden Retaining Walls

Wooden retaining walls are usually made of redwood or rough cedar. These woods weather best in contact with soil and can be used without painting the exterior face, if desired. It is always wise, however, to treat those wood faces that come into contact with the soil with a wood

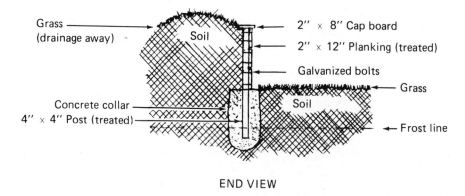

Grass (drainage away)
Soil
2″ × 8″ Cap board
2″ × 12″ Planking (treated)
Galvanized bolts
Grass
Soil
Concrete collar
4″ × 4″ Post (treated)
Frost line

END VIEW

Figure 3-17. Wooden retaining wall.

preservative. Wood offers a great deal of flexibility from a design standpoint, but the basic construction is similar in each case.

Support for a wooden retaining wall normally comes from posts anchored in the ground with concrete. The size of these posts depends on the height of the wall, but they should be at least 4″ × 4″ and should be set in the ground with at least 2′ extending below the frost line. Bolted to the posts are 2″ × 12″ planks. Recommended spacing of posts is 3′ maximum for a 2′ high wall, 2½′ for a 3′ high wall, and 2′ for a 4′ wall. Four feet is the maximum height recommended for a wooden wall. Bolts used in these walls should always be galvanized to resist rusting. Figure 3–17 shows the end view of a typical wooden retaining wall of very simple construction.

To enhance or vary the appearance of a wooden retaining wall the posts can be placed on the outside of the wall. This results in an even stronger structure. Also the size of the posts and the width of the planking boards can be varied. One-inch boards can be nailed to the outside of the planking to create the look of diagonal siding. It is important to note that one-inch boards cannot serve as the planking, however, because they do not have the strength to withstand the pressure of the backfill.

Planking should be put on with some space between boards, so excess water can seep out from behind the wall. Even so, it is advisable to drill weepholes about every 4′ in the base of the wall. Otherwise, when water builds up behind the wall, the boards will swell and the gap between the planking may temporarily swell shut.

Two bolts should be put in each plank as it intersects with each post. This ensures that the planks will not warp as they weather.

Figure 3-18. Wooden retaining walls built with redwood. Note the tiny weepholes at the bottom of the wall in the foreground.

Patios and Sidewalks

Properly designed and carefully constructed patios and sidewalks add to the usefulness and aesthetic value of any landscape. Patio size should be of paramount importance. Many times a builder will construct a beautiful house, and, expensive as it is, he will pour a 10′ × 12′ concrete patio behind it. Place a picnic table in the middle of it and there is no more room! When designing a patio, each piece of furniture should be planned for in advance, and plenty of room allowed for free circulation among the pieces of furniture. The patio must be kept in scale with the furniture, flower pots, or other intended accessories to ensure that the area has a comfortable appearance. Other considerations include the amount of entertaining planned for the area, and whether the patio will be used as an access route to the house on a regular basis. Obviously, the more entertaining and the larger the groups being entertained, the larger the patio must be. Regular access to the house via the patio will demand a more open and direct route from the yard to the door. An old rule of thumb is to plan 125 square feet for each family member, but this is only valid if all of these other factors are considered at the same time. The patio should be viewed as an outdoor room and should be planned in the same way that an interior room would be.

The spaces around the patio must be considered also. Packing shrubbery, retaining walls, benches, or other structures around the edge of a patio has the effect of reducing the size of that area. The patio should at least partially open onto a lawn, to accomodate overflow, if necessary.

Many types of materials are available for patio construction. The most commonly used types are concrete, brick, patio blocks, and flagstone. Each type can be made attractive, if the material selected mixes well with materials used on the house and with surrounding area features.

Concrete Patio and Walk Construction

Without doubt, concrete is the most popular surface for patios and walks. Although the use of concrete is often disdained by designers, it is a very useful material and can be quite attractive. If a little imagination is used in design and construction, many variations are possible.

Five steps are involved in pouring a concrete surface: excavation, forming, pouring, finishing, and cleanup. Let us look at each step in detail.

Excavation. Excavation is simply the act of removing the amount of soil necessary to make room for the concrete. For most patios and walks, the concrete is poured to a thickness of 4″. Two inches of sand or fine gravel is usually placed under the concrete to provide a solid base and to allow the concrete to "float" somewhat on the surface. Assuming that the top of the concrete surface is to be the same elevation as the ground level, 6″ of soil would have to be removed to allow for the concrete. This excavation may be done by hand or by machine (depending upon accessibility), but it should be as close to the correct depth as possible. Removal of soil is expensive, and the excess removed must be replaced by sand or concrete, so it is important to be accurate. The subsurface drainage is also an important consideration. Water must not be permitted to collect under the patio or seep into the basement through the foundation. Excavation must extend far enough beyond the boundaries of the patio to allow for the forms to be constructed freely, and enough soil should be left for backfilling after the forms are removed.

Forming. *Forming* is the erection of borders around the patio or walk edges in order to hold the concrete in place until it hardens and provide a means for leveling the surface of the concrete as it is poured. Forms are usually wooden 2″ × 4″ boards for square or rectangular areas, or either 1″ × 4″ boards or ¼″ masonite strips 4″ wide for curved edges. These forms are held in place by stakes, usually 2″ × 2″ or 1″ × 2″, which are driven into the ground and nailed to the forms. All forms are placed on the outside of the area to be concreted, so they can be removed after the concrete hardens, leaving a smooth surface on the edge of the patio or walk. Stakes are placed on the outside of forms, usually 2′ to 3′ apart for 2″ thick forms and as close as 1′ apart on 1″ curving forms.

Since the forms provide the basis for the level of the concrete surface, their elevation must be checked closely. The surface drainage of a concrete area will depend entirely upon the height of the forms at various points. These elevations can be checked by use of a builder's level, transit, or hand level (discussed earlier in this chapter), or they can be checked with a very straight (no warping) 2″ × 4″ board and a carpenter's level. The carpenter's level can be placed on the edge of the board, which is stretched from the top of one form to another. At the lowest form, the edge of the board is elevated until the bubble shows that the carpenter's level is level. The distance from the bottom edge of the board to the top of the form is then measured to see if the elevation has dropped the proper amount for adequate drainage. At least a 1% grade is required for adequate drainage on a concrete surface.

The forming process also includes the preparation of the subsurface of the patio. As mentioned earlier, the addition of 2″ of sand or fine gravel beneath the concrete is desirable. Usually this sand or gravel is watered with a fine spray to thoroughly settle and compact it.

Most concrete structures are reinforced with steel to strengthen them and minimize movement. For patios and sidewalks, this reinforcing is usually accomplished with a 6″ × 6″ wire mesh. Before the concrete is poured, the mesh, which comes in rolls, is cut to fit the area and laid on top of the sand or gravel base. If a patio or walk is poured next to a concrete foundation or adjoining piece of walk, patio, or driveway, it is advisable to drill holes into the existing concrete every two feet and place lengths of ⅜″ rebar into the holes, extending out into the area where the new concrete will be poured. This will help prevent the new concrete from pulling away from the old as ground movement occurs from freezing and thawing. It is also wise to insert a piece of *expansion joint*, which is a felt strip, between old and new concrete to allow expansion and contraction without separation.

Sometimes, forming might include the installation of dividers, which will remain a permanent part of the patio. Normally these are redwood 2″ × 4″ boards, which are placed at heights consistent with the outside forms. Intersections of such dividers are usually made by notching one board halfway up from the bottom and the corresponding board halfway down from the top, so when placed together, the two boards fit snugly and the top of each is equal in height. Six- or eight-penny nails, driven about one-third of the way into the sides of such dividers about 1′ apart, help keep the concrete from pulling away from the dividers. These nails should have a box head on them, and they should be galvanized.

Pouring. Pouring concrete is laborious work, regardless of whether the concrete is hand-mixed, machine-mixed, or ready-mix. The concrete is placed in the preformed area, lifting the mesh so it rests one-third of the way up in the concrete thickness, and tamped to eliminate voids. Next, the concrete must be leveled by a process called *screeding.* A *screed board,* usually a straight 2″ × 4″, which will reach from form to form at the widest point, is selected. The edges of this board are placed on the forms at one end of the area being concreted, with one man at each end of the board. With a back and forth action, the workers move the screed board across the concrete, filling all voids in front of the board and removing the excess concrete as they go. This process is usually repeated two or three times, until the concrete is properly compacted and its surface even. Now, the workers must wait until the concrete chemically sets sufficiently to be finished.

Figure 3-19. Screeding freshly poured concrete. Note that the area has been divided by a temporary form to make screeding more manageable.

Finishing. Unfinished concrete is unattractive and not nearly as strong as finished concrete. Finishing may be done in several ways. For example, concrete can be float finished, trowel finished, broom finished, or it can have an exposed aggregate finish. Actually, it might be more proper to state that these are stages of finish because floating is a prerequisite to a trowel finish, and both floating and troweling are prerequisites to a broom finish.

After concrete has been poured and screeded, it has a wet, somewhat shiny appearance until it begins to cure. When it begins to lose this shiny appearance, it is ready for the first stages of finishing. *Floating* is a process by which moisture is brought up through the concrete, and the concrete is further settled and compacted. A wooden or metal device, known as a *float*, is moved over the surface several times, usually in a circular motion, until the surface is a consistent series of bubbly and very moist ridges. Since the concrete cures fastest along the outside edges, floating begins along the edges where the first concrete was poured.

Edging should begin when the floating is well underway or as it is finished. *Edgers* are metal devices that allow the concrete to be formed into gently rounded edges along the forms. (See Figure 3–20.) This process gives a neat appearance to the concrete and also helps eliminate crumbling.

Troweling is a process by which floated concrete is made very smooth and somewhat shiny. *Metal trowels,* which are flat instruments, are used in much the same fashion as floats; that is, when the floated concrete begins to lose its sheen, metal trowels are used, first at the edges, starting at the end first poured. *Power trowels,* which are large, motor-driven machines, are useful for large expanses of concrete. The concrete must cure longer to enable these machines to be used.

Large pieces of concrete surfacing are subject to cracking. In order to control the location and results of this cracking, *score marks* are drawn periodically in the concrete slab. A *score marker* is a metal device that has a V-shaped projection down its center, usually about ⅜" deep. To score a slab of concrete, a straight 2" × 4", or some other straight edge, is laid across the slab from form to form. The score marker is run across the slab, keeping one edge of the marker tight against the straight edge. This results in the formation of a ⅜" deep trench in the concrete, with gently sloped edges. This score mark weakens the concrete at that point, causing the cracks that inevitably follow any weakness. But instead of a bunch of ugly, wandering cracks, the concrete will be broken up by a group of decorative score marks. Score marks are usually placed every 8'

Figure 3-20. Assorted tools for working concrete. Floats, trowels, edgers, score markers, knee pads, and a shovel with a notch cut in the lower edge are shown. The notch is used to hook re-mesh and pull it up into the concrete.

Figure 3-21. Troweling concrete to a smooth finish.

to 10′ in patios, although the distance can vary for design purposes. For walks, distances between score marks are normally 3′ to 5′.

Broom finishes are often used for decorative purposes or to afford better traction on a trowel-finished piece of concrete. (Trowel finishes make the concrete surface stronger and more resistant to weathering than float finishes, but the result is a slick surface with poor traction.) The process is begun as a troweled piece of concrete begins to set, but before it gets hard. The broom is drawn lightly over the surface, either in a straight line or in gentle swirls, digging small grooves with its brushes. Excess concrete should be cleaned from the bristles before each pass is made.

Exposed aggregate finishes are those with a pebbly aggregate protruding from the surface of the concrete. There are two ways to achieve this effect. If desired, the aggregate may be used as an ingredient in the concrete mix in place of the gravel normally used, or an amount of the aggregate may be "seeded" on the top of the screeded concrete and packed into the surface. Either way, the aggregate is worked into the concrete surface, and the floating process serves to cover the aggregate completely with concrete.

As the concrete begins to set, a washing and brushing process is begun: a very fine spray of water, coupled with a light brushing, removes some of the concrete on the surface and exposes portions of the aggregate rocks. Less than half of the individual rocks should be uncovered, or they will subsequently loosen, come out, and leave holes in the surface. Aggregate rocks are usually rounded, water-worn pebbles, sufficiently colorful to contrast well with the concrete. Sharp, pointed rocks will not hold well in the surface, nor are they pleasant to walk on.

Brick and Patio Block Patios and Walls

Paving bricks, like those seen in old city streets built before the advent of asphalt and concrete, make excellent patios and walks. Other brick-type blocks, such as colored patio blocks made from a concrete material, involve the same type of construction. All materials of this type can either be constructed dry (without concrete) or mortared (using a concrete binding). We will discuss both methods.

Dry brick or block patios and walls. In the initial excavation and forming phases, dry brick or block patios and walks are constructed much like concrete structures. Because of the need to conform to the length and width of the bricks or blocks, however, the length of all forms must be determined by measuring the size of the materials accurately, or physically laying out courses of them on the subgrade. If this is not done, many bricks or blocks will have to be cut in order to conform to the size of the forms. This results in unnecessary work and a less pleasing appearance.

Sand or gravel fill can be used on the subgrade, but fine gravel has an advantage because it provides firmer resistance when weight is placed on one corner of a brick or block. The gravel used should be of a fine

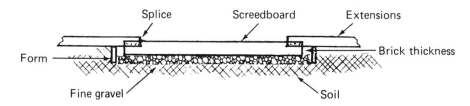

Figure 3-22. Special screed board for subgrade screeding.

consistency so it will pack well. To make a patio of this type absolutely even, it is best to screed the subgrade gravel. This can be accomplished by cutting a screed board that is about 1' short of reaching the forms on either side. Short boards are then nailed to each end of the screed board so that when these short boards are placed on the forms, the screed board will extend down into the patio area the depth of the bricks or blocks, minus ⅛". When screeded, the surface of the gravel will allow the bricks or blocks to extend ⅛" higher than the top of the forms. When the bricks or blocks are thoroughly settled, they will be level with the top of the forms. To prevent outside bricks or blocks from collapsing, the outside forms are made of redwood and installed permanently.

After the forms are placed and the gravel packed and screeded, the bricks or blocks are placed in a predetermined pattern, taking care that each one is level as placed. Fine sand is then worked between the bricks or blocks by sweeping with a broom and watering with a fine mist. It will be necessary to sweep the sand across the surface several times, followed by fine watering, to thoroughly fill the voids. In subsequent weeks following construction, the sweeping and watering processes should be repeated as the settling continues. The patio's strength and solidity depends on the proper packing of the subbase and the thorough filling of the joints. Soil sterilant can be applied to the subbase and to the surface of the patio to prevent weed and grass growth between the blocks or bricks for a long term if desired, or the surface can be periodically sprayed with a contact killer as the weeds appear.

Brick or block patios can be built in many different patterns, each of

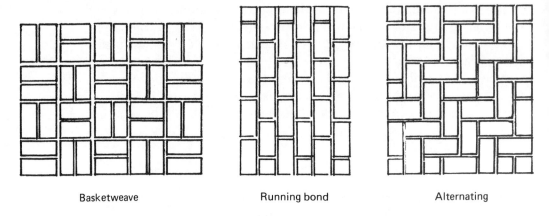

| Basketweave | Running bond | Alternating |

Figure 3-23. Patterns for brick patios.

Figure 3-24. A dry brick patio built in a running bond pattern.

which results in a different appearance and texture. Three popular patterns using *modular* bricks—those that are twice as long as they are wide—are represented in Fig. 3–23.

Mortared brick or block patios and walks. Brick or block patios and walks with mortared joints are built by first constructing a concrete patio in place of the subgrade. This patio can be float-finished and left fairly rough in texture, so the mortar placed on top of it will adhere well.

The bricks or blocks are then mortared into place, using any of the patterns available for dry patios, with a thin layer of mortar beneath the bricks or blocks, as well as on all sides. The mortar joints are finished as the mortar begins to set. These patios tend to be somewhat stronger than dry brick or block surfaces because of the strength of the concrete subgrade, but they are also proportionately more expensive.

Flagstone Patios and Walks

Types of flagstone vary considerably from one part of the country to another. Generally, flagstones are flat pieces of rock, cut to the same thickness, but quite irregular in shape. The varying colors and shapes of flagstone make it a natural for a patio or walk surface.

Flagstone patios, like brick patios, can be constructed either dry or with mortar. The construction methods are the same, except that the irregular sizes and shapes of the flagstone dictate some changes. The edges of a flagstone patio should be constructed first in order to ensure fairly straight lines. Then the work proceeds toward the middle. (Brick

Figure 3-25. A flagstone patio.

patios normally start at one end, and the work proceeds toward the other.) Flagstones can be broken as necessary to provide pieces to finish the center of the patio or walk. Because flagstone is irregularly shaped, the joints between individual pieces will also be irregular. (On a brick or block patio the joints are uniform.) The arrangement of these irregular pieces and the corresponding irregular joints between them can contribute greatly to the appearance of the surface.

Flagstone patio construction methods are also used in the construction of slate surfaces. Slate is normally thinner and more brittle, so it must be handled with caution.

Fences

Fences are of two general types: privacy and enclosure. Privacy fences must be solid enough to preclude an open view into or out of a private area. Enclosure fences are merely designed to prevent access to or exit from an area. Obviously, a privacy fence may also serve as an enclosure. Wood fences are normally best suited for privacy, while chainlink fences are very popular for enclosure purposes.

Wood Fences

Every fence must have a structural framework. Some wood fence designs allow for the framework to be covered and, therefore, are referred to as *two-sided fences*. Others, with the framework covered on only one side, are referred to as *one-sided fences*. Let us examine the construction methods of some of each.

Solid one-sided privacy fences. A *solid, vertical board fence* is one that has vertical boards all on the same side of the framework. The framework consists of posts and rails. Normally, the space between posts is 8'. Either two or three rails, to which the fencing is nailed, extend between the posts. These fences are normally either 5' or 6' tall, and the boards on the fence can be any width, up to 12". Posts should be at least 4" × 4", and should be 7' long for a 5' fence, and 8' long for a 6' fence. The rails should be 2" × 4".

The first step in building a solid, vertical board fence is to set the posts. Holes for the post should be 8" to 10" in diameter for a 4" × 4" post. Posts should extend into the ground below the frost line. They must be aligned with others in the same row and plumbed in both directions before the concrete is poured around them. To align the posts horizontally, the corner posts are set first and braced plumb with the help of a carpenter's level. Two diagonal braces nailed temporarily to the posts and angled into the ground will hold the corner posts in place. A taut string line, drawn between the two corner posts, will provide a line to follow in setting the other posts. Each post should be similarly plumbed with a carpenter's level and supported with two diagonal braces. When all of the posts have been plumbed in a straight line, the holes are filled with concrete. After the concrete is tamped securely around each post, it must be given adequate time in which to cure before further work is done on the fence.

Rails can be installed either vertically, with the 4″ dimension of the rail extending up and down, or horizontally, with the 4″ dimension extending across the width of the fence. A vertical position provides more strength to support the weight of the fence, while a horizontal position provides more lateral strength against wind. In either case, it is wise to cut notches ¼″ deep into the posts at the point of rail attachment. Allowing the rails to extend ¼″ into the post is good insurance against the rail slipping downward. Galvanized nails are used to secure the rails to the posts. If the rails are positioned vertically, two rails are necessary for a 5′ fence, and three rails for a 6′ fence. When rails are installed horizontally, three rails should be used for both 5′ and 6′ fences. Horizontal and vertical positioning of rails are shown in Fig. 3–26.

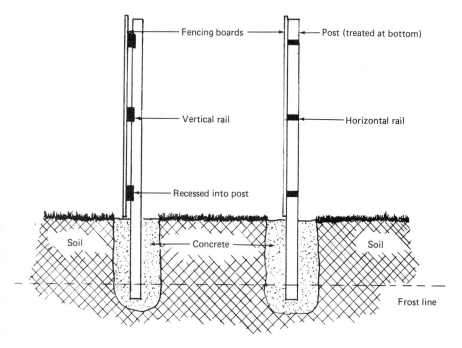

Figure 3-26. Positioning of rails.

If two rails are used on a 5′ fence, the bottom rail should be placed 1′ above the bottom of the fencing boards, and the top rail 1′ below the top of the fencing boards, with a 3′ gap between them. If three rails are used, the bottom rail should be 6″ above the bottom of the fencing boards, the top rail 6″ below the top of the fencing boards, and the middle rail should be located halfway between the bottom and top rails, regardless of whether the fence is 5′ or 6′ tall.

The fencing is begun at each end or corner post. One board is attached to each post at the proper height. (Make sure the board is plumb.) A string line can then be attached between these top boards to provide a quick reference for height on the remaining boards. On a long stretch of fence, intermediate boards will have to be placed to support the string line and minimize sag. The cutting of a spacer block, which is the thickness of the desired spacing between boards, is also desirable. Each fencing board can be placed on the fence quickly and easily, using the string line at the top as a guide to the height, and the spacer block as a guide to the spacing. One nail can be quickly driven into the top rail and one into the bottom rail to hold the boards satisfactorily until they are all placed. The nailing can be completed easily later. To prevent

Figure 3-27. A solid, one-sided, vertical board fence.

warping, each fencing board should be secured with at least one nail on each side of the boards at the points where they intersect with rails. Unless the length of the fence is such that an even number of boards will fill the space, it will be necessary to ripsaw at least one board to fit the final space. If the need to ripsaw is anticipated, it looks better if the final two or three boards are ripped. Then all the boards will be more uniform in size.

If the bottom of a fence must follow a fluctuating terrain, the top of the fence may have to be left uneven until the entire fence is constructed. Then, a level line can be marked across the top of the fence, and each board can be crosscut sawed to level the top of the fence. A fence always looks better if the top is level, at least in increments.

A *solid, horizontal board fence* is also a one-sided fence. The rails are eliminated, however, since the fencing boards can be nailed directly onto the posts. Since the fencing boards are only 1″ thick, the spacing between posts should be reduced from 8′ to 6′ to provide lateral strength against the wind. The horizontal fencing boards should be long enough to encompass three different posts. This will contribute to the strength of the fence and allow the ends of the boards to be joined on alternate posts, which makes a nicer looking fence.

Two-sided wooden privacy fences. A *vertical board-on-board fence* is a two-sided fence, which at least partially hides the framework from view on either side. This type of fence is sometimes called a *shadowbox* fence, because it forms a pattern of shadows caused by alternating fencing boards.

Figure 3-28. Fences can be built in all sorts of imaginative styles.

Figure 3-29. A vertical board-on-board fence. Note the dry rock wall retaining the soil beneath the fence.

The post and rail structure is exactly as described for the solid, vertical board fence. The rails are normally installed in a horizontal fashion, so the fencing boards will also enclose the posts.

Fencing boards are installed on alternating sides of the rails. The result is a fence that looks the same on either side. Because of the 4″ gap between the sides of the fence, the edges of the fencing boards must be overlapped. Otherwise the fence would afford little privacy when viewed at an angle. If 12″ boards are being used, an overlap of 1″ on each edge is usually sufficient, making the effective space covered by each board only 9⅝″. Using a spacer board of 9⅝″ width, it is possible to nail all of the boards on one side of the fence, then the other, as in the procedure described earlier. Another method is for two men to nail on the fencing boards simultaneously, one on each side of the fence.

The construction of *horizontal board-on-board fence* is similar to that of a solid, horizontal board fence, except that, again, the fencing boards

Figure 3-30. A horizontal board-on-board fence.

are alternated on either side of the fence. No rails are necessary, but the spacing of the posts should be reduced, and the boards must overlap to decrease the gap between them.

Another popular type of two-sided fence is the *basketweave*. This fence is a cross between the horizontal board-on-board fence and the solid, horizontal board fence. It requires no rails, and the boards are nailed on in a horizontal fashion. But in this case, the end of a board is nailed to one side of one post, then bent around the other side of the next post, bent again to be nailed to the third post on the same side as the first, and so on, alternating sides. The next board above is nailed to the opposite side of the first post, then subsequently bent around each post so that it is always nailed on the opposite side of a post from the board above it and below it, like the weaving of a basket. In between the posts, where the boards are bent, a small board is placed between the fencing boards and nailed to them. This keeps the bends in the boards consistent and keeps them separated. (See Figure 3–31.)

Figure 3-31. A basketweave privacy fence.

Staining or painting fences. Many fences are constructed using redwood or cedar woods, which weather to a nice dark gray and do not absolutely require a finish. If pine, fir, or other types of lumber are used, it will be necessary to paint or stain the fence to protect the wood.

Linseed oil is an excellent material for preserving wood. Liberal applications of this oil will prevent the wood from drying out, cracking, and splitting and will aid in preserving a consistent appearance. Because of its preservative qualities, linseed oil is also added to oil-based paints.

Paints are often used on fences, particularly those not built with **redwood or cedar. One disadvantage of painting an outside surface is that** the process must be repeated often. Paint will not last long on fences, decks, retaining walls, or other surfaces that are exposed to weathering from all directions. If paint is used, the oil-based paints tend to act as better preservatives than the latex paints because they are readily absorbed by the wood. But the latex paints are easier to work with and to apply.

Stains work well on outdoor surfaces because they soak into the wood and are usually more earthtone in color. *Sealers*, which are a type of stain, are often applied to make the wood weather to a natural gray, while preserving the wood and preventing mildew. Since sealers are nearly clear, they do not need to be reapplied nearly so often as paints. One advantage of stains is that, unlike paints, they will not chip.

Chainlink Fencing

Chainlink fencing is strong, long lasting, and manufactured for easy installation. As with the other fences discussed, setting the posts is the first task. Since the posts are all 2½″ in diameter or less, the size of the holes can be reduced to 4″ to 6″ in diameter. Posts should be set at a depth of 2′, with a concrete collar around them.

Chainlink fencing systems have a piping, called a *toprail*, around the top of the posts. This piping contributes greatly to the strength and stability of the fence. Most contractors set the posts in the ground and attach the toprail before the concrete is poured. This serves to brace the posts while the concrete is setting up.

Figure 3-32. Chainlink fence installation. Attaching mesh to tension bar before stretching.

After the toprail has been attached and the posts set in concrete, the concrete must be allowed to harden before the fence is completed. Mesh can then be stretched on the framework and tied to the posts and toprails with wire ties. The mesh is connected to end or corner posts by slipping tension bars through the ends of the mesh in a weavelike fashion. Clamps are fitted around the corner and end posts and then bolted on the back side of the tension bars. Thus, the tension caused by stretching the fence is absorbed by the tension bar and not by individual loops in the mesh. All parts of a chainlink fence are usually galvanized or covered with vinyl to resist rust.

Rail Fences

One more type of wood fencing warrants attention. Rail fences are not solid enough to keep anyone in or out of a yard. They are primarily decorative in nature. Rail fences can either be *rustic* or *formal*. *Rustic* fences are usually split cedar and are very uneven and rough in texture. Formal rail fences are made from smooth sawed domestic lumber and have a much more regular appearance.

Figure 3-33. A rustic cedar split-rail fence.

Split-rail fences are manufactured in components. Corner, end, and line posts all have the proper holes in them to accept the ends of 10′ rails. Rails are inserted in the posts at the same time the posts are set. The crew starts at one end of the fence, digging holes to set posts as they go. As each post is set, the ends of the rails are inserted. Because the rail ends must be inserted in the posts, it is not possible to set all the posts

Figure 3-34. One of many types of formal rail fences.

and insert the rails later. Split-rail fences come in two- and three-rail heights. Because there is very little wind resistance from a split-rail fence, it is often installed without concrete collars around the posts.

There is little difference between the framework construction of formal rail fences and most of the wood fences discussed earlier, except that, in this case, the framework is the entire fence. Posts are set, usually 10′ apart, and the rails are notched into the posts. Often the rails are the same size as the posts, both being 4″ × 4″, for example. Rail fences are usually not as tall as other wood fences, since they are strictly decorative in nature.

Wooden Decks

Decks and patios serve much the same purpose, but each has certain advantages and limitations that must be considered. Decks can be built at any height (at second-story level, for example), while patios are restricted to the ground level. Decks offer a contrast to patios in texture, color, and type of surface. Water drains through the surface of a deck, so the deck can be built exactly level. But in the construction of a patio, drainage patterns must be carefully considered.

The size of a deck is an important factor. Since a deck is often built high off the ground, it must be self-sufficient; that is, there can be no provision for spillover onto a lawn area. Also, a railing or bench is necessary as a safety precaution. But keep in mind that a railing or bench will further restrict the size of the structure. Planning the size of a deck is similar to planning the size of a room. Consideration must be given to the furniture to be used and to any activities that may be anticipated.

The construction of decks is highly variable because the size, height, and designs are quite different. All decks are only as good as the support under them. This support usually comes from posts or from an extension of floor joists from within a house. If the joists from within the house are to be used, this must be done as the house is being built. The 2″ × 10″ joists that support the flooring in a second story are extended out to as much as 8′ beyond the outer wall of the house. These joists are usually 16″ apart. Since decks are exposed to the weather, redwood is normally used for the joists that will be extended for a deck. Pine or fir will be used for the other floor joists in the house. In order to provide enough strength to support a deck extending 8′ from the wall on the house, a second 2″ × 10″ is nailed alongside the joist, doubling the width, and effectively making each joist a 4″ × 10″. This type of deck is said to be *cantilevered* from the house. If the deck needs to extend further out from the house than 8′, posts must be added on the outer edges to support it. In this case, the deck would no longer be cantilevered.

Decks that are not cantilevered can also be supported by concrete *piles*. A concrete pile is a small diameter core of concrete that extends into the ground below the frost line and has a flat surface on the top. If the height of the deck must extend considerably above the height of the piles, posts must be anchored to the top of the piles. If the deck is to be 1′ or less higher than the piles, ledger plates are bolted to the piles. Usually small angle irons are used to bolt the posts or ledger plates to the concrete piles. Fig. 3–35 shows examples of concrete piles with ledger plates and posts attached.

Notice that the piles are wider at the bottom than at the top. This adds to their stability and prevents any further settling. The ledger plate (i.e., the board extending across the top of the posts) supports the weight of the deck because all of the joists are attached to it, and the decking is supported by the joists. Where the deck attaches to the house is either another set of posts with a second ledger plate, or, if possible, a second ledger plate attached directly to the house. The size of these ledger plates in part determines the number of posts required. Also, whether or not the ledger plate can be attached directly to the house is another factor in determining the number of posts needed. If a 2″ × 10″ or a 2″ × 12″ ledger plate is used with 4″ × 4″ posts, a maximum span of

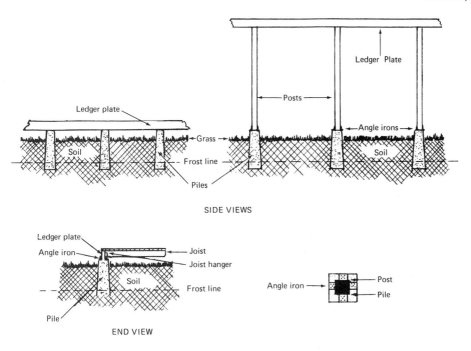

Figure 3-35. Deck supports.

10′ between posts is possible. If smaller ledger plates are used, the span between the posts must be shortened. If the ledger plate near the house wall can be attached directly to the wall by lag screws secured to the foundation or to the floor joists on the house, no posts are required for support. If the ledger plate can be attached to the wall of the house at about every two feet, instead of being secured only at the posts, it will be much stronger. Of course, the ledger plate extending between the posts can be strengthened by doubling its width, making it a 4″ × 10″ or a 4″ × 12″, if excessive sponginess exists.

Joists are hung between the ledger plates, which support the decking, and the length of the span of each joist will determine the size joist required. Joists should be spaced 16″ to 24″ apart for proper floor strength. A 2″ × 6″ joist will span up to 6′, a 2″ × 8″ joist will span up to 8′, and a 2″ × 10″ joist will span up to 10′. Joists can be nailed directly to the ledger plate, which is bolted to the posts or piles, or joist hangers, which are metal U-shaped hangers, can be nailed to the ledger plate to support the joists.

Decking is nailed directly to the joists, usually with galvanized finish nails. The boards should be arranged so splices occur at alternating joists, and care should be exercised to keep the nails in straight lines. These measures enhance the good appearance of the deck. At least two

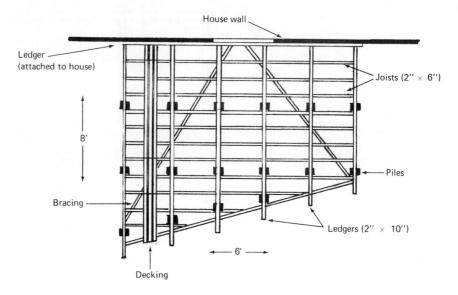

Figure 3-36. Simple deck design.

nails, one in each side of the decking board, should be used at each joist in order to prevent the deck from warping. Decking boards are usually either 2″ × 4″ or 2″ × 6″. The 2″ × 6″ boards are stronger. To ensure proper drainage and to accommodate swelling when the boards become wet, a spacing of ⅛″ to ¼″ between decking boards is recommended.

Different patterns can be made by changing the direction of the decking. Decking can run across the deck, with the deck, diagonally across the deck, or in a herringbone pattern. The joists must be planned to accommodate the decking pattern desired. A simple deck design is shown in Figure 3–36.

Deck Railings

For safety purposes, railings are usually installed on decks that are more than a couple of feet high. They are also used to enhance the beauty of a deck. Railings are normally built 30″ to 36″ high. If posts are used to support the deck, it is possible to extend the posts above the deck to provide corner and intermittent support to the railing, but other short posts, extending from the top of the deck to the top of the railing will be needed also. The spacing of posts on a railing is usually 4′ to 6′. If support posts for the deck are 10′ apart and if they are extended above the deck to become part of the railing, a short post might be added between them, making the spacing between posts on the railing 5′.

Figure 3-37. One of many styles of deck railings.

Railings are constructed in the same fashion as the post and rail structure of a wood fence, except that the top rail is usually placed on top of the posts.

Deck Benches

A bench is sometimes built as a supplementary part of a deck, often substituting for a railing. Deck support posts can be extended above the deck to provide partial support for a bench, with other short posts added. The simplest bench is built by spacing posts every 4′ along the edge of the deck. The posts are set in 6″ from the edge of the decking and measure 14″ to 16″ from the deck surface. Boards, 2″ × 6″ × 18″ are then bolted on each side of the post's top, creating a "saddle" effect. For variation, the lower edges of these boards can be bevelled. When decking boards are nailed on the top of the saddle boards, the result is a bench surface 18″ wide. An example of such a bench is shown in Fig. 3–38.

Another popular bench is the *triangle frame bench*. In this type of bench construction, deck support posts are not used. Instead, a triangle-shaped support is built on top of the decking. A backrest is one valuable feature of this bench.

Supports for the backrest are cut on an angle. They are bolted to the ledger plate on the side of the deck, rising at an angle to a height of 42″

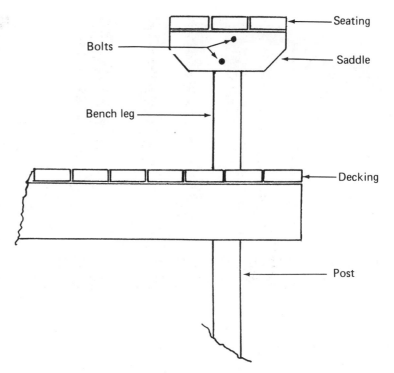

Figure 3-38. Saddle bench—end view.

Figure 3-39. A redwood deck with a saddle bench. Overhead beams are decorative.

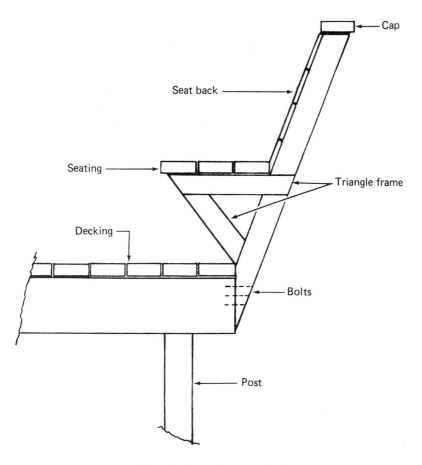

Figure 3-40. Triangle frame bench with backrest.

above the decking. At a height of 16″ above the decking a 2″ × 4″ is bolted onto the backrest support. It extends forward 18″, parallel with the surface of the deck. A third 2″ × 4″ is then cut to connect the end of the 18″ board with the base of the backrest support, at the point where it rises above the surface of the deck. This completed triangle forms a base to which the benching boards can be nailed. Backrest support boards can be nailed to the backrest supports. The tops of the backrest support boards are cut at an angle. This ensures that the cap board, which is nailed to those ends, will lay level. Figure 3–40 is a schematic drawing of such a backrest and bench combination.

Decks can be built in almost any configuration. They need not be limited to square or rectangular shapes. Often, a deck is combined with a patio. The result is not only practical (more space), but esthetically satisfying.

SUMMARY

Landscapers frequently offer construction services. The installation of retaining walls, patios, sidewalks, fences, and wooden decks can be an important aspect of a landscaping operation.

A topographical survey is necessary before a retaining wall can be designed. Instruments commonly used for surveying include the builder's level, the transit, and the sight level. All must be used with a target rod. Each of these devices allows level sighting at all times, so the changing elevations are recorded as the target rod is moved from one location to another.

Surveys are normally made by dividing an area into a grid system and taking sightings at each grid intersection. The sightings are then converted into relative elevations.

Retaining wall design depends upon the consideration of three criteria: the shape and substance of the wall, the positioning of the wall for minimum soil movement, and surface water drainage both above and below the wall. Ideally, the amount of soil removed at the base of a wall to create a fairly flat area will be placed above the wall; soil will not have to be removed from the site or brought in.

Rock retaining walls can be built solid—with mortar in the joints, or dry—with no cementing agent. A mortared wall requires concrete footings, an occasional deadman ballast, and weepholes for drainage. Dry walls depend upon a solid base, the amount of batter put on the front of the wall, and leveling and solidifying of individual rocks with small chalk rocks. *Batter* is a term used to describe the movement of the face of the wall backward as the wall increases in height. A minimum of 2″ batter per foot of height is required for a successful dry rock wall.

Post walls are built by digging a trench, setting posts in the trench in an upright position, plumbing them straight in both directions, and pouring concrete in the trench to hold them in place.

A railroad tie wall gives an excellent rustic appearance. It does not require a footing, but must be securely staked together. It must have an occasional deadman ballast or be stepped back with a batter.

Wooden retaining walls are very flexible in appearance. They should not exceed 4′ in height, and the wood should always be treated with preservative materials to prevent rotting or termite invasion.

In the design of a patio its size, shape, and proposed uses are important considerations. Open space must be maintained around patios to evoke a feeling of spaciousness and to provide for any overflow traffic. Patios and sidewalks are commonly constructed of concrete, bricks or blocks, and flagstone.

Five steps must be followed in the construction of concrete patios and walks: excavation, forming, pouring, finishing, and cleanup. Specialized tools are also required. For example, a screed board is essential when leveling concrete between two forms; floats are used to settle concrete and bring moisture to the top; trowels are necessary to smooth and seal the surface; edgers are used to finish the edges of a slab of concrete; and score markers weaken the concrete so it will crack in an orderly fashion.

Concrete may be float finished, troweled, troweled and broomed, or finished with an exposed aggregate finish. A trowel finish is strongest.

A thoroughly packed gravel base is vital to the success of a dry brick or block patio. Forms must be carefully measured to eliminate any needless cutting of the bricks or blocks. If a brick or block patio is to be mortared, a concrete patio is poured underneath for the subgrade.

In order to maintain a straight line along the edges, a flagstone patio is constructed from the outside edges in. Joints are irregular in size and shape. A flagstone patio also requires a concrete subgrade.

Most fences are built to ensure privacy or to enclose a particular area. Some rail fences (e.g., the split-rail and formal rail) serve only decorative purposes. Privacy fences include the solid vertical board fence; solid horizontal board fence; vertical board-on-board fence; horizontal board-on-board fence; and the basketweave fence. (These can be used for enclosure.) A chainlink fence is used exclusively for enclosure.

One-sided fences, including the solid, vertical board fence and the solid, horizontal board fence, have all of the structure on one side, with the framework exposed to the other side. Two-sided fences, including the vertical board-on-board, the horizontal board-on-board, and the basketweave, look the same on either side, with the framework at least partially hidden.

The framework of wooden fences consists of posts and rails. Rails may be installed either vertically or horizontally. Rails should be notched slightly into the posts to prevent their slippage.

In the construction of a chainlink fence, the toprail should be installed before the postholes are filled with concrete.

The posts must be set as the rails are installed on a split-rail fence, whereas the posts are installed first in the construction of a formal rail fence.

Wooden decks may be cantilevered from floor joists during the construction of a house. Otherwise, they must be supported by piles or posts, or both. Ledger plates, which absorb the weight of the deck and spread it evenly over the supports, may be attached directly to the piles, to posts, or to the wall of the house. Joists extend between the ledger plates, and decking is nailed directly to them.

Raised decks are normally bordered by railings, benches, or both. If a deck is properly designed, the posts that support it can be extended upward to provide part of the support for the railing or bench.

SUMMARY QUESTIONS

1. What is a survey?
2. Differentiate between raw survey sightings and relative elevations.

3. What is a topographical map?

4. What is the height of instrument?

5. What three criteria must be considered in the design of a retaining wall?

6. Name the two methods for constructing rock retaining walls.

7. What is a deadman?

8. Why are weepholes necessary in a mortared wall?

9. What is batter? Why is it important?

10. Why are weepholes unnecessary in a post wall?

11. Why are new railroad ties seldom used in retaining wall construction?

12. Why must the wood in a retaining wall be chemically treated on all surfaces that come into contact with the soil?

13. Name the five steps in the construction of a concrete patio or sidewalk.

14. What is a screed board? How is it used?

15. Why is it necessary to draw score marks in a concrete surface?

16. What is a modular brick?

17. How does the construction of a flagstone patio differ from that of a brick patio?

18. What are the two general types of fences?

19. Distinguish between a one-sided fence and a two-sided fence.

20. What is a cantilevered deck?

21. Which deck component spreads the weight of the deck evenly over the supports?

CHAPTER 4
The Mechanics of Landscaping

Coordinating Activities

Beautiful and functional landscaping does not just happen. It is the culmination of efforts on the part of the designer, plant grower, material suppliers, job foreman, salesperson, laborers and property owner. A functional landscape of great beauty can only result from the cooperative efforts of all involved.

First, the owner of the property, the salesperson, and/or the landscape designer must reach an agreement that such landscaping is necessary and that a landscape plan or sketch is a prerequisite for proper design. They must then decide the criteria by which the landscape will be designed. Preliminary sketches and estimated costs might be required before a final design is decided upon. Once the design has been finalized and the price agreed upon, the landscape installation begins, a process that can decide an area's future appearance and usefulness.

The growers of the plant materials to be used in a landscape do not wait until a landscape has been planned and then grow the plants. Instead, they try to project the needs for various plants in advance and produce them for sale at a later date. The quality of the material produced and the availability of varieties greatly affect the quality of a landscape, as does the care with which the plant material is handled by the grower during the harvesting and shipping procedures. The grower, then, is at least partially responsible for the success of a high-quality landscape.

The production of a high-quality landscape is equally affected by the ability of other suppliers to provide materials on a timely basis. A supplier's failure to ship needed materials can delay other operations, cause inefficiency, and result in a lower quality product.

Perhaps the most important contributions to landscape development are those made by the installers, the job foreman and his laborers. The best of all possible designs will pale if not installed and cared for properly. On the other hand, proper installation methods, followed by excellent maintenance, can make an otherwise ordinary landscape appear quite extraordinary.

Landscape Plans and Sketches

Formal landscape plans are usually drawn to a measurable scale, which aids the installation crew during the layout. Plans drawn at a scale that can be easily measured by a steel tape measure are particularly easy to read on the job. For that reason, many residential landscape plans are drawn at a scale of ⅛″ = 1′. If landscaping sketches are not drawn at a measurable scale, layout of the landscape usually must be done by the designer or salesperson, or notations on the sketch must be sufficient to allow the foreman to know exactly the desired placement. Of course, a plan done to scale is only as accurate as the measurements taken prior to its drawing, so the accuracy of the lot size and house location should always be checked before layout begins.

Each landscape designer has his own style of delineation and graphics. It is important that the plan be readable and that adequate notations be made to ensure its proper implementation. The scale should be such that the printing is not extremely small nor easily smudged. The printing style should be clear, simple, and unadorned. Some graphic styles, while elaborately beautiful, are not easily read and should be avoided if possible.

Specifications accompany most landscape plans that are prepared by a designer. They are written to direct the installers in the production of a landscape of predictable quality. Even the best written, best conceived specifications cannot ensure the highest quality materials and workman-

TABLE 4-1. Materials Assembly List

XYZ Nursery						
Job Name _____			Job Location _____			
Material	Size	Quantity	Supplier	Date ordered	Date Rec.	Location

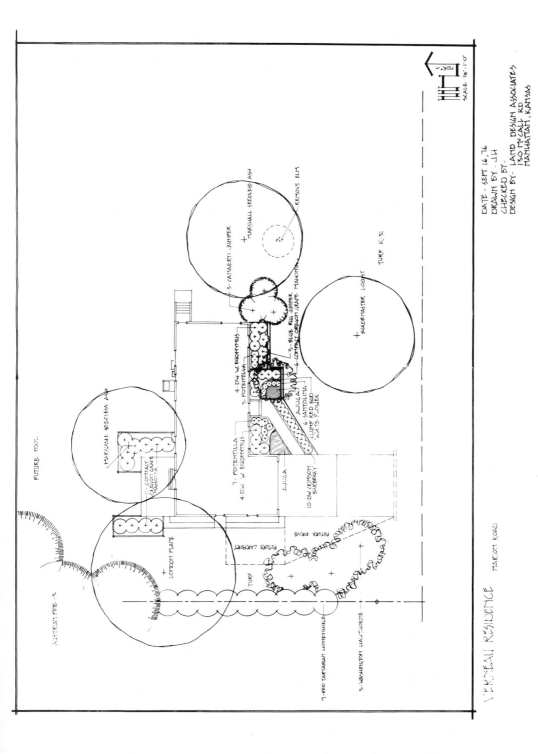

Figure 4-1. A well-labeled landscape plan.

99

ship, however, because all landscapers simply do not have the same capabilities. Still, specifications are the best insurance available to the property owner when bids are let for landscaping; but the designer must provide for an adequate system for checking to see that the specifications are followed.

When the purchaser contracts for a landscaping installation, he is led to expect certain qualities and styles by the salesperson, or from the specifications and plans. To achieve customer satisfaction, it is necessary for the installers to equal or exceed those expectations. As a result, all involved must adhere to consistent goals. This begins with the preparation of job documents and the processing of necessary materials.

Job Documents

Job documents include the plans and specifications, but also the job sheets, materials assembly lists, and estimate or bid contracts. Job sheets, which will be discussed in more detail in Chapter 10, contain directions for the completion of the job and usually a materials list for future billing. Materials assembly lists are forms that can be used internally to order needed materials for a job. These are sometimes called "dig lists" if they are used primarily to order plants dug from a nursery. They record not only the plants and hardgoods required, but the sizes, quantities, the name of the supplier, the date of ordering, and the date received. They should also contain the location of the materials after receipt to ensure accessibility by the installation crew. Table 4–1 is one such materials assembly list, although each company should devise the form to fit its own needs. Estimate or bid contracts are the binding agreements by which jobs are done, and it would be unwise to initiate installation without them. All of these forms are normally filled out by the salesperson, who is the only person familiar with the job at the time the sale is made. But once the job documents are completed, the job scheduled, and materials ordered and secured, the foreman should be assigned to study the documents before any work is initiated.

Work Order Analysis

An analysis should be made in advance of doing the job, which will reveal a logical pattern for completion. Construction work, such as retaining walls, will have to be completed before plants are installed. Plants in a gravel bed should be installed before the gravel, whereas in a groundcover bed, it may work better to install both shrubs and groundcover simultaneously. Should grass be planted before the trees are planted, or afterward? All of these factors should be considered well in advance of beginning the job, so a smooth agenda can be planned for the most efficient job progress.

Stakeout

Immediately prior to startup, or simultaneous with startup, the designer, salesperson, or foreman should stake out plant locations, bed delineations, wall locations, or other landscape features, so less time will be lost by the crew. This staking can be done in several ways. Wood, wire, or metal stakes may be placed in the ground, with names of plants or other information written on them. Or they might have no writing on them and be used to indicate location only with the plan supplying the information. Regardless of method, the staking must be done in order to make sure the entire composition of the plan is correct. If planting is started at one side of a bed and continued until the other side is reached, it is possible for a mistaken measurement on the plan to distort the bed completely out of the desired shape or dimension. Staking prevents such happenings, since corrections can be made before the plants are actually installed.

Bed Preparation

Assuming that the aforementioned processes have been accomplished prior to job startup and all necessary construction work has been completed, the next task facing a landscaping crew is bed preparation. Not only does the preparation of planting beds affect the appearance of a completed landscape, but it also affects the livability and growth potential of the individual plantings. The proper preparation of these planting beds involves four processes: stripping sod, establishing the drainage, amending the soil, and edging the bed.

Stripping Sod

Stripping sod from a bed area can be fairly simple, if the firm owns a sodcutter, or difficult, if it does not. But this stripping must be accomplished to facilitate further soil amendment in the bed and to keep

Figure 4-2. Preparation of a planting bed. When edging is to be installed, a straight, vertical trench is cut.

unwanted grass from resuming growth within the bed. Simply rototilling the bed area, without stripping the sod first, means leaving clumps of grass, which are difficult to work with, and, given water, can continue to grow. If a sodcutter is unavailable, the sod can be stripped with a sharpened, flat-bottomed shovel. One man inserts the shovel just under the sod while another pulls the edge of the sod back, keeping pressure on the sod at the point where the shovel is being forced under it. The combined pressure of pulling up the sod and the sharp edge of the shovel against the roots makes the sod release rather easily. The bed can then be cultivated without the interference of any remaining grass clumps.

Drainage

The next step in the process depends upon the type of bed being prepared. If plantings and gravel are to be installed, further excavation beyond the sod stripping will be required. Adequate drainage must be provided at the time the excavation is done. The sodcutter can be run over the area to be excavated a second time, and although the soil will not roll up like sod, the cutter will still cut to an even depth, allowing laborers to shovel the soil up evenly, leaving an even surface in the bed. A rototiller will serve the purpose of loosening the soil for easy removal, if a sodcutter is unavailable.

Since gravel beds must be excavated to a depth of 2½" to 3", assuming the bed is to be left even with the lawn, good bed drainage is necessary. Otherwise, the bed will become a quagmire. If the bed is against a house, fence, or other structure, the slope should run away from that structure. This permits only a small amount of water to accumulate next to the edge of the bed; all excess water runs into the yard. This small accumulation near the edge is not harmful; it soon soaks away. To achieve a minimum slope of 4% to 5%, it is sometimes necessary to actually fill soil near the structure. Such filling will be helpful in two ways. First, less soil will have to be hauled away, reducing the labor on the job, and second, the increased slope of the bed will make it more visible from a distance, normally a desirable feature. If the bed is located out in the yard, the center of the bed should be the highest point, and the bed should slope to both sides. As the bed is excavated, care should be exercised to cut the edges sharply vertical in the proper line or curve. This will save valuable time later when the edging is installed. Any soil removed from the edges of the bed can be placed in the center.

Further excavation is not necessary for a groundcover bed. In fact, if the sod stripped was significantly thick, it might even be necessary to fill in some soil to achieve the proper level within the bed. As long as proper drainage can be provided, soil need not be added because the height of the groundcover as it becomes established will compensate for the soil loss.

Soil Amendments

Soil amendments as recommended by experts in each locality should be added to a bed at the time it is cultivated. Peat moss, gypsum, bone meal, or lime are the most common amendments. Peat moss increases the moisture retention capabilities of the soil and provides organic material, ultimately enriching the soil. Gypsum is sometimes recommended to loosen a tight, clay soil. Bone meal is a high phosphorous fertilizer used mostly in flower beds containing bulb plants. Lime sweetens an acid soil and should only be added when soil tests indicate that it is necessary. Other possible soil amendments include: compost, to add organic material; sand, to loosen and aerate the soil; aluminum sulfate, to add acid to an alkaline soil; or Perlite, Buildex, or any of a number of inert loosening materials. These soil-amending materials are spread over the bed area in the amounts recommended locally, then mixed into the soil with a rototiller to a depth of 3" to 4". Any soil amendment should always be mixed very thoroughly. If there is a layering of materials, water movement and root growth can be impeded.

Edging

Edging should clearly define the bed but not dominate its appearance. Commonly used as edgings are: redwood, flexible steel, bricks, flexible PVC, or plastics, corrugated aluminum, and railroad ties. Ideally, besides defining the edges of the bed, the edging will retain the material within the bed, prevent grass from growing into the bed, and provide an edge against which the grass can be easily trimmed. Because of soil movement, particularly in the winter as a result of freezing and thawing, edgings need to be anchored or retamped periodically if they begin to rise out of the ground. Redwood edging, for example, since it expands when it gets wet, has a tendency to float out of the ground. A redwood stake, $1'' \times 2''$, can be placed in the ground every three to four feet and can be attached to the edging by galvanized nails. This will help hold the edging in the ground. Many of the flexible metal and plastic edgings are anchored with heavy wire stakes. Each stake has a hook at the top designed to be secured over the top of the edging. Such hooks, while effective, are somewhat distracting in appearance. Railroad ties may be anchored to the ground by drilling holes through the ties, then driving a length of rebar, $\frac{3}{8}''$ in diameter and $2'$ in length, through the hole and into the ground below. Brick edgings may be set in a sand- or gravel-based trench; sand between the bricks allows them to move with the soil. Or they may be set in mortar, with mortared joints. If the latter is used, a footing of concrete, extending below the frost line, will be required under the edging to prevent the mortar from cracking and crumbling as soil movement occurs. A heavy metal edging, $\frac{1}{8}''$ thick or more, will not require staking, but each spring it may need to be pressed down to compensate for minimal floating.

Edgings should be set so the top edge is just slightly higher than the ground level beneath the grass. When the lawn is mowed, the mower can lap over the edging, eliminating much trimming. The edge of the bed will be crisp and clean, and the transition from lawn to bed will be smooth and satisfying in appearance. If railroad ties, redwood, or bricks are used and if they are set just higher than the ground outside, trimming can be achieved very easily by lowering the mowing height on one side of the mower $\frac{1}{2}''$ to $1''$ and then placing the wheels of the lower side on the edging as the grass is mowed. The reduced height on one side of the mower will trim the grass nicely along the edging. Also, when the edging is placed almost completely into the ground, soil will secure the outside edge and either soil, gravel, bark, or other groundcover will stabilize the interior edge. A properly installed edging is shown in Fig. 4–3.

Figure 4-3. A well-edged planting bed.

When edging is installed, it is important to cut the outside edge of the bed clean and vertical. This ensures that the outside edge of the edging can fit snugly against the soil. Otherwise the space between the outside of the edging and the grass will have to be filled with soil and sod, which will be difficult to water and sustain. Since the soil filled in is loose, settling can occur, and the edging may even buckle. Fig. 4–4 shows the proper and improper way to install edgings.

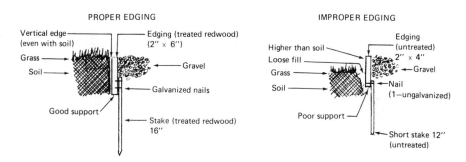

Figure 4-4. Proper and improper edging installation.

Sometimes, particularly in a groundcover bed, the edges are defined by merely cutting a straight or curved edge with a shovel. This method can be very effective, but the procedure must be repeated often to keep the edge sharp and well defined. Such edges break down with nothing to support them.

The proper edging of a bed is vital to the good appearance of a landscape. Crooked or ragged edges detract from, rather than enhance, the beauty of the landscape.

Planting

There is a great deal of shock involved in transplanting a plant from one location to another. That shock can either be minimized or maximized by the methods used during transplanting. Many factors influence the success or failure of transplanting, including the plant's root structure, its health and vigor, the harvesting procedure, the time of transplanting, and the quality of care after transplanting. Let us look now at possibly the most important factor in the transplanting process: the actual planting of the plant.

Installing a plant includes six operations: the preparation of the hole, the addition of soil amendments, the placement of the plant in the hole,

Figure 4-5. A landscaping crew unloads trees in preparation for planting.

backfilling with soil, tamping, and watering. Pruning might be considered part of the planting process, but, for reasons to be discussed later, I consider it part of the overall job.

Preparation of the Hole

The size of the hole has been a subject for much discussion over the years, and even a cursory reading of specifications for planting will reveal that there is no consensus of opinion. It is generally agreed, however, that the hole must be large enough to permit the soil around the root system to be thoroughly tamped; that is, no air pockets must remain. Specifications often indicate that the hole should be 6″ to 1′ wider on each side of the root extension and 6″ to 1′ deeper than the root system. Perhaps the most desirable hole would extend several feet beyond the root spread, so the roots would have loosened, amended soil to grow into, but such a practice is too expensive to be practical. The soil type is another consideration. In loose, fertile, well-drained soil, a large hole is not required. But installing a plant with loose, amended soil around it in tight, poorly drained soil, however, is like placing the plant in a bucket with no drainage. The amended soil and the plant's root mass require frequent waterings, but the tight, clay soil will not allow excess water to drain away; water stands in the root zone and drowns the plant. This type of situation can sometimes be alleviated by drilling a small drainage hole in the bottom of the planting hole. Water can then seep through the tight clay into a better draining soil stratum below.

Shovels or augers are most frequently used to dig holes for plants. Both implements tend to leave the edges of the hole sheer and slick, and the soil tightly compacted. Gouging into the sides of the hole with a shovel will relieve the compaction and eliminate the sheerness. Then the plant's roots can penetrate these edges more easily, and water can satisfactorily drain from the sides of the hole. If the edges of the hole are left sheer and compacted, the plant's roots will turn and curve around the interior edge of the hole just as they curve around the interior edge of a container.

The bottom of the hole should be loosened to at least a depth of 6″ to 1′ lower than the extent of the root mass. This is done to allow excess water, which will nearly always be present to some degree, a place to accumulate until it can drain away. Roots that grow downward are then afforded the same opportunities to begin growth as those on the side. Although the soil beneath the plant must be loosened (or replaced with loose soil), care must be exercised to retamp the soil to adequate firmness; otherwise severe settling of the plant might occur as it is watered.

If the soil removed from a hole is to be used around the plant, it should be chopped and texturized as it is removed. Satisfactorily texturizing a sizeable pile of soil all at once is a difficult task. The soil on the top of the pile will have an adequate texture, but the soil at the bottom will contain many large clods. Large clods in the backfill result in air pockets, which are the plant's worst enemy. It is best to use burlap, plywood, or wheelbarrows to store the soil in from the time the hole is dug until the soil is backfilled around the plant. A cleaner appearance and a more professional looking job will result.

Sod taken from the top of the hole should be stored separately and should either be placed back around the plant to be properly mowed and trimmed or disposed of entirely. Chopped up pieces of sod, if placed in the backfill, cause air pockets; they can continue to grow and will soon become maintenance problems. Sod pieces placed on the top of the backfill or in the saucer are distracting and ugly.

Finally, a few notes about shovels and plant holes. A sharp, clean shovel digs faster holes. Since the digging of plant holes is at best a time-consuming task, everything possible should be done to expedite the process. Each worker should carry a small putty knife in his or her pocket, frequently cleaning the blade of his or her shovel. Shovels should be sharpened often, so they will cut quickly and cleanly through soil, roots, and grass. Soil can be removed from a planting hole more quickly and with less effort if it is first loosened to shovel depth and if only small "bites" are taken with each shovelful. Workers should be taught to pry back on a shovel at an angle, instead of straight back, which puts more pressure on the shovel handle, often causing it to break.

Mixing Soil Amendments

Types, amounts, and methods of incorporation of soil amendments are subjects of debate. At one time it was thought advantageous to mix peat moss, sand, or other amendments to the soil used to backfill plants, but further research has shown that may not be the case.

It is extremely important that soil amendments be mixed thoroughly and completely with the soil. Pockets of pure peatmoss, sand, or other foreign substances can cause problems for the plants, primarily because of differing water attraction and retention capabilities. A layer of sand or peat moss, for example, will not absorb any water until the surrounding soil is thoroughly saturated. In all probability, roots will not penetrate these pockets, but if they do, they might die later from a lack of water. If such a layer stretches completely across the hole, all the soil below might be deprived of water for long periods of time, causing the death of all roots in that area. In order to achieve a thorough mixing of the soil amendment with the soil, it is necessary to thoroughly pulverize the soil, leaving no clods of any size.

Soil amendments can be introduced and mixed in several different ways. If plants are being planted in shovel-excavated holes, the amendment will most likely be mixed with a shovel. The amendment will be spread in the right proportion on top of the soil, then shovelfuls of amendment and soil will be turned over until the mixture is homogenized. If the plant holes are drilled with an auger, the soil amendment can be filled back into the hole along with the excavated soil. Subsequent redrilling with the auger will serve to mix the amendment and the soil. A third method, particularly applicable for mixing a soil amendment in a groundcover or shrub bed, involves spreading the proper amount of soil amendment on the surface, then mixing it into the soil with a rototiller. Finally, soil and amendments may be shoveled into a cement mixer, where they will emerge after a few minutes thoroughly mixed. Other methods may be devised to suit a set of working circumstances, but the important thing to remember is that the mixing must always be thorough.

Special soil amendments are sometimes required for certain plant varieties. For example, the pH of the soil dictates the color of bloom on hydrangeas. If blue blossoms are desired, the soil needs to be slightly acid; for pink blossoms the soil must be slightly more alkaline. Aluminum sulphate can be added to the soil to produce the acidity required for blue blooms; calcium carbonate will make the soil more alkaline. Other specific amendments might be necessary to adjust the texture, drainage, or moisture-retention capabilities of the soil for special varieties of plants.

Plant Placement

The first matter of concern is the size of the hole itself. Moving a plant in and out of a hole more than necessary can be damaging. Balled and burlapped or container-grown plants can become loose, allowing air inside of the root ball, which can ultimately cause the plant's death. The hole should be carefully measured, and corresponding measurements made of the plant's root system, to make sure the hole is deep and wide enough to accept the plant properly. These measurements can be made with a tape measure, a stick, or a shovel handle.

The type of preparation given to the bottom of the hole depends upon the particular kind of plant being installed. Balled and burlapped or container-grown plants require a flat bottom, sufficiently firm to resist settling and level enough to allow the plant to sit upright. For bare-root plants, the soil should be placed in the shape of a cone in the bottom of the hole. Then the crown of the plant can be placed on the cone, with the roots extending down the sides. The construction of this cone prevents the formation of air pockets beneath the plant and assures firm contact between the roots and soil.

Whenever possible, plants should face the same direction they faced in the nursery field. Often though, it is impossible to tell which direction the plant faced in the nursery. There is a certain amount of shock involved if the plant is turned; that is, the side that heretofore faced north is suddenly facing south, exposed to heat and hot winds. On the other hand, trees that have developed a curvature in the leader from prevailing winds in the nursery might well be turned so that the curve faces the prevailing winds at the planting site. Given time, the leader will be straightened as a result.

Workmen should always make sure that a plant is set so it appears level on the top and straight up and down. A plant set crooked will detract from the plantings surrounding it. Repeated attempts to straighten it might result in a loosening of the root mass, causing injury or even death. Small evergreens and shrubs can only be set straight by walking completely around them and viewing them from all angles. A tree can be plumbed by sighting a line through the edge of the main trunk, in reference to the corner of a house or other object known to be plumb. A plant should be straightened before the backfilling is begun. Straightening requires the lifting of one side of the plant base, and if backfilling has begun, an air pocket might be left under one edge of the root ball.

Backfilling, Tamping, and Watering

Backfilling and tamping must be discussed together, since they occur simultaneously. After the plant is set, the backfilling is begun. Care should be exercised to avoid jolting the plant to one side, which would result in a crooked planting. Soil should be backfilled in even layers, completely surrounding the plant. If the plant is bare-root, the soil should be carefully worked in among the roots by hand, as the backfill is added. When about 4″ to 5″ of backfill has been placed, it should be thoroughly tamped to an equal firmness. A shovel handle, baseball bat, or any other narrow, but blunt, instrument can be used for the tamping. The objectives of tamping are to eliminate air pockets, achieve close contact between the plant roots and soil, and firm the soil to eliminate settling. Tamping should not compact the soil too much, though, or more harm than good will be done. The moisture content of the soil must be gauged during the tamping process. If a soil is wet, excessive tamping results in extreme compaction, whereas powder dry soil may completely resist compaction.

Backfilling and tamping should continue until the hole is about two-thirds full. Then the remaining one-third of the hole is filled with water. After the water has completely soaked away, the remaining backfill can be added, but no tamping should be done. The watering has changed the moisture level of the soil so that further tamping would result in compaction. Instead, the surface should be firmed with the worker's foot only.

Saucering

Remaining soil should be used to make a saucer around the top edge of the backfilled hole to permit water to be held in place until it can be absorbed into the hole. The appearance of this saucer should not be overlooked. Sloppy workmanship will result in an ugly saucer, which will detract from the good features of the landscape. More importantly, a poorly built saucer may not function property, and sufficient water may not be able to penetrate to the plant's root system.

As soon as the saucer is constructed, the final watering should be given, filling the saucer full. Any soil spilled in the area around the plant can be cleaned up with a rake at this time, so the grass will not be adversely affected.

Pruning

Some pruning of new plants is always required. Pruning eliminates broken or bruised branches, compensates for root loss, equalizes plant sizes, and improves the shape of the plants. All plants of a single variety must be installed before their sizes can be equalized. Even though typically all plants of one variety on a job will be within the same size range, minor differences become apparent when they are planted side by side. Eliminating this disparity contributes greatly to the appearance of the overall project.

Bare-root plants stand a much better chance of survival if the tops are pruned back. This reduces the potential leaf surface by at least one-third. The quicker establishment, and subsequently more thrifty growth exhibited by the plant, will more than make up for the temporary decrease in size. Pruning the tops of balled and burlapped trees (particularly large ones) will compensate for the significant root loss during harvesting. Although the primary objectives of this pruning is to reduce the potential leaf surface, the future shape of the tree can be enhanced at the same time; scaffold branches—those that permanently dictate the form of a tree—can be established, others eliminated, and wider, stronger branches can be developed by pruning to outside buds.

Pruning plants for shape is important; it might be the last pruning they receive for many years. Once installed, the plant's future care depends totally on the property owner. Even if the owner is conscientious about attending to his plants, he might not know the proper technique. Shaping plants properly when they are installed at least gets them off to the right start.

Staking Newly Planted Trees

Because tree branches and leaves offer wind resistance, newly planted trees need help to remain firm and straight. Until new roots are well established, *staking* or *guying* help prevent unnecessary movement. A stake, usually 2″ × 2″ × 8′, is driven into the ground diagonally, immediately adjacent to small tree trunks. A soft plastic tie, flexible garden hose, or cloth is then used to tie the tree trunk to the stake. The material should be tied in a figure-eight fashion, so the stake and the tree trunk do not rub each other. Another method of staking involves setting a stake on each side of the tree, with a short pieces of board connecting them, to which the tree trunk is tied.

Guying is a system reserved for trees 2″ in caliper or larger. Three stakes, usually 2″ × 4″ × 24″, are driven into the ground equidistant around the tree. Heavy gauge wires are then looped from these stakes around the trunk at its juncture with the lower branches. Pieces of garden hose cover the wires at the point of contact with tree branches, to prevent injury. Turnbuckles, attached to the ends of the wire, are used to tighten the wires, so each is equally firm. In lieu of turnbuckles, the wire can be twisted until tight. This tree guying method is demonstrated in Fig. 4–6.

Wires or stakes must not be allowed to rub directly against the bark of

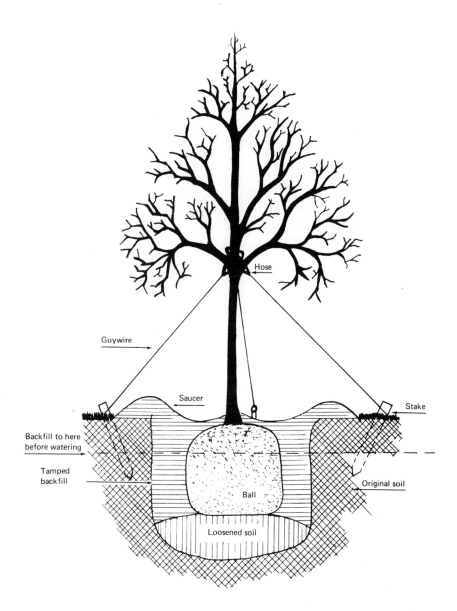

Figure 4-6. Planting.

a tree. As the tree grows, all ties must be loosened occasionally, to prevent girdling. As soon as the tree has rooted sufficiently to support itself, the stakes or guy wires should be removed.

Finishing and Maintenance

Figure 4-7. A completed planting bed, showing groundcovers, trees, shrubs, and edging properly installed. Sodbed has been prepared in the foreground.

The finishing touches are important in a landscape installation. Cleanup of all debris tops the list, of course, along with removing all tags from plants. Any necessary final touches should be given to planting beds, making sure the edges are neat and well trimmed and that the shape of the beds conforms to the design plans.

Maintenance recommendations. As mentioned earlier, even the best of landscapes must have adequate care after installation in order to look good. The care given by the property owner cannot be satisfactory unless he possesses the correct information, most of which must come from those installing the landscaping, the salesperson, the designer, or all three. Information about watering predominates, since that is basically the only care involved initially. It is difficult to state exactly how often people should be told to water plants; the climate and time of year as well as size and variety of plantings are all factors to be considered. The soil type is especially important; newly installed plants in a light, well-drained soil in a warm climate might require daily watering, but the same watering practices would literally drown plants in a tight, clay soil that did not drain properly. The only advice that can be given here is to know the soil type in an area and make recommendations accordingly,

Figure 4-8. A well-maintained lawn and landscape.

Figure 4-9. A home very similar to that shown in Figure 4-8, but poorly landscaped and maintained. What a difference!

keeping in mind that it is just as disastrous to overwater newly installed plants as to underwater them. The customer should be informed that fertilizer is usually not recommended the first year, nor is pruning required.

Since the maintenance of planting beds is so important to the overall appearance of the landscape, recommendations concerning their up-keep should be carefully explained to the property owner. Nothing destroys the appearance of an otherwise attractive landscape more quickly than unsightly, poorly edged planting beds, weeds growing up around plants, or sloppy trimming around the edges of beds designed to have clean, sharp edges. The methods for maintaining these beds, and the importance of doing so, should be stressed to the customer.

The reputation of any landscaping firm depends, among other things, upon the appearance of the work they have completed. In that sense, every job serves as either positive or negative advertising for that business. Any and all avenues to the establishment and continuation of a beautiful and functional landscape should be explored. The costs are so low, and the benefits are magnificent.

SUMMARY

The creation of a beautiful and functional landscape depends on the performance of the designer, salesperson, plant grower, hardgoods supplier, job foreman, laborers, and property owner. A breakdown on the part of any of these individuals can result in inefficiency, at the least, or a totally ineffective job, at the most.

Landscape plans should be drawn to a scale that can be measured with any common tape measure. Plans should be readable and should contain adequate information to ensure the proper installation of the landscape.

Specifications are written to protect the property owner. They specify uniform qualities, regardless of who performs the work or supplies the products. Specifications are only as effective as the checking system employed to make sure they are being followed.

The landscape installation begins with the processing of job documents. Plans, specifications, instructions, material orders, and contracts should be in order before a crew is assigned to the job.

A job analysis, in which a step by step approach is outlined for the logical and efficient completion of the job, must also be prepared before job startup.

Staking out locations of plants, beds, and other landscape features should be completed before any planting or construction begins. Measurements can then be confirmed, and any costly changes resulting from earlier mistakes can be avoided. Staking can be done in a number of different ways, each effective.

Bed preparation involves sod stripping, establishment of drainage, amendments to the soil, and edging. Beds should not contain clumps of sod and must have at least a 4% to 5% slope to drain properly. The edge should be cut vertically and should correctly follow the planned line of design.

Many edgings can be used for beds, including redwood, flexible steel, bricks, flexible PVC, plastics, corrugated aluminum, and railroad ties. Most require some type of staking to keep them in place. To facilitate mowing and trimming, all should be placed so the top of the edging is just barely higher than the soil under the adjacent grass.

Methods used in the installation of plants contribute greatly to their future survival. The installation of a plant involves six operations: hole preparation, soil amendments, plant placement, backfilling, tamping and watering.

Holes should be large enough to accommodate the root extension of the plant and to allow backfilling to be done without air pockets. Sides of the hole should not be sheer, and the bottom should be loosened, then refirmed. In tight soils, provision should be made in the bottom of the hole for excess water to drain away. Clean, sharp shovels facilitate faster hole preparation.

While the value of soil amendments is a subject of current debate, thorough mixing of any amendments added is absolutely necessary. Several methods for mixing are available, depending upon the circumstances of the job. Special soil amendments are sometimes required for specific varieties of plants.

The condition of a plant's root system determines how it should be placed in its hole. Solid bases, which leave the plant sitting in an upright position, are important for balled and burlapped plants or for container-grown plants. Bare-root plants require a cone of soil over which the roots can be spread for close contact. Before placing the plant, careful measurements should be taken of the hole. This precaution will minimize the number of times a plant will have to be moved, thereby minimizing the risk of root system damage.

When backfilling and tamping occur simultaneously, the result is close root to soil contact, without unnecessary soil compaction, and an elimination of air pockets. When the backfilling is two-thirds complete, water is applied, after which the remaining backfill is placed and firmed, but not tamped. Saucers are constructed to catch and hold water until it can soak into the plant's root system.

Pruning newly installed plants eliminates bruised or broken branches, compensates for root loss, equalizes plant sizes, and improves the shape of plants.

Proper cleanup and finishing touches are extremely important to the success of a landscape installation.

Good information must be given to the property owner for future care of a landscape. The appearance of a landscape depends on good maintenance practices, and the landscaping firm's reputation relates directly to the appearance of its finished work.

SUMMARY QUESTIONS

1. How does the supplier of hardgoods affect the efficiency of a landscape installation?

2. Why must a landscape plan contain notations concerning the installation procedures, even though such information is in the specifications?

3. Why does the sale of a landscaping job initiate the installation procedures?

4. What is a materials assembly list? How is it used?

5. Why is a job analysis done prior to startup?

6. Why is it necessary to stake out the locations of plants and other features prior to startup?

7. Why should sod always be stripped from bed areas?

8. Describe the two-man method of stripping sod, if a sodcutter is unavailable.

9. What is the minimum slope required within a gravel bed for proper drainage?

10. Why is it important to avoid hauling off any more soil than necessary during the excavation of a gravel bed?

11. Describe the easiest method of incorporating soil amendments into a groundcover bed.

12. What are the primary reasons for using an edging around a bed?

13. Why does a mortared brick edging require a footing?

14. Why is it not desirable to fill in the area between edging and existing soil with soil fill and sod?

15. What five factors affect the success or failure of transplanting a plant?

16. Why should the sheer sides of a plant hole be gouged with a shovel?

17. Why should soil be texturized as it is removed from a planting hole?

18. Why is it necessary to thoroughly homogenize soil amendments with soil?

19. Why is it dangerous to the health of a plant to adjust it after backfill has been added?

20. How does the soil moisture level affect the amount of tamping done?

21. Name four reasons for pruning newly installed plants.

22. Why is a poorly maintained landscape considered "negative advertising" for the company that did the installation?

CHAPTER 5

Plant Materials: Use and Handling

Landscape design and the growing of planting materials are well-documented subjects. Their importance to a successful landscaping operation has long been recognized. Yet there are specific considerations that warrant further attention. The quality of a nursery owner's landscape designs will affect the profitability of his operation, the profitability and usefulness of the landscaping for his client, and the firm's reputation in future years. Also, the use of proper and efficient methods for handling and caring for plant material is not only vital to the health of individual plants but to the firm's continued good standing in the community.

So, while this chapter will not tell you everything you need to know about landscape design or about the growing of plants, hopefully, it will add to information available from other sources.

Landscape Design

Many different authorities have offered definitions of landscaping. Additionally, laymen seem to have many ideas of their own about the term's meaning. Some think of landscaping as a method of grading soil; others think of it as "exterior decoration"; still others think of a landscape only as an oil painting of the countryside. The Random House Dictionary defines *landscape* as: (1) a section of scenery that may be seen from a single viewpoint; (2) a picture of such scenery; or (3) to improve the appearance of (an area of land, etc.), as by altering the contours of the ground.

I would like to offer still another definition of a landscape, as it applies to real estate. *Landscaping is the arrangement of space and features on a property so they are at one time both functional for the needs of that property and pleasing to view.* In such a definition, the *needs* of the property may be those of the land itself, the buildings on that land, or the owners or frequenters of that land. The *features* of the property may be those originally in existence or those added later and may range from plants and grass to retaining walls, fences, garden pools, and outdoor lights. Since beauty is said to be in the eye of the beholder, the *pleasing to view* stipulation of the above definition might be the hardest portion to pin down. No landscape is going to please all who view it. Those who own the property or otherwise have the most interest in its beauty are normally the ones who must be pleased.

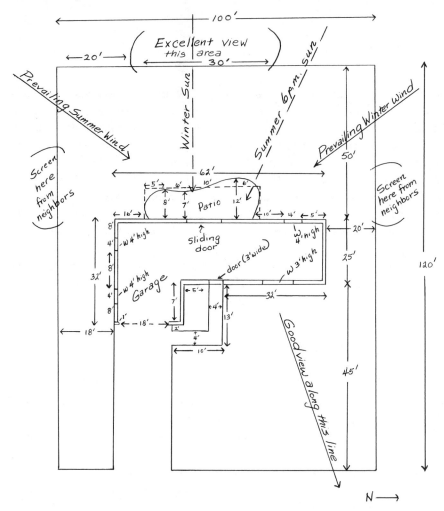

Figure 5-1. Quick diagram of needs and measurements.

A good designer analyzes the features and space of a given property, studies the needs of the property and its owners (or those who frequent the property), adds some features, subtracts some, and ultimately causes the property to function properly, while enhancing its appearance. Not an easy task, right? Yet there are some basic rules by which landscape design can be simplified, especially from the viewpoint of the landscape nurseryowner.

1. Provide for the basic environmental needs of the property.
2. Accent only the good features of the property, de-accentuate the bad features.
3. Accent only the good features of buildings, de-accentuate the bad features.

4. Do not try to bend the rules of nature.
5. Landscape with the surrounding area in mind.
6. Do not suggest anything without a purposeful basis.
7. Design landscaping with today in mind, but with an eye to the future.
8. Design landscaping for those primarily concerned with the property.

By elaborating on each of these points, their importance can be more easily understood.

Provide for the basic environmental needs of the property. Among the most important tasks of landscaping is to make a property more comfortable by providing shade, wind protection, and screening. With decreasing energy supplies and correspondingly rising energy costs, shade and wind protection become more important from an economic standpoint. Properly planned environmental landscaping can cut the property owner's energy costs considerably and conserve valuable energy resources at the same time.

The first task of any landscape designer should be to study the sun and wind patterns of the property. At the same time, the desirable and undesirable views should be analyzed. A good knowledge of the area is important in making these determinations. The directions of the prevailing winds (often different for different times of the year) must be known, along with the sun's path, which changes during the year. Shade trees should be positioned to block the sun during the hottest times of the year, yet not impede desirable sun's rays during the wintertime.

A quick diagram of the property is helpful. It should show these prevailing patterns and also indicate the good views to be left open and any that require screening. Other notations can also be made on this diagram; for example, property measurements, customer requests, and any reminders about adjoining properties. If the landscape design is to be completed away from the property, these notes will prove valuable and will usually eliminate a return trip before the plans are complete. It is also advantageous to take a photograph or two of the property with an instant-developing camera so particular building features will not be forgotten.

Shade is usually provided for with trees. A large, well-placed shade tree might lower the temperature of an area as much as 15 to 20 degrees on a hot summer day. Unfortunately, it takes many years to grow a mature shade tree. But shade can also be provided by other means. A patio can be shaded by a wooden trellis, a roof made of wood or metal, or an arbor on which grape or other types of vines can grow. Awnings can be used to good advantage on the south and west exposure windows, as can exterior shutters that can be closed over the windows. If any of these suggestions are implemented, some adjustments will become necessary during the cold winter months. The sun becomes a valuable asset then, because passive solar heat has great impact on energy requirements. In a trellis roof over a patio, panels can be made removable; then the sun can shine in during the winter to heat a window or sliding glass door leading to the patio. Vines can be pruned back on an arbor to permit the warmth of the sun's rays to penetrate. (The vines will grow back over the arbor before the hot summer season the next year.) Also, a skylight built into a patio roof is a good source of light and heat during the winter. In the summer the skylight can be covered underneath by a shade.

The shade value of small trees should not be overlooked. Ornamental varieties, such as redbud, crabapple, hawthorne, goldenraintree, and many others, will shade an area quite well if they are placed properly. Since they never achieve great height or spread, they simply must be placed closer to the desired shady spot. These trees are usually started at a size that is more proportionate to their mature size than shade trees. Since they also develop faster, their shade potential is more quickly realized.

Wind protection can be provided by trees, shrubs, fences, or soil. Often, the most interesting landscape designs will incorporate several of these means. Seasons must be considered because, although deciduous trees and shrubs will be of some help in breaking a winter wind, evergreen foliage will be much more effective. Wind protection does not necessitate planting trees in straight rows like a windbreak, either. In fact, a flowing planting, using several varieties of trees and shrubs, in layers, is not only more effective, but more pleasing to look at. Most of the plants used will look best if planted in masses of odd numbers.

Fences will look and function better for wind protection if plantings are arranged on both sides of the fence. Neighbors' plantings, which appear above the fence line, can be used to good advantage by alternating plantings to fill gaps inside of the fence. Since a fence can only be 6' or 7' tall, any wind above that height will continue to blow, unless impeded by plantings. The appearance of a fence is greatly enhanced when its length is cut with plantings. Conversely, a fence provides an excellent background for the plant material.

Care should be taken not to cut the wind so severely that there is no breeze in a yard. A planting can be developed to the point that it totally envelopes an area, precluding any air movement. When this is done, the area becomes uncomfortable, to say the least, but it also becomes a haven for fungus diseases, which thrive on moist, muggy conditions. Further care must be taken not to plant winter wind protection too close to the north side of a driveway in snow country. The plants act like a snow fence in such cases, causing heavy drifts across the drive.

Screening can often be coordinated with the wind protection. Only when the direction of the prevailing winds also happens to be the direction of a desirable view, does a problem arise. In such a case, those property owners must ultimately decide whether it is more important to save the view or shut out the wind.

Privacy is essential to most people. Some screening must be devised to make at least one part of a landscaped area private. We want our houses to be private, but we also want windows for an outward view. Similarly, the landscape must not be entirely closed in. Screening selectively provides both the necessary privacy and the desirable outward views. This should always be considered early in landscape development, along with shade and wind protection. All are closely interrelated. The position from which the view is desired must be studied. If a family room window looks out into a backyard, and the occupants of the house feel that this is their most important viewpoint, then screening should be aligned from that point. If more than one such important viewpoint exists, then each should be considered, and compromises might be in order.

A well-placed mound of soil, with plants and/or grass planted on it, can function very well for screening and wind protection. It can also serve the shade function, by placing trees at a higher starting point, and can serve to deaden sound, if noise screening is necessary. When designing mounds, it is essential to keep drainage in mind and blend such mounds into the surrounding terrain. A good height-to-spread ratio must also be considered, so the mound does not take on the appearance of a freakish bump.

Building mounds can be quite expensive on an established property, if the soil must be hauled in. But properties upon which construction is in progress are a different matter. Often, builders are forced to haul away excess soil that could be used to add contour and interest to the property.

Accent only the good features of the property, de-accentuate the bad features. Every piece of property has its good features and its bad features. Look for the good features first. A steep slope, for example, might contain a unique rock outcropping which can be further exposed. Or it might afford the opportunity to build a series of terraces using retaining walls. The appearance of some existing trees on the property might be enhanced if supplementary plantings are supplied to make them look as if they belong. A rolling terrain might lend itself to some natural mounding, around which other landscaping can be designed. A small wooded area might provide a private haven for a secluded patio, sitting area, or children's fort. Two existing trees might be perfect for a hammock, and the surrounding area could be planned for relaxation. A flat space might be ideal for a play area, for croquet, or other lawn sports. Existing trees might serve to screen the service area of the yard. By selecting the best features of the lot first and working with them, the landscape design becomes more effective and easier at the same time.

Problem areas or uninteresting aspects of a property can also be dealt with successfully. If a yard is too flat, artificial mounding might be added, or more likely, the area can be cut up into segments with plantings to make it more appealing. At the same time, each of the areas can have a specific use. Every property needs public, private, and service areas.

Air conditioning condensers, gas meters, and phone jacks are generally unsightly or downright offensive. But designers must be careful in their treatment of these intruders. Placing one shrub in front of a gas meter to hide it might only serve to draw more attention to it. It would be better either to extend a line of shrubs around the front of the meter or to do nothing at all. An air conditioner, if it is close to the patio area, might serve as a useful table if a redwood box was built over it. Always remember that good air circulation is essential for the operation of these condensers, and that all of the meters and appliances must be read and serviced. Easement rights to meters and other utilities must not be infringed upon without permission. Most of these companies are very cooperative if they are contacted before anything is done on their easements.

Accent only the good features of buildings, de-accentuate the bad features. Buildings are necessarily constructed with sharp lines and angles. The surrounding landscape, however, is largely flowing lines and rounded forms. Because of this, buildings stand out from the landscape; they do not blend with it. The design of a good landscape involves measures to tie the building into the surrounding landscape, enhancing both to a maximum. This can be accomplished by accenting the best features of a house, for example, the entrance, interesting window trim, or the roof, and de-accentuating the sharp lines and angles on corners and garages. Properly executed, such a design can not only make a house seem more inviting, but also can make it seem larger.

Most houses are designed to draw the most attention to the entrance. By themselves, they fail to do this, because the sharp lines and angles at the corners and the impact of the garage doors tend to attract more attention. Landscaping can solve this problem by softening the corners and accenting the entrance. The *funnel* approach is quite popular for this purpose. Plantings at the corners are designed to extend at least half to two-thirds of the distance from the ground to the eaves, and the plantings become correspondingly lower toward the entrance. This technique funnels attention toward the entrance, while softening the lines and angles at the corners of the house. Using a plant with strong features further serves to accent the entrance. An example of a typical funnel planting is shown in Figure 5–2.

Tree placement is another important factor in determining how to de-accentuate the less attractive features of a house. Trees, placed off the front corners and forward of a house, can aid in softening the lines and angles on the house, while framing the view of the house. At the same time, if the sharp lines on the corners of a house are obliterated by a tree so they cannot be seen from a front view, then the mind can imagine that the house continues, instead of stopping at the corner line. In this way, landscaping can make a house seem larger.

Shade trees behind a house can help frame the view, soften the roof line, and add background to the view of the house. These trees will also function for shade and wind protection in the backyard.

A well-placed tree to one side and forward of the entrance can serve to draw the desired attention to the entrance. At the same time, this tree can get tall enough to cut the roof line, thereby making the house more attractive.

Trees can also be used to *level* a house and snug it into the terrain. Split-level houses, which are a half-story higher on one end than the other, appear less segmented if trees of proportionate height are planted

Figure 5-2. The funnel effect.

at the corners, ultimately causing the top of the plantings to be level with the top of the house.

That portion of the concrete foundation which shows beneath the siding on a building is best covered by plantings. The siding and trim, instead of the bare foundation, will then dominate the view. In many cases, this foundation planting also functions as part of the funnel effect and should not generally draw strong attention to itself. If kept in good proportion to the house, it helps snug the house into the terrain.

Do not try to bend the rules of nature. Even the best landscape designers cannot make water run uphill, create a natural-looking forest, or change the climate in an area. Nature's rules are largely unbending. A designer who goes against these rules will be forced to deal with problems later.

A good designer must know the climate in his area well and must only use plant material that is well-suited to that climate. Even though an exotic plant may survive several winters in an unsuitable climate, ultimately it will be severely harmed or killed. Sometimes, a plant that has survived several seasons but finally succumbs will cause great problems in a landscape because in the interim all surrounding plants have grown to a size that cannot be matched by a new replacement planting. Climatic zone maps are available to guide the proper selection of plant material in each area. Wholesale nurserymen are a good source for this information, and horticultural extension bulletins are also available.

Grading should never be taken for granted. In some locations, it is virtually impossible to determine slope direction by viewing the terrain with the naked eye. Surveying equipment must be used to assess whether or not the terrain will accommodate the proper drainage.

Since a designer cannot design a natural-looking forest or prairie, which, when planted, will look like the real thing for the thirty or forty years it takes nature to develop it, probably it is better not to try. A flat lot, in the middle of a treeless subdivision, can be better landscaped by more contemporary means than by trying to duplicate nature's efforts in other places. This brings up the next point for consideration.

Landscape with the surrounding area in mind. Anything that greatly differs from its surroundings will stand out. A stark, desert-type landscape in the midst of green lawns and shrub beds filled with groundcovers will truly be outstanding. But it might not be desirable, standing out that much from its surroundings. Such a sharply defined landscape will make the property seem smaller. Many people would feel quite self-conscious about such a unique landscape. It might make the property less marketable in the future. A formal English garden with clipped hedges and formal flower beds might look as out of place in an Arizona desert subdivision.

Using materials that are indigenous to an area enhances a landscape. This is the reason that desert-type landscaping looks appropriate in Arizona, but not in New England. Japanese-type landscaping looks great in small backyards, but is often difficult to establish in the rambling yards of suburban America. If, for example, rock outcroppings are frequently seen in an area, they can be used very effectively in the construction of retaining walls. Similarly, tree and shrub varieties that grow well in nearby woods can be selected for landscapes in that area, but any material actually used must be nursery grown. Material collected from the wild will often not transplant well and has not been inspected for disease and insect pests.

Do not suggest anything without a purposeful basis. Every part of a landscape design should have a distinct purpose. That purpose might be as practical as the environmental considerations discussed earlier or as simple as a customer's request for a particular type of flower, but in either case, the purpose is clear. The plants are fulfilling a need. Designing landscaping without a clear purpose results in overplanting and a poorly functioning property. Some possible needs for plants, besides those already mentioned, are: color, groundcover, erosion control, definition of areas, and food production.

Design landscaping with today in mind, but with an eye to the future. While overplanting is undesirable, underplanting is just as bad. Overplanting can best be described as a situation in which plants are installed too close together and later must be removed. On the other hand, if all plants are planned for their ultimate growth and are spaced accordingly, it will be many years before most landscapes present a reasonably good appearance. Since we live in a relatively mobile society, this often means that the original property owners, who are responsible for the landscaping, never get to see or enjoy the final product of their efforts. Consequently, they might be unsatisfied with the results and the landscape designer.

As a compromise, it is possible to provide a more quickly maturing landscape without overplanting by spacing plants of the same variety closer together and separating those of different varieties to their mature spacings. In other words, within a mass grouping of five plants of the same variety, the mature size might require a spacing of five feet. By spacing these plants only three feet apart, the maturity time of the planting can be cut in half. This solution does nothing to diminish the ultimate appearance of the planting and does not require that some of the plants be removed later simply because they are all of the same variety and appearance. An adjacent planting of a different variety, however, must be spaced according to the mature growth of the two varieties. If the two varieties grow into each other, the appearance of the landscape will be distorted. Trees should always be spaced for ultimate growth unless a forested appearance is desired, or a hedge-type screen is planned for several trees of one variety.

It is wrong for anyone to think of a landscape, or at least some parts of it, as being permanent. Some plants—upright evergreens are a good example—are used in locations for which they ultimately become too large. It would be nice if plants grew to enough different mature sizes to suit all uses, but unfortunately, they do not. Consequently, the landscaper and the customer must both realize that landscapes must be rennovated from time to time. This should not distress anyone. After all, people repaint and redecorate their houses periodically. Mostly, they do this to maintain the home, although they also enjoy changing its appearance. Why should the exterior of the house be any different? Relandscaping an older home can be exciting and fun and can profit both the landscaper and the homeowner.

Design landscaping for those primarily concerned with the property. Designing landscaping is fun; especially when one is allowed to do the design to suit one's own taste. However, if a professional landscape nurseryman wishes to satisfy his customer and hopes for a recommendation of the firm's services to others, he must consider the customer's desires before his own. This does not mean that the landscaper should do an inferior landscape design to suit a customer's poor taste. It simply means that the landscaper should endeavor to find out about the style of landscaping the customer likes best and provide a well-done plan for that style.

Before designing the landscape, the designer should visit with the owners of the property to determine their preferences. As they make suggestions, the designer can discuss with them the feasibility of their ideas and begin steering them toward a well conceived landscape. If the customers have had bad experiences in the past with, for example, thorns on plants, this is the time to find out—not later, when the designer has plastered mentor barberry all over their plans.

The questions asked by the designer are very important at this time. The designer should find out how many family members there are, what use they plan to make of the yard, what needs they have in the way of a service area, what their favorite plants are, which plants they dislike, and whether they entertain much, and, if so, how large the groups are.

All of these considerations will guide the designer toward proper decisions concerning patio size, area definition, and landscaping style.

Delineation of a Landscape Plan or Sketch

Sometimes there is a tendency for uninformed persons to think that any landscape plan characterized by good drafting is a well-designed plan. Anyone well-versed in landscape design should know better, of course, but professional-looking delineation does add credibility to a plan. Actually, design and delineation have little to do with one another. A person can be an excellent designer, but because of a lack of training, experience, or artistic skills, might not be able to draw a professional looking plan. Conversely, a fine draftsman may be a poor designer. Landscape nurserymen are most likely to fall into the first category.

If a landscaper knows from past experience that he is a good designer but is unable to represent these plans adequately on paper, a couple of remedies are available. Draftsmen can be hired, and, although they may not know anything about design, they can turn crudely delineated designs, scribbled on paper, into beautifully represented plans. Anyone with artistic talents can be hired to do this work, although the plans must always be carefully checked before they are shown to customers, to make sure the details were not lost in translation.

Rubber stamps, imprinted with plant representations, can be purchased for designing landscapes. These stamps work very well and, when blueprinted, look professional. Similarly, plant representations can be purchased on transfer-type materials, which stick to paper after being rubbed off with a pencil. Lettering is also available in transfer letters or ink stamps, which can be used to make a professional looking presentation. All that remains is to draw the boundary lines and the floor plan of the house on the paper with a pencil.

A qualified landscape architect is, of course, an ideal solution. Many landscape nurseries do a large enough volume of plans to be able to employ several landscape architects. Some firms utilize these persons as salespeople as well as designers, while others prefer to separate the two functions, hiring specialists for each. While almost all landscapers would like to hire the services of landscape architects, many have not, largely because they have been reluctant to pass on these charges to their customers. There is justification for this reluctance. Many customers have felt that, since the landscaper hopes to sell plants and services, he should be willing to provide design services free of charge. A good design service, however, is a separate endeavor, with a value of its own.

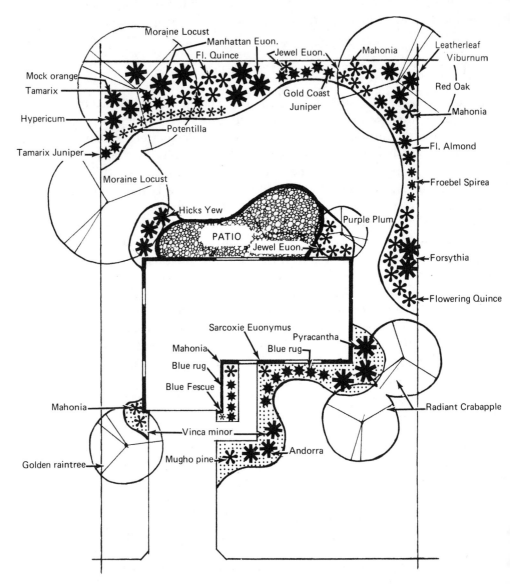

Figure 5-3. Plan using transfer symbols.

Some of the firms that charge for their plans either make a straight per-plan charge or an hourly charge with no discount. Others charge a fee for their plans, then offer discounts to their customers based on the amount of purchases they make. By this discounting system, the landscaper is able to protect the value of his design services, while rewarding his customers when they make purchases. As an example, not to be considered average, a landscaping firm might charge $100 for a landscape plan, then discount $50 of that cost when the customer's purchases exceed $500 during a specified time period, and discount the remaining $50 when the customer's purchases exceed $1,000 during that period.

Regardless of the methods chosen for the rendering of, or charging for, landscape plans, it is important to realize that customers are unlikely to place much value on those plans unless the landscaper himself feels they are valuable. They must appear to be professional, and the landscaper must treat them in a professional manner.

Handling Plant Materials

The physical care and handling of plant materials is of the utmost importance to the landscape nurseryman. The methods used affect his reputation, his profit margin, the efficiency of his operations, and the way he and his employees feel about the firm. Most landscape firms have to handle large volumes of plant material; their success is related in many ways to the success of that plant material.

Storing Plant Materials

A shipment of plant material sometimes goes directly from the wholesaler to the jobsite, where it is immediately planted. This is fine when it occurs, but more often, the landscaper must store the plant material for a period of time before he can plant it. This storage is important, both in terms of the cost of the material and its livability.

The condition of the plant material upon arrival governs its care to a large extent. Plant materials can be balled and burlapped (b&b), bareroot (br), container-grown (pot), or packaged, which includes peatballed plants. These are known as conditions of the material, and each requires different treatment.

Balled and burlapped plants, if they are to be held for a long period of time, should be healed in with straw, shingle-tow, or some other moisture-conserving material. They should be watered frequently and never allowed to completely dry out. Too much water, on the other hand, will cause the burlap to deteriorate more quickly. Once the ball is thoroughly wet, as it should be shortly after it arrives, the mulch is applied. As the mulch begins to dry, short waterings will keep the ball moist, but not saturated. Overhead sprinklers work best for b&b material, since the burlap will not allow the moisture to be absorbed quickly.

If b&b material is to be stored for long periods of time, the burlap might have to be overlaid occasionally with a new layer of burlap or rot-proof burlap might have to be applied upon arrival, before storage. After a long-term storage in sawdust or some other medium, roots from the ball will project into the medium. Care should be exercised not to cut off more than necessary of this root growth as the plants are re-moved. These new feeder roots can increase the trees' chances of survi-val after transplanting and can enhance subsequent growth. New burlap should be wrapped around the ball as it is readied for transplant to prevent the roots from drying out.

If bare-root material is to be held in a dormant state, it can be stored in cold storage; if not, it can be *puddled-in*. Puddling involves laying the plants in a ditch or trench, then backfilling over the roots with soil, straw, or other mulch to conserve water. The trench protects the roots from the wind and aids in keeping the root system wet. Neither cold storage nor puddling will last indefinitely. The plants will suffer a greater shock if they are held by these methods for long periods, then exposed to more severe drying conditions after transplanting. Mist sys-

Figure 5-4. A temporary holding area for plants that are to be installed within a month. The lath fence protects these plants from the wind. Note the pulsating sprin-klers on top of the fence.

tems are sometimes used in cold storage to water and to control the humidity of the atmosphere. Plants held by puddling are usually hand-watered.

Container-grown plants are often stored on bare ground, with no mulch, since the container does supply some insulation. These plants can be watered by an overhead sprinkler, by hand-held hose, or by individual drip tubes. Drip tubes are small tubes leading from a larger pipe into the individual containers. Container plants must be watered daily when temperatures are high and frequently when it is cool. The containers are designed for good drainage, since the plants would easily drown if they were not. If containers are being stored for long periods of time, the sides should be split to allow roots to grow into a surrounding mulch. This prevents the plants from becoming root-bound. The addition of mulch around the containers will make watering easier over the long haul.

Packaged plants are normally wrapped with plastic to prevent the shingle-tow, peat moss, or other material mulching the roots from drying out. These plants do not dry out quickly and should not be watered often. When they are watered, the water should be applied sparingly, so the bag does not end up being full of water. The moisture level in the mulch can be checked by loosening the top of the bag and feeling the mulch inside. Moisture in the mulch is readily discernible to the touch.

Lath fences or lath roofs can aid in plant storage keeping the wind and sun from hitting the plants directly. They provide a mini-climate most suitable for holding the plants. When the plants are finally moved to another location, and no longer have the lath protection, they often require special attention for a period of time to minimize the shock of the wind and sun's full attention. Often, they will wilt during the hottest part of the day, even though there is plenty of soil moisture. When this happens, a syringing with the hose may be necessary to temporarily slow their transpiration rate. Soon, they harden to the new conditions, achieve new root growth, and are able to fend for themselves.

Carrying Plants

Moving plants from one location to another or loading and unloading affords an excellent opportunity to either kill or maim even the most hardy plant. Each time a plant is picked up, there is a chance that branches will be broken or scarred or the root system will be loosened. Proper handling methods minimize this risk and make the handling easier at the same time.

Balled and burlapped plants should always be handled by the ball. The ball is heavy in proportion to the remaining weight of the plant. If the plant is picked up by the branches or foliage, it can be severely damaged. The plant's branches and foliage can be bruised or even broken. Although this damage might not show up for some time, it will surely show up. Carrying a balled and burlapped plant by the ball provides further support to the ball, ensuring that it will not crack or break, either of which is most damaging to the plant. If a plant cart is unavailable, a piece of burlap serves nicely as a sling for those b&b plants that are too heavy for one person to carry. The burlap sling can be laid on the ground, and the ball rolled onto it. Then one person on each side grabs two corners of the burlap and lifts it straight up. The sling provides a secure base for the ball and makes the plant easier to carry.

Plant carts, dollies, or hand trucks are essential for the movement of large b&b material. The combination of leverage and wheels make it possible for one person to maneuver large plants without undue effort. Hand trucks carrying very heavy balls can be rolled up planks onto trucks or trailers and unloaded. By using a block and tackle, or some other rope and pulley system, this loading can be done with a minimum of effort and a maximum of safety.

Figure 5-5. An experienced, careful tractor operator loads a large balled and burlapped tree onto a trailer using a front-end loader. Note the tire chain sling being used around the ball.

Truck-mounted cranes and slings can be used to good advantage for loading b&b material. Cranes are manufactured that mount on the sideboards or to the floor of a truck and are operated by hand-operated hydraulic jacks, electric motors, or some other mechanical means. The crane is hooked to a sling. The sling may be custom-built or it may be a tire chain for a large-size tire. The crane lifts the ball to a height level with the truck bed, then swivels before setting the plant down.

A tractor with a front-end loader may also be effectively used to load large b&b material. Once more, a sling is used to cradle the ball, and a log chain is hooked at one end to the sling, at the other end to the loader. Safety precautions must be carefully observed, so the chain does not break loose while a worker is underneath the ball. A good, experienced tractor operator is necessary for this delicate operation.

To move a large ball a rope is secured at one end to a solid object, such as a metal post driven well into the ground, and wrapped around the ball; when men pull on the other end of the rope, the ball begins to roll. One or two men must guide the direction of the roll to ensure that the ball does not roll off of the rope and head the wrong way. To perform this operation, it is necessary that the ball be extremely solid and reinforced with tight burlap, woven twine or rope, or wire wrapping. A soft, uneven ball will break or crack, causing damage to the plant.

Container-grown plants must be carried by the can, not by the branches or foliage. Special pliers, which work like ice tongs, are popular for moving container plants. Many landscapers have devised or purchased pallet-carriers for the three-point hitch on their tractors, primarily for moving several container plants from one location to another.

Plant Guarantees

Most nurseryowners offer plant guarantees, ranging from 100% replacement on down and ranging in duration from one growing season to one year. Usually, the guarantees stipulate that the nursery will warrant the plant to be true to the name by which they are selling it, to be free of disease or insect pests, and to be in a healthy state at the time of the sale. The "limited warranty" given by many nurseryowners also states that the nursery will not be liable for replacement of a plant that is damaged by fire, storm, insect or disease infestation, neglect, or other acts of God. In this way, the guarantee is meant to protect the customer from transplanting death only, but not from those other occurrences over which the nursery has no control. For making a replacement planting, labor is usually charged at current rates.

Plant guarantees are difficult to administer. Although most nurseries attempt to avoid replacing plants for reasons other than transplanting shock, in reality, it seldom works that way. It is very difficult to tell a customer that his plant died because he did not water it often enough, and still keep the customer happy, even if the nurseryowner knows absolutely that insufficient watering was the cause of death. Consequently, most nurseries make plant replacements with very little quibble, almost regardless of circumstances. The cost of offering a guarantee is included in the price of plants, so, unfortunately, the customer ends up paying more because of it.

Consumers are "guarantee conscious" in the marketplace today. People are reluctant to buy anything without a guarantee, even though it ends up costing them more. Manufactured items, like cars, probably should have guarantees, since they are assembled by people, and people do have their bad days. Guaranteeing a car to run, however, is not the same as guaranteeing a plant to live.

Plant Insurance

Some nurserymen have discontinued offering plant guarantees, and offer instead, an insurance policy that can be purchased along with a plant. This serves as an alternative for those good gardeners who are highly successful at starting transplanted plants and do not wish to pay the extra cost of the guarantee. Such an insurance policy might be helpful in making customers realize that plants are living, breathing entities that are definitely perishable, if not given the proper care.

SUMMARY

The landscaping of real estate is the arrangement of space and features on a property so they are, at one time, both functional for the needs of that property and pleasing to view.

Since beauty is in the eye of the beholder, the landscape must be pleasing to the view of those who own or frequent the property most often.

A quick environmental diagram, when property measurements are taken, is helpful in designing wind protection, shade, and screening. While shade is essential in the summer, provision should be made to let the sun in during the winter, in cold climates. Wind protection and screening must be well coordinated, lest one should interfere with the other.

Look for the best features on a property or building and landscape to accent these. After that, try to distract attention from the property's or building's worst features. A building looks best when the landscaping "snugs" it into the property. When its sharp lines and angles are softened, the building blends in more readily with the rounded contours of the surrounding terrain.

A designer might be able to go against nature for a short period of time, but he surely will have to pay for it later.

Planting with a definite purpose in mind helps avoid overplanting and aids in the creation of a functional landscape. Underplanting is just as bad as overplanting because the landscape develops so slowly that the first occupants seldom see the results.

A good designer will try to find out as much as possible about his client's needs and desires for landscaping, then proceed to design to suit those needs and desires.

A professional looking plan representation will help convince clients that the design is also professional. Rubber ink stamps or transfer symbols are suggested as aids to those without graphic talents or those who cannot hire landscape architects or other capable design personnel.

Care for plant material that must be temporarily stored before installation will depend largely on whether it is balled and burlapped, bare-root, containerized, or packaged.

Plants maintained under a lath screen or in cold storage must be given special care for a short period after transplanting to ensure a proper adjustment to the new "climate" in which they are planted.

Methods used to handle and load plants will greatly affect their health and vigor. Balled and burlapped plants should always be carried by the ball, while container-grown plants should always be carried by the container. Hand trucks and burlap slings aid in carrying b&b material; special pliers are available to carry containers.

Large b&b material may be comfortably and safely loaded and unloaded using hand trucks with ropes and pulleys, or cranes or front-end loaders with either custom-built slings or large size tire chains.

Plant guarantees, while intended to guarantee only against transplanting death, validity of name, and health at the time of the sale, are in reality often a guarantee against anything. Guarantees vary in duration and in amount.

SUMMARY QUESTIONS

1. What characterizes a good landscape designer?
2. Describe four ways of providing shade in a landscape.
3. Why is it inadvisable to protect a yard completely from wind?
4. In what ways must the designer be careful in his or her "camouflage" of gas meters, air conditioners, and like objects?
5. Why is it that buildings do not blend well with their surroundings without landscaping?

6. What is the principle behind the funnel-effect–type of landscaping?

7. Name four uses for trees in a landscape.

8. Why should landscaping be in keeping with the area in which the property is located?

9. What is overplanting?

10. Why should landscaping not be thought of as permanent?

11. Why is it important for a designer to find out as much as he can about his client's needs and desires before designing a landscape?

12. Why must a landscape design look professionally done?

13. Why should a balled and burlapped plant always be carried by the ball, instead of by the branches or foliage?

14. Why should packaged plants be watered infrequently and sparingly?

15. Describe a method by which a large ball can be rolled, using a rope and a metal stake or post.

16. What is the major distinction between a guarantee for an inanimate object and a guarantee for a plant?

CHAPTER 6
Lawn and Landscape Maintenance

Perhaps *maintenance* is the wrong term to use in describing the efforts of landscaping firms to care for lawns and landscapes. *Maintenance* means "to keep in a specified state or condition." In reality, most landscaping firms involved in maintenance work seek to improve the lawns and landscapes, rather than just maintain them. Maybe *betterment* or some other, more positive term would be more descriptive of these efforts. Nevertheless, in our discussion we will use the term *maintenance* because of its wide-spread acceptance.

The maintenance of lawns and landscaping is an area of vital concern. Whether a firm is specifically in the maintenance business or merely performs maintenance functions along with other services, its maintenance practices largely affect the reputation of the entire landscaping industry. This is because the benefits of good landscaping are only visible when the landscape is well maintained. Poorly maintained landscaping and lawns will do little to stimulate public belief in their value or even in their necessity.

Lawn Maintenance

In chapter 2, the lawn was identified as being the most important feature in any landscape. It follows then that the lawn should also be the first maintenance consideration. Most people feel that lawn grasses are the most difficult plants to maintain. Trees, shrubs, and groundcovers seem to fend for themselves much better. Of course, people do not walk on trees, and it is safe to guess that there has never been a football game in a tree. We do not mow off the new growth on a tree with regularity. Furthermore, the roots of a tree, deeply embedded in the ground, are well insulated against man's follies and the ravages of nature.

Mowing

Lawngrasses must be mowed with some regularity, or they cannot be considered a lawn. If allowed to grow, a lawn eventually will revert to a more natural prairie existence. Mowing is probably the most abused of all maintenance measures. The health and vigor of lawngrasses relates directly to the methods used for mowing it.

Each time grass is mowed, some injury results. There is no way to cut a leaf into separate pieces without some bruising, tearing of tissue, and shock. Good mowing practices involve minimizing this injury.

The most common mistakes made in mowing are: mowing with a dull blade; allowing the grass to get too tall between mowings; mowing too short; and mowing grass in a weakened condition. While a sharp mower blade will cut cleanly, it still will bruise the grass blade at the point where it is cut. But this bruise will be slight, almost unnoticeable, and the plant's reaction will also be slight. A dull mower blade will tear the grass in half, causing a tissue die-back of several millimeters and resulting in a much more severe shock to the plant. Similarly, with the exception of the warm-season grasses that thrive on short mowing, mowing too short will severely shock the grass plants. When grass is shocked, it responds by not growing immediately, and it becomes subject to infestation by insects and diseases that prey on weakened plants with low resistance. Allowing grass to become too tall between mowings also serves to shock the grass plants in a way that is similar, though usually not as severe, as mowing too short. Mowing grass in a weakened condition adds more shock, where shock is already present, further weakening its condition.

Mower blades can be sharpened on a power grindstone or by hand with a file. Commercial maintenance firms are more likely to use a grindstone for efficiency. Constant sharpening must be done with care,

| too little bevel | too much bevel | just right |
| (blade dulls quickly) | (edge is brittle) | (durability and sharpness) |

END VIEW

Figure 6-1. Proper sharpening of mower blades.

in order to keep a straight cutting edge on the mower blades and maintain the blades in proper balance. An unbalanced blade, turning at high speed, can be hard on the mower's engine. The more bevel (the angle back from the sharpened edge) a blade has, the sharper the blade will be. If the bevel is extremely acute, however, the edge on the blade becomes thinner and weaker and consequently can be dented or dulled more easily. Sharpening mower blades properly is a practiced skill, learned more by "feel," than by study. Inexpensive balancing spindles are available to check the balance of the blade.

Most cool-season grasses, like bluegrasses, fescues, and ryegrasses, thrive at mowing heights of from 2½" to 3½". These tall mower heights allow the grasses to tiller properly, making them very thick and allowing them to manufacture large food supplies. Also, the root system is well insulated because the long grass blades provide an excellent barrier between the hot sun in the summer or the cold air in winter and the ground below. Increased chlorophyll production under higher mowing heights stimulates the dark green coloring of these grasses. For special-purpose uses like golf courses, these grasses are mowed shorter, but they are also more rigorously maintained under such circumstances.

Warm-season grasses, which grow low to the ground and spread by stolons, rhizomes, or both, respond better to low mowing heights. These grasses will not do as well when mowed at the heights recommended for cool-season grasses.

Mowing frequently reduces the shock, because less of the total grass blade is cut off. Additionally, the clippings will disintegrate quickly, returning to the ground as organic material. Although some experts still insist that it is necessary to remove clippings by bagging or raking, many now agree that if grass is mowed frequently so clippings are short, there is no harm in leaving them on the lawn. Some view this decomposition of organic material as a way of returning nitrogen to the soil. However, nitrogen is also required for the composting process, so nitrogen produced by composting might only balance nitrogen consumed.

Generally, as long as one-third or less of the total leaf blades are being cut, the mowing can be considered to be of sufficient frequency, and the clippings can be returned to the turf. At one time most experts thought that these clippings contributed to excessive thatch, which is an accumulation of dead leaf and stem material on the surface of the ground. Now, most agree that small clippings will decompose quickly and will not contribute to an adversely dense thatch layer.

Mowing grass that is wilted or otherwise in a weakened condition will further intensify the damage. Sometimes, if grass is severely weakened, the pattern left by the mower wheels will be visible as a light brown streak for days. Also the grass is much more susceptible to secondary infestations of diseases. Dollar Spot and other fungus diseases seem to be able to attack the grass more easily when its defenses are down. For best results, mowing should be done during periods when the grass blades are all turgid with water, showing the characteristic dark green color of healthy grass. If possible, it is best to mow in the morning or evening, when the weather is not extremely hot. The grass might be under stress, even if it has adequate moisture during the hottest part of the day.

Mowing grass in alternating directions each time improves its appearance by causing the grass blades to stand upright. Subsequent mowings leave the lawn with a criss-cross pattern that also contributes to its pleasing appearance.

Mowing efficiency. Commercial mowing requires efficiency. Because a business must charge higher rates than a neighborhood youth using Dad's mower, the business must do a superior job in less time. Typically, a maintenance firm might send two-man mowing crews, equipped with mowers, edgers, power trimmers, extra blades (and tools to change them), brooms, rakes, and other miscellaneous gear, out for a day's mowing in a company vehicle. This is quite an investment! Only if the crew is efficient can the company realize a fair return on its investment.

Efficiency begins with good scheduling. Mowing assignments should always be arranged for easy access and a minimum of travel time. Many firms schedule a day's mowing for a crew in one quadrant of a city, then another day's mowing in another quadrant, to keep travel to a minimum. Careful time checks should be made by the crew dispatcher to ensure that little time is lost between jobs.

When clippings are being collected in a catcher bag, the mowing crew can increase its efficiency by carrying an $8' \times 10'$ tarpaulin that can be spread out in the immediate area in which they are mowing. Clippings can be deposited on the tarp, allowing trips to the truck to be made only as the tarp is full, not with each full bag of clippings.

Trimming and edging are both required of a commercial firm, and both are time consuming. As discussed earlier, if the ground under the grass is just lower than adjoining sidewalks, drives, or curbs, the edging can be facilitated by lowering the height setting by ½" on the outside of the mower while making the first pass around the property. The ½" will be unnoticeable, except that it will trim the edge much more neatly, often eliminating the use of an edger altogether.

Trimming around plants, fences, walls, and other obstructions has been greatly reduced by the advent of the fishing line power trimmers. These machines, available in either electric or gasoline-powered models, are very effective and easily operated. Extreme caution must be used around plants, however, because these machines can cut through the bark and the cambium layer on a plant trunk, girdling the plant and causing its death. When operating these machines, safety goggles should always be worn.

Equipment care. Mowing crews should be carefully educated about the care and handling of their equipment. A careless crew can cause expensive damage to equipment; mowers can be dropped from trucks, hand tools and catcher bags can be buried under grass clippings (never to be seen again), or engines may be operated with insufficient engine oil or dirty air filters. This type of carelessness can negate the entire profits from the crew's operations.

Many firms control the maintenance of their lawn mowing equipment by attaching to each mower a record sheet on which the hours of operation are recorded. At the end of a specified period of operation, the mower is serviced; oil changed, filter cleaned, bolts tightened, and so forth. This service period is then recorded on the record sheet. Other firms service the mowers daily, believing the regularity ensures that the service will be properly carried out. Some firms have a shop mechanic who does the service work; others require crew members to perform the service. Regardless of the method, small machines do require regular maintenance, and a system should be instigated that will ensure that service.

Mowing safety. Power mowers are dangerous machines. The manufacturers have taken great strides in trying to make them as safe as possible, but any machine that small with a sharp blade rotating at high speed is inherently perilous. Below are some safety rules that always should be followed to the letter.

1. Debris can be picked up and thrown by the mower. Always check to see that the area to be mowed is debris-free.
2. Before starting the mower, place one foot firmly on top of the mower deck and make sure the other foot is on solid ground, well away from the mower.
3. Make sure the catcher bag or deflector shield are firmly attached before starting.
4. Make sure the area is free of children or other onlookers, before starting.
5. Never remove the catcher bag while the mower is running. Besides being dangerous, this practice will damage the grass in the area where the mower is left running.
6. Do not fill the mower with gas while it is running. A spark could cause an explosion. The mower should be filled off of the lawn area; any gas spilled on the grass will kill it.
7. Always mow a slope on the sidehill, never up and down.
8. Always push the mower in front, never pull it.
9. Shut off the engine whenever someone approaches the mower.
10. Disconnect the spark plug wire before working on the mower.

Watering

Except for a newly seeded or sodded area, lawngrasses should be watered as infrequently as possible. Frequent watering encourages shallow rooting, because, although roots do not grow toward water as is popularly believed, they will continue to grow deeper as long as they have adequate moisture. If excessive moisture is present in the top layer of soil, the root's need for water will be satisfied, and the roots will not grow further.

When water is applied, it should be applied in quantity. During the summer months, the operation of a sprinkler for four hours might deposit an inch of water to the area. This type of water application will reduce the frequency of watering and will result in a reduced water cost. Since all sprinklers are different, and the water requirements are different in various areas, local determinations must be made about the length of sprinkler settings. To determine the amount of water applied by a sprinkler, place a flat bottomed, straight sided pan or other container under the sprinkler for a period of operation. At the end of the period, measure the amount of water in the container as the equivalent in inches of precipitation.

Grass wilts when it is dry; the leaves take on a bluish green cast and instead of standing straight, they curl inward. Grass should not be watered until it begins to show the symptoms of wilting. By the same token, if a green, lush lawn is desired, the grass should not be allowed to dry beyond the initial stages of wilting. Beyond that stage, most grasses go into a dormant state, the stand of grass thins out, and weeds begin to intrude.

Timing water applications to a lawn area is important. Early morning is generally the best time because the temperature and wind are low, which reduces evaporation, yet the leaves dry quickly after the watering ceases. Late evening watering is a poor choice during the warm time of the year because the leaves stay wet, creating high humidity at the level of the grass blades. That humidity, coupled with warm temperatures, produces an ideal condition for the growth of fungus diseases. Watering during the hot time of the day is alright if necessary, although evaporation from the sun and wind will reduce the efficiency considerably.

Commercial watering. Watering lawns commercially involves doing the job right, as efficiently as possible. The type of equipment selected and the personnel efficiency are the deciding factors. Sprinklers should be selected that will cover the largest possible area evenly and without needing to be moved frequently. Depending upon the water pressure and volume available, and the size of the area, the large pulsating, traveling sprinklers work well for sizeable areas. The watering can be completed with a minimum number of return trips to move the sprinkler from one location to another. Smaller sprinklers will be required for smaller areas and should be selected to cover a variety of area sizes and shapes. Each location to be watered should be serviced by the maximum sprinkling equipment possible at one time, so return trips to make settings will be held to a minimum. Again, the water pressure and volume will dictate the number and type of sprinklers available at one time.

Individuals in charge of commercial watering must be highly organized. The watering must be completed in the shortest possible time, and all areas must be adequately covered. For safety reasons, they must be extremely careful about sprinkler settings. Auto accidents have been caused by drivers swerving to avoid the water spray from a misdirected sprinkler or jerking the steering wheel in response to an unexpected cold spray of water.

The timing of commercial watering often involves consideration of working hours and days. If a landscaping firm in charge of watering commercially must pay its employees overtime on weekends, it might want to start the watering early in the week, before the grass actually shows a need, in order to complete watering before the weekend. Allowing the grass to go through the weekend without water might cause wilting to proceed to dormancy, in which case it will take a long time to restore its color and health.

Fertilizing

Most lawns require commercial fertilizer to prosper in a thick, lush, dark green condition. The selection, timing, and method of application of these fertilizers are important. The grass species, location, and soil fertility will govern the amount and timing of fertilizers, along with the type of fertilizer selected.

Soil fertility tests are a good idea, particularly in an area that is unfamiliar. These tests can be provided for by both public and private agencies. Samples are taken from random parts of the area to be tested, mixed together, and then submitted to a soil-testing lab. In due time, a report is issued by the lab, detailing the nutrient requirements. A fertilizer can then be selected to supply these nutrients.

Nitrogen, which governs the growth rate and the green color of grass, is the most important requirement. Nitrogen moves in the soil, leaching out of the root zone as water is added. Consequently, it is also the most frequently required nutrient. In smaller amounts, phosphorus and potash are needed. Trace amounts of other elements, such as sulfur, magnesium, and iron, are also required, although these are normally present in most soils.

Fertilizer amounts are often gauged by the amount of nitrogen (N) per 1,000 square feet. Fertilizer analysis is recorded on the package by the percentages of nitrogen, phosphorus, and potash they contain, in that order. Hence, a bag of fertilizer containing an analysis of 23-6-4, for example, will consist of 23% nitrogen, 6% phosphorus, and 4% potash. The remaining 67% of the material will contain a few trace elements, but mostly inert carriers to give the fertilizer bulk and carry it properly through the spreader.

Calculations for applying the proper amount of fertilizer will depend upon the results of soil tests and the requirements of the local area. Generally though, cool-season grasses require three to four applications of fertilizer during the year, each designed to apply 1 lb. of actual N/1,000 square feet. Thus, if a 50-lb. bag of 23% N fertilizer is being used, each bag will contain 11½ lbs. of actual nitrogen and will cover 11,500 square feet, when applied at the rate of 1-lb. actual N/1,000 square feet. These applications to cool-season lawns should be made in early spring, late spring, early fall, and late fall. Fall applications should contain some phosphorus and potash to encourage root growth during the fall.

Warm-season grasses require monthly fertilizer applications of from 1 lb. to 2 lbs. actual N/1,000 square feet each month from April through July. No fertilizer should be applied to these lawns at other times of the year.

Fertilizer materials are not all alike, even though their formulation analysis may be similar. The sources for the nutrients and their compounding regulate the speed with which nutrients are released, and consequently, the length of time a fertilizer material will feed a lawn. The formulation also governs the possibility of fertilizer "burn." Selection of fertilizers must be made carefully to realize maximum results.

Fertilizers can be applied successfully by either broadcast- or drop-type spreaders. Directions for their use must be followed carefully and they must be set according to the fertilizer manufacturer's recommendations. Fertilizer should not be broadcast by hand or by any other method, since it is impossible to achieve even coverage.

Liquid application of fertilizer materials has become a big business in recent years. Liquid fertilizer materials can be custom-mixed to serve a specific area, and other pest control materials can be mixed into the solution. This solution is then sprayed onto lawn areas in less time than is required for dry material application. Many liquid application lawn maintenance companies have franchised their operations. This permits aspiring business owners an excellent opportunity to enter the field with a lower investment and less expertise. Training programs for new franchisees greatly speed the learning process.

Pest Control

It would be impossible to itemize all of the diseases and pests that could possibly ravage lawns and landscapes or to adequately describe all the available chemical controls. Nevertheless, some general remarks on pest control as it applies to both lawns and landscape plantings may prove valuable.

A valid comparison might be to visualize pest control as one would visualize good police work. In both cases, the diagnosis must be accurate in order to preclude any control measures that cause additional, nonrelated problems. Only the minimum necessary force for control should be applied in each case; again to avoid creating additional, nonrelated problems. When control is necessary, it must be exercised accurately, firmly, and with the proper timing, so the problem can be quickly controlled.

Police agencies first try to quell disturbance by talking to the individuals involved and trying to help them resolve their differences. Similarly, if a pest is present in the landscape, the first order of business is to identify it and determine the severity of the problem. If the pest is a chewing insect, known to have a short life cycle and to cause little damage (except some holes in leaves), perhaps it is best left untreated. On the other hand, a severe infestation of bagworms, for example, can riddle an entire evergreen population in fairly short order. Such an infestation requires treatment.

When discussion fails to quell a disturbance, the police make a show of force, hoping to convince the perpetrators that if push comes to shove, the police will win. When force becomes necessary, the police use as much restraint as possible in order to prevent turning a small disturbance into a riot. Similarly, when chemical controls are necessary, the landscaper should use the chemical that will do the job with the least toxicity and the least residual effect. If everyone would follow this advice, we would have good control over plant pests and be able to maintain the quality of life quite well.

Timing is critical. If the police are five minutes late in arriving, they may face a full-scale melee instead of a minor dispute. If bagworms are not killed when they are extremely small, much stronger chemicals with a longer residual effect will be required, and not all of them will be killed. Proper diagnosis involves not only identifying the pest correctly, but also determining the pest's stage in his life cycle, so chemicals can be applied at the correct time for control.

Police agencies study situations carefully and develop regulations to govern their actions for each type of disturbance encountered. Chemical pest control is a studied science also. Chemical companies develop and test their chemicals to make sure they are safe and effective. Colleges test them further and recommend the most appropriate chemicals for the control of each pest. But the users of these chemicals control how they are utilized. If the label directions are followed and the chemicals used are those recommended by the experts, the environment can be safely protected, while pests are effectively controlled. *Always follow the label directions exactly for any pest control chemical.* More is not better. More is simply foolish and dangerous, and less will not accomplish control.

Maintenance of Landscape Plantings

In a properly designed landscape, maintenance requirements are minimal. The plantings are designed to grow to their maturity and are well suited to the climatic zone in which they are planted. Still, some main-

Figure 6-2. A well-maintained lawn area is not only useful, but beautiful as well.

tenance is required, especially if betterment, rather than maintenance, is the real goal.

Watering

Mature plantings require little, if any, watering to stay alive. New plantings, on the other hand, will require regular watering as described in Chapter 4. Mature plantings will grow and prosper, however, with regular watering during dry periods. These plants will grow faster, look better, and will resist invasion by diseases and pests better because of their healthy status. Leaves of well-watered plants will be larger and will have better color.

Watering mature plants deeply, either by means of a root feeder or a slowly trickling hose, should be done no more often than weekly, even in a porous soil, in dry, hot weather. Frequent, shallow watering will result in a shallow root system, which will require water more often and will not provide the plant proper support.

Since most plants have the majority of their feeder roots near the drip-line, at the edge of their foliage, water should be applied at this point. Additionally, although deep watering encourages a root system that will be deeper, most of the feeder roots, even on the largest trees, will be in the top 1' of soil.

Fertlizing

Plants require nutrients too. Trees and shrubs in a landscape will benefit from fertilizer materials applied to the lawn surrounding them, but they will benefit more from fertilizers applied directly in their root zone. As in the case of watering, the application of fertilizer will improve the overall health of the plants. To be sure, it will also increase their rate of growth.

Numerous fertilizers are available for trees, shrubs, and groundcovers. Some are dry formulations, designed to be applied directly to the ground, poured into holes drilled into the root zone, or flushed into the root zone in liquid form by means of a root feeder. Many of these fertilizers have been formulated for particular types of plants.

The timing of fertilizer application for trees, shrubs, and groundcovers is important. Trees can be fertilized in the early spring and summer when growth is taking place. They can also be fertilized in late fall to encourage root development and prepare them for the next growing season. They should not, however, be fertilized in late summer or early fall. To do so might encourage too much growth just before a hard frost, at a time when the tree should be slowing its growth and preparing for dormancy. Roses require regular feedings during the blooming season. Each other type of plant has its own fertilizer requirements, which can be obtained through extension service bulletins or fertilizer company recommendations.

Pruning

Possibly the most misunderstood aspect of landscape planting maintenance is pruning. That it is misunderstood is evidenced by the fact that plantings all over are continuously pruned to look like anything but the plant in its natural growth habit. Plants look best when they are allowed to grow in the form that is natural to them and are selected to suit a landscaping need because of their form, size, color, and texture. There are exceptions, of course. Clipped hedges certainly have their place, as do formally pruned evergreens in a formal landscape. But formally pruned plants in a landscape that was planned to be informal are definitely out of place.

Pruning is done to restrict size, improve plant structure, rejuvenate growth, improve flowering, or increase fruit-bearing capacity. Since fruit tree pruning is an entire science in itself and is well documented elsewhere, we will not discuss it here.

Pruning evergreens. There are two basic types of evergreens: broadleaf evergreens and narrow-leaf–type evergreens. Most of the narrow-leaf evergreens fall into three categories of growth: upright, spreading, and prostrate. Upright evergreens have a conical shape, spreading evergreens are normally more wide than tall, and prostrate evergreens are very short, with branches remaining close to the ground and spreading several feet.

When upright evergreens are used in tight quarters, such as the front foundation planting of a house, they are normally sheared into a tight, formal form. These plants are misused to a large extent because they draw so much attention, and they are often placed where attention is undesirable. They can, on occasion, be used in a formal scheme, to draw attention properly. A more suitable purpose, however, to use these evergreens, in their natural shape as part of a windbreaking or screening planting.

Upright evergreens are naturally conical, having a series of longer and shorter branches that give them a layered appearance. Proper pruning involves cutting back the longer tips of foliage and allowing the shorter tips to replace the longest ones. Overall, such pruning will reduce the size of the plant temporarily, but the natural shape will be retained.

Pruning of the other juniper-type narrow leaf evergreens is done in similar fashion; that is, always shortening the longer tips of foliage and allowing the shorter tips to replace the longer ones. The natural layered shape of the plant will be preserved. It is often impossible to tell when pruning has been done, even though the plant is some 6" to 8" smaller on all sides.

Most broadleaf evergreens have rounded forms, but again, in the natural state, some branches are longer than others. Pruning that leaves all of the branches the same length formalizes the plant and makes it appear unnatural. Again, the longer branches should be pruned back, leaving the shorter branches to dominate, while effectively reducing the size of the plant. Each cut should be made as close as possible to a lateral bud, since the stem remaining above the last bud will dry up anyway. Cutting close to the bud allows the plant to quickly heal the wound and reduces the chances of infection by disease organisms or infestation by insects. New branches will be generated at the point of the lateral bud, thickening the density of the plant foliage.

Evergreens may be pruned at virtually any time of the year, except when they are frozen. It is best, however, to prune them during their spring and fall growth periods; they will recover more quickly.

Pruning deciduous trees. Trees, like other woody ornamentals, grow by terminal buds. This means that if a small tree has its lowest branch extending from the trunk at a height of 3' off the ground, that branch will remain at that height for its entire life. When pruning young trees, it is important to remember this fact and leave only those branches that are ultimately to remain on the tree. Do not, however, immediately remove all of the branches from a 6' tall tree, just because ultimately it is desirable to have a 6' span between the ground and the first branches. The young tree needs those branches and the leaves on them to produce food for its survival. As the tree grows, the branches can gradually be removed.

The gap between branches on a tree narrows as the tree develops, because each branch enlarges in diameter. (Each branch does not grow further from those adjacent to it.) Gradually, the branches should be thinned to a spacing which is ultimately suitable for a mature tree.

Branches can be "aimed" in the right direction during the pruning process. A lateral branch, which is growing downward when it would be more desirable for it to grow upward, can be aimed in that direction. This is accomplished by pruning the branch back to a lateral bud on the top of the branch. As the new growth ensues from that bud, it is started in an upward direction. Selective pruning might need to be done later, since growth might begin from more than one bud at the point of the initial pruning cut. Small wounds on trees, which result from pruning cuts, need not be treated with any dressing; they will heal quickly. In fact, authorities are in some disagreement about the feasibility of dressing any pruning cut, because the dressing, while it protects, slows the healing process. Cuts should always be made as close as possible to the remaining branch or trunk to allow the cambium layer and bark to grow back over the wound as quickly as possible. Where it can be done, the wound should be cut at the closest possible angle to straight up and down, so it will effectively shed water.

Most trees are best pruned in late winter or early spring, in advance of spring growth. They should not be pruned while the wood is frozen.

Pruning deciduous shrubs. Although most deciduous shrubs have a growth pattern similar to the broadleaf evergreens and can best be pruned in the same manner, there are some other considerations to be made. Many of the deciduous shrubs are planted for their flower and must be pruned at the proper time to realize their maximum potential for flowering. Spring flowering shrubs, for example, should be pruned in the late spring, after blooming. Pruning later might mean the loss of some of the buds that will produce the flowers for the next spring. Likewise, fall flowering plants should be pruned in late fall, after their blooming period.

Pruning for rejuvenation is a process often followed on old, woody, flowering shrubs. In the late winter or early spring, many varieties of deciduous shrubs can be cut back very severely, even to the ground, and will respond by issuing new, leafy growth. The flowers might be lost for the year, but the renewed condition of the shrub is worthwhile. Often, only the older, more woody stems are cut clear back, while the smaller stems are left.

The pruning of a formal hedge requires some mention. In order for a hedge to remain full of foliage from top down to the ground, the base must be pruned to be wider than the top. Otherwise, adequate light will not reach the lower leaves. Consequently, the lower branches will die out, and the hedge will become leggy.

Pruning equipment should always be kept clean and sharp. Disease organisms can be transferred from a diseased plant to a healthy one by pruning shears. Hook and knife type shears are preferred to the knife and anvil type; the former cuts cleanly, close to adjacent twigs or buds, while the latter crushes a portion of the wood left behind and will not cut as close.

SUMMARY

Maintenance, if well done, stimulates greater consumer interest in the other services offered by a landscaping firm. Lawn maintenance is generally considered more difficult than landscape planting maintenance.

Grass plants are injured to a certain extent each time they are mowed. Common mistakes that contribute to a greater degree of injury are: mowing with a dull blade; allowing the grass to get too tall between mowings; mowing the grass too short; and mowing grass in a weakened condition.

Most cool-season grasses should be mowed at a height of 2½" to 3½", while warm-season grasses respond to shorter mowing heights.

When grass is mowed frequently, cutting off one-third or less of the leaf blades, there is no problem with returning the clippings to the turf where they will decompose.

Mowing crew efficiency is regulated by the scheduling of jobs for quick and easy access and through proper training and equipment. Mower maintenance is a very important part of commercial mowing.

Lawn mowers are inherently dangerous. Rules for safe mower operation should always be followed strictly.

Water should be applied to an established lawn heavily, infrequently, and evenly to encourage development of a deep root system and healthy grass. Water should only be applied when the beginning stages of wilt appear—a bluish green cast to the foliage and a curling of the leaves.

Commercial watering firms should select equipment that will cover a variety of shapes and sizes. Such equipment should be set for maximum coverage allowed by the available water pressure and volume. This reduces the number of return trips to make new sprinkler settings.

Watering during the early morning hours is best. Evening watering is not recommended because it creates an overnight condition of high humidity surrounding grass leaves, which can lead to an infestation of fungus diseases.

Fertilizers are identified by their analyses: the percentages of nitrogen, phosphorus, and potash contained in the material. Some are slow to release the nutrients, allowing them to feed over a longer time; others release quickly. The quick-releasing fertilizers are more likely to burn the grass.

Soil tests are advisable to guide fertilizer selection. Generally, cool-season grasses require 1 lb. actual nitrogen per 1,000 square feet, three or four times a year. Warm-season grasses require 1 lb. to 2 lbs. actual nitrogen per 1,000 square feet, once a month from April through July.

Dry fertilizer materials can be applied with either broadcast- or drop-type spreaders, following manufacturer's recommendations for rates and methods. Liquid fertilizers can be sprayed on a lawn. The liquid application business is growing and developing steadily.

The safe chemical control of pests in the lawn and landscape involves careful and sure diagnosis, determination of whether chemical measures are really necessary, application of chemicals having minimum toxicity and residual effect, and proper timing for best results. Label directions on chemicals should always be followed exactly.

Although mature plantings often exist without regular watering, they will respond to infrequent, but deep, waterings with improved appearance, growth, and resistance to pests. Water, like fertilizer, should be applied at the drip-line, where most of the plant's feeder roots are located.

Trees may be fertilized to good advantage in the early spring or late fall. Other plants require fertilizer at various times of the year for maximum growth, health, and appearance.

Plants should always be pruned to their natural growth habit. Clipped hedges and formal plantings have special uses and are exceptions. After each plant is analyzed for its growth habit, pruning should be accomplished to remove the longer growing tips, leaving the shorter tips to replace the longest ones, and thereby reduce the plant without changing its appearance.

Trees and shrubs grow from terminal buds. This means that a branch will remain at the same height on the tree where it first appears. Pruning should reflect that fact, leaving only those branches that are ultimately desirable. To aim a branch in the proper direction, the landscaper must prune to a lateral bud on the side of a branch that is headed the right way.

Flowering shrubs should be pruned shortly after they complete their bloom. This ensures that the next year's flower supply will not be diminished. This type of deciduous plant can be rejuvenated by cutting the large, woody canes out in early spring or cutting the entire plant down close to the ground.

A hedge must always be trimmed wider at the bottom than at the top to allow light to reach the lower leaves. Failure to do so will result in a top-heavy hedge, with few leaves at the bottom.

SUMMARY QUESTIONS

1. What are some of the reasons that grass is more difficult to maintain than trees, shrubs, or groundcovers?
2. What are the four most common mowing mistakes?
3. Why is it better to mow during the morning or late afternoon in the hot summertime?
4. Why should a mower blade be balanced?
5. Describe one method of facilitating edging by mower settings.
6. Why are fishing line trimmers sometimes dangerous to plantings?
7. Give two reasons for not leaving a mower running while the catcher bag is emptied.
8. Describe a safe mower-starting procedure.
9. Why should grass be watered as infrequently as possible?
10. Do roots actually grow toward water because they are attracted to it?
11. What regulates the number and size of sprinklers that can be set on a property at one time?

12. How does safety enter into commercial watering?

13. What nutrients do the three numbers in a fertilizer analysis represent?

14. Which nutrient is most likely to leach out of the root zone?

15. What is meant by the *minimum force necessary* in pest control?

16. Why is timing critical in pest control?

17. What are the five reasons for pruning plants?

18. Why should pruning cuts be made as close to the nearest branch or bud as possible?

CHAPTER 7
Selling the Product

All business activity begins with sales. No matter how effective the management of a business is, without adequate sales, profits will not occur.

Sales are generated by a customer's *need* or *desire* for goods or services. We all buy groceries, heating fuel, clothes, and many other essentials for living because we need them, although we may often desire them at the same time. On the other hand, many sales are generated by a desire for a product when a need for the product does not exist. Large pleasure boats are normally sold more from the standpoint of desire than need.

Often, products and services fall into categories in which both a need and a desire are present, although one usually outweighs the other. Landscaping is a good example of one of these categories. Those who know the value of landscaping recognize the need consumers have for it. Often, the consumer himself does not recognize this need, however, and if he considers purchasing landscaping at all, desire stimulates him to do so.

Active and Passive Sales Approaches

A business generates sales through either an active or a passive sales approach. A *passive* sales approach might best be described as one in which the firm advertises its services and lets the business come in as it will, with no further solicitation. Call-in orders over the telephone often are passive sales. Many route salesmen have a passive approach; they write their customers' orders each week, but make very little attempt to sell them anything new. An *active* sales approach is one in which the business and its salespeople energetically pursue potential sales that might not be generated by a passive method. Extensive advertising, personal solicitation of sales, and aggressive pursuit of customers are hallmarks of the active sales approach.

Although some businesses are much more aggressive in their pursuit of sales than others, most utilize both the active and passive sales ap-

Figure 7-1. Salesman shows landscape plans to customers. In this case, they are in the plant sales area having a first-hand look at suggested plantings.

proaches to a certain extent. Nearly all well-established businesses will receive some orders for goods or services without active solicitation on their part. The general sales approach of a firm becomes apparent, however, by its reaction to a normally passive sale, a call-in order, for example. That business which has generally an active sales approach will try to recognize each opportunity to add to the sale, while a firm of passive persuasion will take the order and look for no further business from it.

Attributes of a Good Salesperson

Salespeople are of many types. Anyone who makes sales by any method on a regular basis can be considered a salesperson, even though they might have many other duties as well. Although they come in all sizes, shapes, colors, and gender, there are basic attributes that a potentially good salesperson should have. These are described in the following list, not necessarily in order of importance.

1. A good salesperson will be knowledgeable about his or her products and services. A large part of any sales success must be attributed to the salesperson's ability to answer the customer's questions knowledgeably and to present the products or services in an appealing manner.

2. A good salesperson must be an educator. The ability to teach a prospective customer about the goods or services offered allows the salesperson to establish the needs or desires that will eventually motivate the customer to buy.

3. Anyone desiring to become a good active salesperson must be aggressive. Sales must be pursued energetically, so the customer knows that the salesperson is anxious to serve him. Being aggressive does not mean being obnoxious, however. The customer knows that the salesperson is desirous of making the sale, so there is no reason to try to hide that fact behind an unenthusiastic approach. Instead, the salesperson needs to approach the customer with a positive enthusiasm, indicating that the sale will be good for both parties.

4. A salesperson must be honest. No one can consistently make good sales in a community over a long period of time without a reputation for honesty. Those who keep their promises to customers about price, quality, or delivery date are the ones who will be successful in sales. Being honest is its own reward anyway, because of a sense of well-being that accompanies it. One broken promise has a most lasting effect on a customer than ten promises that are kept.

5. A good salesperson will be articulate. Everything said should be expressed clearly, concisely, and with a respect for the English language. It is not necessary to have a "tongue of silk," nor is it always desirable, but a customer must always be able to understand everything the salesperson says. Incorrect grammar must be avoided; it can be distracting to the customer.

6. Cleanliness and good grooming are essential for any aspiring salesperson. It is not necessary to wear a fine suit of clothes, though. The clothes worn by a salesperson should be in keeping with the types of products sold. While a salesman of men's clothing might be wise to wear the latest fashions, a landscaping salesman might look out of place in a three-piece business suit. It is best to dress conservatively, since flashy clothes might be a distraction, and it is important to keep the client's attention focused on the sales presentation.

7. A good salesperson will be sensitive to his or her client's feelings. An initial negative response on the customer's part will not deter the salesperson from trying to complete a sale, either now or in the future, but care must be exercised not to become a pest. Negative responses have different connotations, as will be discussed later in this chapter, and the person making sales must learn to judge these responses, so the customer will not be offended.

8. A good salesperson will always be grateful to his customers, who provide, in large part, his livelihood. A simple thank you, expressed

sincerely, is very meaningful. Once expressed, it need not be repeated; people can be overwhelmed with gratitude.

9. A good salesperson will never forget a client. A customer does not think about all of the others who also make purchases from a salesperson and will be disappointed not to be recognized at a later date. Always remember that a customer who makes purchases today might have need for further goods and services later.

10. Finally, a good salesperson will be loyal to his or her employer. The opportunity to continue making sales is totally dependent upon the relationship between the salesperson and employer. Customers frown upon disloyalty also.

As mentioned, salespeople fit many molds. Some are able to operate with a high-pressure approach, while others are very subtle in their approach. In making sales some depend upon their product knowledge almost exclusively, while others depend on outside activities that establish them as "nice" people to do business with. Regardless of the individual approach, a good salesperson must possess the characteristics just described to ensure continual success.

Prospecting

As the miner prospects for gold, so does the business prospect for potential customers. *Prospecting* can be described as the activity of a business to attract customers, who might then purchase goods or services from that business. Prospecting can be accomplished through various means of advertising or by personal contact. It is usually most successful when several methods are used in combination.

Advertising

Advertising is the most commonly used means of prospecting. Signs, telephone directory listings and ads, business cards, newspaper ads, radio and television spots, direct mail pieces, and magazine ads are all types of advertising that can be used to develop prospects. Any means of presenting the company name, address, phone number, and business services available to potential clients can be considered advertising. The use of a welcoming service, such as "Welcome Wagon," is also a type of advertising used in prospecting. In all cases, such advertising is designed to make potential clients either call or visit the place of business, indicating a desire for more information about its products and services. These "prospects" can then be contacted by salespeople for further development.

Direct Contact

Prospecting can also be accomplished by direct contact. In those areas where door-to-door sales approaches are restricted by law, it is sometimes necessary to precede a personal contact with some form of advertising, often a direct mail piece or welcoming service, offering homeowners a gift or other incentive to have a salesperson call on them. In areas not so restricted, salespeople will usually ring doorbells, introducing themselves and the business they represent to the residents. The object of such a visit is not usually to make an immediate sale, but to generate interest in the company's products and services. Such an approach is called a "soft sell," because no pressure is put on the residents to buy anything immediately. The salesperson merely introduces himself or herself to the residents, briefly tells them about the services and products represented, presents a business card, and leaves. This type of approach exudes confidence in the landscaping company's workmanship and product quality. Hopefully the prospective clients will check on the firm's reputation, determine their own needs and desires, then call the salesperson back for a second visit.

The impressions made by a salesperson during an initial prospecting visit can be enhanced by either showing pictures of previously landscaped properties or, if possible, leaving a brochure with pictures and descriptions of goods and services offered.

The personal visit method of prospecting utilizes the personality of the salesperson, the reputation created by the firm, and advertising in the form of a business card or brochure to good advantage. Personal contact, when properly handled, is always more impressive than nonpersonal advertising methods alone.

Presentation of Bids and Estimates

When a prospect asks for an estimate or bid, the salesperson must respond properly, or the company's image will suffer. A request for a price for seeding a lawn, for example, should be met with sound estimation procedures and a firm price or price range. The temptation to toss off an estimate too quickly without measurements or proper calculations, regardless of the salesperson's previous experience, will reduce the credibility of the salesperson and the business as well. The best salespeople will take careful measurements as needed and make price calculations in the presence of the customer, so the customer knows that the bid or estimate given is accurate. Prices should be given in writing, and both the customer and the salesperson should retain a copy. The work and materials needed should also be specified. Even though the salesperson might keep very accurate records of all prices given customers, he or she cannot depend on the client to do the same. If the customer knows that copies of all conditions of a bid or estimate are owned by both himself and the business, misunderstandings are less likely to occur. Many businesses use a work estimate form, which serves the purpose of providing copies of prices given and also can be utilized to specify other conditions of work, such as guarantees.

Prices given to customers should be stated in definite amounts or definite price ranges. A salesperson should never say, "I think it will cost about this much." The customer is not interested in approximations. He wants a definite price for a bid and a definite price range for estimates. Even price ranges are of somewhat equivocal value to the salesperson, because often the customer will only remember the lower of the figures given.

The Sales Education

The customer should have a reason for each purchase. The identification of these reasons by the salesperson is often the primary motivation for the customer to buy goods and services. The education of customers concerning the reasons for making a purchase should be the primary function of the salesperson.

Landscape nurseries are often called to a new home to make suggestions for landscaping, although the homeowner may not have a clear understanding of the reasons for doing it. He may feel pressure to do some landscaping just to "keep up with the Joneses," but might not understand that it is also necessary for shade, wind protection, screening, area definition, simplification of maintenance, area usage, and beautification. The salesperson has a duty not only to educate a client concerning these needs but to cultivate his desires in the proper directions as well. When both desire and need are present, the impetus to buy is much stronger.

While educating the prospective client about the need for landscaping, the salesperson should keep in mind that the customer is primarily interested in only those products or services that apply to his particular situation. Discussion of services offered by the firm that do not apply to the customer's situation should be avoided, except to mention the availability of such services, if there is reason to suspect that need for them will arise later.

The education should be thorough. For example, when showing a customer a landscape plan that was prepared for his property, each plant should be discussed in detail. This includes presenting a thorough physical description of the plant along with pictures and the reasons for selecting the plant for that location. Flowering sequences, screening arrangements, shade angles, design elements, and area designations should all be discussed, but not to the extent that the customer becomes bored. It is not necessary to render a client expert in the field of landscaping. The purpose is, instead, to impress upon him that you have taken care to see that the best of all possible landscapes has been designed for his property. All construction features, such as decks, patios, fences, and retaining walls need to be carefully explained. The client must know that they were designed to serve *his needs*.

The customer's needs should always be emphasized. If a prospect calls a landscape firm to his house to help him "decorate" the front of the house, and the salesperson wishes to convince him of the necessity of a landscape plan, he or she can do so by establishing needs. The prospect is told that well-placed shade trees are needed to cool the house and reduce utility bills, that screening plants can make the yard more private and eliminate the need for a more expensive fence, and that properly designed landscaping can make the house seem larger, more attractive, and, consequently, more valuable. This information can then stimulate the customer's desire for the landscaping. The salesperson must then explain the necessity for a formal design, indicating that adequate time must be spent to properly consider all of the needs of the property and to accurately assess all costs. Most prospects respond to such an education in terms of their own needs with increasing desire for such services.

A sales education becomes a sales "pitch," when the salesperson begins to chatter nervously, changing voice inflection, being too polite, or making wild claims about the results to be expected. A sales presentation should always be made in a relaxed, conversational tone, with plenty of time allowed for questions. Questions should be encouraged, since people are more apt to remember something said in response to their question.

Part of the sales education is the presentation of prices. Because of a fear or rejection, salespeople are often nervous about presenting a price. If the salesperson feels that the price given might be considered too high by the customer, he or she may become nervous. This nervousness is quickly sensed by the customer who may then begin to doubt the fairness of the price. One of the primary rules of salesmanship is never to try to decide whether a price will suit a customer. The customer alone is able to determine the suitability of a price to his own budget. The salesperson, confident that the price is fair for his or her business to offer, should state prices firmly, with no hesitation and no qualification.

Making a Sale

Selling to an Individual Homeowner

Methods of making sales will be dictated, in large part, by the size and composition of the group to whom the sale is being made. Selling to an individual differs considerably from selling to a couple or to a committee. Making sales to a homeowner involves different strategy than making sales to a businessman.

When making sales to an individual, only one set of likes and dislikes will be encountered. It is the job of the salesperson to uncover those likes and dislikes as quickly as possible, so the objections raised by the customer can be dealt with while those features he likes can be accentuated.

The salesperson can learn much about an individual by observing the style and type of furnishings used in his house. The type of automobile owned by the customer is also worth observing. If an individual's home is well furnished, with many expensive pieces of art about, the salesperson might well pursue the sale from the standpoint of beauty. On the other hand, if furnishings, car, and so forth, have been selected by the homeowner for their durability and practicality, perhaps it would be best to pursue the sale from that standpoint.

Small talk with customers is fine, since most people use such talk to establish a comfortable atmosphere before talking business. However, the salesperson should not discuss inflammatory subjects, such as politics, because a difference of opinion between salesperson and customer can negate the chances for sales. As soon as the customer indicates that he is ready to discuss business, the salesperson should do so and should not wander off the subject thereafter.

Most of the time, objections will be raised by a customer during a sales presentation. Although the salesperson might feel that objections are a source of discouragement to him or her, nothing could be further from the truth. If the customer does not feel even remotely interested in purchasing, he will not usually bother to voice all the objections he might have, but will instead, try to end the conversation as quickly as possible. When the customer voices his objections, this affords the salesperson an opportunity to counteract them. The customer is saying, in effect, "If you can answer my objections satisfactorily, you have a chance to make the sale."

The four objections most commonly expressed by individuals are as follows:

1. "The price is too high."
2. "I don't think I can adequately take care of all of that."
3. "That appears to be overplanted."
4. "I really had something a little different in mind."

The primary rule for answering these objections is for the salesperson to always be positive. Negative statements like, "You don't know what you're talking about," may be true enough, but they surely will not induce the customer to purchase. Some suggested responses to these objections follow:

1. "Mr. Smith, I know that costs are surprising these days, but all of our goods and services are priced competitively, in line with our costs. We offer only the highest quality, and I'm sure you would find our prices to be fair were you to check around."
2. "Systematic plant maintenance can be quite simple. A plant need only be watered once a week, if watered thoroughly. We will build soil saucers around the plants to help catch and hold the water, and I can suggest some tools, such as a root feeder, that can be used to reduce the amount of time spent watering."
3. "The reason the plan seems to be full of plants is that we have drawn the plants at the sizes they will reach upon maturity. Of course, they will be separated much more when planted, but such planning avoids overgrowth later. Also, since we use more dwarf and compact varieties, which will result in a more permanent landscape, we must use more of them to adequately cover a given area."
4. "Apparently, I misunderstood your desires, Mr. Smith. I'm sure if we talk a little more, I can revise the plans to suit your needs. I will be most happy to do that for you."

Each response is made in a positive manner, indicating a genuine desire to please the customer. Of course, there are countless other objections a customer might make. The important thing is for the salesperson to offer positive, feasible solutions, so the objections work to his or her benefit. Many times, a customer is actually hoping the objections will be overcome so he may feel free to make the purchase without qualms.

After the sale and subsequent delivery or installation, it is imperative for the salesperson to make a return call upon the customer. If the customer is well satisfied with his purchase, the call will serve to tell the customer that the salesperson is interested in satisfying him, and that the salesperson has confidence in the performance of his or her company. If problems have arisen, they will be solved much easier at that time than later, after the customer has allowed the problems to fester.

Selling to a Couple

Selling to two people differs from selling to an individual, primarily because there are two personalities involved and possibly two sets of needs, desires, and objections. Also there is more possibility of a personality conflict between one of the customers and the salesperson.

Normally, in a transaction involving two people, one of them will dominate. The salesperson's job is to find out which one will dominate as quickly as possible and satisfy that individual. There are some signs to look for. Which one shows the most enthusiasm? Which one asks the most pertinent questions? Which one shows the most knowledge of the products and services being offered? The person answered in each of those questions is usually the driving force behind the decision to consider the purchase. If properly handled, that person will help make the sale.

The other half of the twosome may be the one who voices most of the objections. These objections must be handled with care. Poor answers will do nothing to change the viewpoint of the one who voiced the objection and could change the other person's mind about the transaction.

Deliberation over a disputed purchase between two customers can turn into an argument. The salesperson must avoid joining the argument or taking sides, for the result of either will be the alienation of at least one of the parties.

Selling to a Committee

Every committee is made up of three distinct parts: the *leader*, the *main body*, and the *anchor*. The leader will often, but not always, be the chairman. This leader is responsible for making the committee decide upon issues, and without him or her, no decisions would ever be reached. The anchor serves the opposite function. This individual drags his or her feet on decisions, taking the negative role. Many of the objections voiced will likely come from this individual. The main body of the committee consists of the remaining members, who will be persuaded by the most convincing argument. The roles often change from one issue to another, with different leaders and anchors for every discussion.

The salesperson's job is to identify the leader and the anchor as quickly as possible and deal primarily with them. Usually the leader is a strong and persuasive person. If he or she is convinced that the purchase is a good idea, the salesperson will have a strong ally in the effort to persuade the majority of the members. The anchor will usually offer ample opportunity for positive, feasible answers to objections, which, if properly handled, can help persuade the main body, but if improperly handled, can reverse the roles, making the anchor become the leader of a negative committee faction.

Close observation by the salesperson will usually reveal the roles of various committee members. The leader will quickly display a positive attitude and will attempt to stimulate discussion and action, while the anchor will continually voice doubts or objections. The members of the main body will discuss in general terms, but will not express feelings in either direction.

Committees will seldom make a decision without private discussion. It is difficult for a salesperson to leave a committee meeting room, knowing that objections to purchasing can be made without proper rebuttal afterwards. A good salesperson will make a strong effort at sales education, parry the objections as well as possible, then leave as the indication is made that the committee must deliberate privately. Successful identification of the committee leader and anchor, and adequate handling of each, should allow the salesperson to predict the decision that will be rendered.

After consummation of the sale, the salesperson must return to check upon the satisfaction of the committee. Again, it is wise to deal primarily with the leader and the anchor. If they are satisfied, the main body of the committee will likely be satisfied also.

Selling to a Business

Businessmen are individuals with likes and dislikes similar to others. Unlike individual homeowners, businessmen have profit as a common goal. A businessman is likely to regard the landscaping of his business in a completely different light than he would for his own home. Therefore, any way the salesperson can attach a potential for higher profits to the landscaping of a business will benefit his chances for success.

Education is a big part of sales to a businessman, who may be interested, but not know the specific reasons. An astute salesperson will point out the need for landscaping and explain that landscaping can be used, for example, as an attention-getting device, as a method for screening from view undesirable sights surrounding the business, and as a way of controlling traffic or defining parking areas. A businessman may not recognize the capability of fine landscaping to serve as a sign for his business—one that might draw more attention than a neon sign. He might not know that by creating nice surroundings, people will be drawn to his place of business. He might not realize that a well-done landscape can contribute to a feeling of well-being and contentment for his employees.

Businessmen pride themselves on being busy people. The salesperson must recognize this fact and take as little time as possible to complete transactions. Acknowledgement of the businessman's busy status is flattering, and he is likely to pay more attention to the salesperson once that fact is established.

Writing all prices and terms of delivery and performance might even be more important when negotiating with businessmen because they are used to dealing in written documents. Terms for payment should be very clear. Many businessmen will use another business's money as long as they can.

One final remark about dealing with a businessman. They appreciate those who do business with them. Whenever possible, the landscaping firm should reciprocate by patronizing those businesses that have made purchases from one of its salespersons.

Measuring Sales Effectiveness

Sales effectiveness, both of individual salespeople and of an entire sales force, should be continually measured. Like any other producing unit within a business, the sales force can be made more efficient, if adequate records are kept.

TABLE 7-1. Sales Effectiveness

Year Number	Salesman A		Salesman B		Salesman C	
	1	2	1	2	1	2
Total sales	$144,000	$140,030	$210,000	$239,775	$160,200	$212,500
Average sales	$300/sale	$335/sale	$500/sale	$575/sale	$900/sale	$850/sale
Contacts/sales	960/480	700/418	700/420	800/417	400/178	500/250
Average sale/ contact	$150/con.	$200/con.	$300/con.	$300/con.	$400/con.	$425/con.

Total Sales Volume and Average Sale per Contact

The most obvious measurements of a salesperson's effectiveness are the total volume of sales and the average sale per contact. If good records are kept for each contact a salesperson makes with a potential customer and the sales that result, simple arithmetic will provide the average sale per contact. Table 7–1 compares the performance of three salesmen for a two-year period.

In Table 7–1, salesman A made fewer contacts, fewer sales, and lower total sales in year 2 than in year 1. His average sale was $35 higher and his average sale per contact was $50 higher in year 2, however. Salesman B sold more total volume in the second year, at a higher average per sale. His average sale per contact remained the same, however, since he had fewer sales resulting from more contacts the second year. Salesman C had a considerably larger sales volume the second year, even with a lower average per sale, because he increased the number of contacts and the resulting number of sales. His average sale per contact increased.

The figures in Table 7–1, while they are interesting and revealing, do not tell the whole story. The comparison of one year to another is not valid unless provision is made to reconcile the economic condition changes from one year to another.

Equivalent Dollars of Sales Volume

In order to properly compare sales figures from one year to another, a calculation must be made to equalize the value of money from one year to another. For example, if the economy becomes inflated by 10% (prices rise by 10% on the average), a business will normally raise its prices by that amount. To properly compare the sales of a given year for a salesperson to the previous year, when the prices of goods and services he was selling were 10% lower, a calculation must be made to equalize the prices of the two years. This is done by multiplying last year's sales volume by a percentage factor plus 100%, in order to arrive at the

TABLE 7-2. Equivalent Dollars of Sales Volume

Year number	Salesman A		Salesman B		Salesman C	
	1	2	1	2	1	2
Total sales	$158,400	$140,030	$231,000	$239,775	$176,220	$212,500
Average sale	$330/sale	$335/sale	$550/sale	$575/sale	$990/sale	$850/sale
Contacts/sales	960/480	700/418	700/420	800/417	400/178	500/250
Average sale/ contact	$165/con.	$200/con.	$330/con.	$300/con.	$440/con.	$425/con.

equivalent dollars of sales volume. This is the amount of total sales volume necessary the second year, in order to equal the first year, when sales were made at lower prices.

For example, assume that the three salesmen in Table 7–2 worked for a company that increased prices 10% from year 1 to year 2. To calculate the equivalent dollars of sales volume necessary in year 2 to equal year 1, the following calculations would be necessary.

$$100\% \text{ plus } 10\% = 110\%, \text{ or a factor of } 1.10$$

$$1.10 \times \text{sales volume (year 1)} = \text{equivalent dollars of sales volume (year 2)}$$

Salesman A sold a total volume of $144,000 in year 1, so in year 2, he would have to sell:

$$1.10 \times \$144,000 = \$158,400 \text{ (equivalent dollars of sales volume)}$$

in order to equal year 1. His average sale was $300 in year 1, so in year 2, he would have to average:

$$1.10 \times \$300 = \$330 \text{ per sale (equivalent dollars of sales volume)}$$

All of the first year dollar amounts in Table 7–1 have been converted to equivalent dollars of sales volume in Table 7–2.

With all of the figures for year 1 converted to equivalent dollars, we find that salesman A still increased his average sale amount and average sale per contact, but the decrease in his total volume is magnified. Salesman B still increased his total sales volume, slightly increased his average sale, but his average sale per contact decreased, instead of remaining even. Salesman C still had an increased volume of sales, though not as dramatic, and his average sale was much lower than last year. The biggest change though was in the average sale per contact for salesman C, which decreased in equivalent dollars, whereas it was thought to increase before the adjustment was made.

Success Ratio

The *success ratio* is the percentage of contacts made by a salesperson to whom sales are made. It is significant because it tells management what percentage of times a salesman will be successful, out of the number of total contacts he makes with potential customers. The formula for calculating the success ratio is as follows:

$$\frac{\text{Sales made}}{\text{Total contacts}} = \%\ \text{Success Ratio}$$

If we apply this formula to the three salesmen discussed earlier, we find the following information.

	Year 1	Year 2
Salesman A	480/960 = 50% success	418/700 = 60% success
Salesman B	420/700 = 60% success	417/800 = 52% success
Salesman C	178/400 = 45% success	250/500 = 50% success

Calculation of the success ratio reveals that salesman A had the highest degree of success in year 2. Salesman B was most successful in year 1. Salesmen A and C increased their success ratios during the past year, while salesman B decreased in efficiency. Many factors can influence the success ratio in a given year, so no valid comparisons can be made on the basis of only two years' results. The territory covered by salesman B could have been affected by adverse conditions not found in the territories of the other two. If the success ratio is calculated over a period of several years, however, it is a valid comparison of the relative efficiency of different sales personnel. As a salesperson gains experience, it should be expected that the success ratio of that individual should increase. A stagnant or declining success ratio indicates a lack of improvement, or regression.

Activity Ratio

Another indication of a salesperson's success is the *activity ratio,* which measures the number of contacts made by a salesperson from year to year in the same territory. The reason for using this ratio is to make sure that a salesperson's efforts to make as many contacts as possible do not decline. Salespeople largely must provide their own motivation, which is difficult to do all of the time. It is easy for a salesperson to allow a dropoff in his or her activity and not even be aware of it. The activity ratio serves as a reminder to him or her and provides a constant goal for more contacts. The formula for calculating the activity ratio is as follows.

$$\frac{\text{Number of contacts (current year)}}{\begin{array}{c}\text{Aver. no. contacts (previous years)}\\ \text{(same territory)}\end{array}} = \%\ \text{Activity ratio}$$

Assuming that salesman A in the previous examples has been with the same business for 5 years, salesman B has been there for 3 years, and salesman C has been there for 12 years (all serving the same territories for their entire tenure), their activity ratios can be calculated given the following information.

TABLE 7-3. Number of Contacts for Each Year in the Same Territory by Salesmen

Year Number	1	2	3	4	5	6	7	8	9	10	11	12
Salesman A no. of contacts	725	775	800	960	700							
Salesman B no. of contacts	675	700	800									
Salesman C no. of contacts	260	250	270	280	320	350	380	375	450	420	400	500

Table 7–3 lists the number of contacts per year generated by each salesman during each year of his employment in the same territory. The first step in the calculation of the activity ratio for each salesman involves totaling the contacts for all years prior to the current year, then dividing by the number of years totaled, to arrive at an average number of contacts per year. Such a calculation for salesman A is as follows:

$$
\begin{array}{rl}
\text{Year 1} & \text{725 contracts} \\
2 & \text{775 contracts} \\
3 & \text{800 contracts} \\
4 & \text{960 contracts} \\
\hline
& \text{3,260 total contracts} - 4 \text{ years} = 815 \text{ con./year}
\end{array}
$$

The average number of contacts made by salesman A during the 4 years preceding the current one is 815/year. By the same method, salesman B is found to have averaged 688 contacts per year, and salesman C averaged 341 contacts per year. Now the formula for the activity ratio can be applied to each:

$$
\textit{Salesman A} \quad \frac{700 \text{ Contacts (current year)}}{815 \text{ Aver. con. (all prev. yrs.)}} = 86\% \text{ Activity ratio}
$$

$$
\textit{Salesman B} \quad \frac{800 \text{ Contacts (current year)}}{688 \text{ Aver. con. (all prev. yrs.)}} = 116\% \text{ Activity ratio}
$$

$$
\textit{Salesman C} \quad \frac{500 \text{ Contacts (current year)}}{341 \text{ Aver. con. (all prev. yrs.)}} = 147\% \text{ Activity ratio}
$$

Salesman C showed the highest increase in activity during the current year, an increase of 47% over the average of all previous years in the same territory. Salesman B also showed a significant increase of 16%, while salesman A demonstrated a 14% decrease in activity.

The activity ratio is a valid comparison of a salesman's efforts in the same territory, as long as conditions do not change drastically within that territory.

Sales territories can be highly variable. In the examples used, salesman A has consistently made almost twice as many contacts as salesman C, and yet salesman C has had the highest volume of sales. This could be a territorial difference. Salesman C might be working an area with large commercial buildings, whereas salesman A might be in a territory filled with low-income housing. Only a salesperson and the supervisors he or she works for can determine if sales performance has been good for a particular territory. The activity ratio and the success ratio are tools that aid them in making such an evaluation.

Again using the three salesmen as examples, it is now possible to draw some conclusions about the respective success of their year in sales.

Salesman A was able to increase his average sale per contact by $35, and the size of his average sale by $5, but he did so only because he made 260 fewer contacts during the year and increased his success ratio with those contacts by 10% (from 50% to 60%). His total sales volume was down in equivalent dollars by $18,370. His activity ratio was only 86%, a result of making fewer contacts during the year than normal.

Since the success ratio increase was the only positive result for salesman A, he and management must decide whether the decline in activity for the year was due to a territorial factor or a decline in effort on the salesman's part.

Salesman B demonstrated an increased activity ratio of 116% for the year by increasing contacts from 700 to 800. But his success ratio of 52% was lower (60% the previous year) because he sold to 417 of those contacts, compared to 420 the previous year. His total volume per sale increased from $550 in equivalent dollars to $575, but his average sale per contact decreased from $330 in equivalent dollars to $300. Total sales increased, however, from $231,000 (equivalent dollars) to $239,775, which is probably the most important of the statistics.

Salesman C had an exceptional year. His activity ratio was 147% because he increased his contacts from 400 to 500, which is remarkable, since he had worked the same territory for 12 years. His success ratio increased 5% by making sales to 250 contacts, and his total volume of sales was $212,500, compared to $176,220 in equivalent dollars for the previous year. His average sale was down from $990 (equivalent dollars) to $850, but that could have resulted from the increased number of contacts that resulted in sales to customers making lesser purchases.

Evaluation of a Landscape Designer

When a landscape designer is employed to design plans from which sales are made, the cost of such plans must be evaluated as a part of the sales cost for the business. The simplest way to make an evaluation of this cost is to keep adequate records of plans drawn, sales made from plans, and costs associated with the landscape designer, and then assimilate these facts by means of a *Landscape Designer's Time and Wages Study*. (This study is very similar to the Foreman's Time and Wages Study discussed in Chapter 12.) Table 7–4 is a sample study for a two-year period.

TABLE 7-4. Landscape Designer's Time and Wages Study—Two-Year Period

	Year 1	Year 2
Regular hours worked	1,774	1,774
Overtime	0	0
Total hours worked	1,774	1,774
Holiday, vacation, sick pay	236	236
Total hours paid	2,010	2,010
Pay rate	$9,000/yr.	$9,450/yr.
Total wages	$ 9,000	$ 9,450
Retirement	$ 450	$ 473
Total wages and payroll taxes	$10,530	$11,057
Actual cost/hour worked	$5.94/hour	$6.23/hour
Total hours charged (except plans)	96	31
Building repair and maintenance	12	15
Equipment repair and maintenance	0	0
Lost time / office work	695	515
Drafting hrs./no. of plans	1,207/ 76 plans	1,449/ 102 plans
Hours drafting per plan	15.9 hrs./plan	14.2 hrs./plan
Total cost of plans	$7,169	$9,027
Average cost/plan	$94/plan	$89/plan
Sales from plans	$96,064	$138,924
% cost of plan sales	7.5%	6.5%
Labor charged—hourly rates	$768	$248
Labor billed for drafting	$1,400	$1,800
Total revenue generated	$2,168	$2,048
Net gain or (loss) on time sold	($8,362)	($9,009)

The time and wages study is divided into three sections. The first section analyzes the cost of the landscape designer's time and the amount of time he spent working, plus the amount of time he was paid for, but did not work. The hours paid, hours worked, and other hourly breakdowns all come from a timecard kept by the landscape designer, from which he is paid. The total wages also come from this source. Retirement fund amounts come from records kept for the retirement program in which each individual's account must be separately maintained. "Payroll taxes" can usually be applied to individual wages by a percentage, by applying the total of these expenses to the total wages. (See Chapter 12 for more detail.) The total wages are added to the retirement funds and the payroll taxes, resulting in the total cost of the landscape designer. This figure can then be divided by the total hours paid to determine a cost/hour for his time.

The second section of the time and wages study consists of a breakdown of how the landscape designer's time was utilized for various purposes. In addition, figures relating to the development of landscape plans are stated: their total cost, revenue received, and the percentage cost of plan sales.

Time-use records, which are forms used by employees to record the utilization of their time, break down the hours into several categories: total hours charged, building and grounds maintenance, equipment repair, and lost time, which includes office work not related to landscape plans. Time-use records are suggested for the entire work force in Chapter 12, but the landscape designer's time-use record should be specialized, so it can also include a column for the amount of time spent drafting landscape plans. Information about the landscape plans must also be kept. The firm must know, for example, the number of plans drawn during the year, the sales made from those plans, and the total charges made for drafting services.

The total cost of plans is calculated by multiplying the total hours of drafting time by the average cost per hour of the landscape designer. Table 7–4 shows that the cost of plans the first year was $7,169 ($5.94/hr. × 1,207 hours of drafting). This figure increased to $9,027 the second year ($6.23/hr. × 1,449 hours drafting), as a result of the increase in both the hourly cost and the number of hours spent drafting. Notice, however, that the average cost per plan actually decreased the second year, because a considerably larger number of plans were drawn ($94.34 to $88.50). The total sales from the plans increased from $96,064 the first year to $138,924 the second, largely because of the increased number of plans, although a quick calculation reveals that the average sale per plan increased from $1,264 to $1,362.

Probably the most important figure on the landscape designer's time and wages study is the percentage cost of plan sales. This calculation is made by dividing the cost of producing the landscape plans by the total sales generated by those plans. In the first year, the total cost of plans ($7,169) divided by the total sales made from those plans ($96,064) yields a 7.5% cost of plan sales. The second year reveals that the cost had decreased to 6.5% of total plan sales. The lower this figure is, the better for the business.

The third section of the landscape designer's time and wages study is a compilation of total charges made for the landscape designer's time and the resulting net gain or loss from his or her services. All labor charged out for the time spent in a nondesigning usage is added to any charges made for drafting services to arrive at the total charges. This figure is then subtracted from the total cost of the landscape designer to arrive at a net gain or loss. Unless charges are made for all plans drawn, without discounts for purchases, it can be expected that the result will be a net loss. The important thing, of course, is for the landscape designer to generate sales through the production of plans, so a net loss on his time charged is not necessarily bad for the business. It serves as a good check to calculate the net gain or loss each year, however, to make sure the total loss does not become excessive in comparison with the amount of sales generated by plans.

Final Notes About Sales

Sometimes, it is best not to make a sale, even though the opportunity for one exists. Successful sales over a long period of time in a community result from good products and services and customers' trust in the judgment of the salesperson. At times, customers are prepared to buy products or services they either do not need or should not have. A good salesperson will advise them against such a move, carefully explaining his or her reasons, in order to serve the customers' best interests. Later, when the opportunity for future purchases arises, the customers are not likely to forget the salesperson's concern for their welfare.

Many times, sales are made, not by talking, but by listening. Good salespeople learn to listen closely to their customers. By doing so, they are able to more clearly define their customers' needs and desires. Sales are then made much more easily.

SUMMARY

All business activity begins with sales. Sales occur because of *needs* and *desires* that customers have for products and services. Although products or services may be purchased because of both a desire and a need, they will never be purchased if neither exists.

There are two general sales approaches that prevail. The passive sales approach is one in which little, if any, effort is made to persuade customers to buy, other than some general advertising to let customers know that the company exists. Active sales are the result of a more aggressive approach in which a business makes every possible attempt to attract potential customers and salespersons make every effort to persuade customers to purchase, or to add to original purchases. Most businesses use a combination of both approaches.

Although salespeople are completely different, they all must possess certain attributes in order to be successful (e.g., sound knowledge of their products, aggressiveness, honesty, and so forth).

Prospecting is the activity of a business to attract potential customers. Prospecting is carried out through various means of advertising, by personal contact, or both.

Customer estimates must always include careful measurements and calculations. Completing the estimate in the customer's presence will satisfy him or her that adequate care was taken in the preparation of the estimate. Prices should always be given in writing, with both customer and salesperson retaining copies.

The education of customers as to the reasons for making a purchase should be the primary function of the salesperson. Careful explanation of the needs for landscaping will lead to sales. Prices should always be given without any qualification, and the salesperson should never try to anticipate the suitability of those prices for the client.

Selling to an individual involves the proper education of that individual and the answering of his or her objections. A customer's objections should be answered in a positive manner, and any counter proposals should be feasible.

If two people are deciding upon a purchase, the salesperson's job is to find out which of the two will play the dominant part in that decision and make every attempt to persuade him or her, while answering the objections of the second party.

A committee consists of three parts: the leader, the anchor, and the main body, which is the remaining members. The salesperson's task is to identify each part, then attempt to persuade the leader to make the purchase, while quelling the objections raised, primarily by the anchor. The main body, which normally controls the majority of the votes, will follow either the committee leader or the anchor, depending on which one is the more persuasive.

Sales to a businessman must be based on the potential for higher profits as a result of the purchase. The salesperson must explore the business' landscaping needs as they relate to increased profits, happy employees, or an improved image.

The effectiveness of a business' sales force must be constantly monitored to remain efficient. The total sales made during a year, the corresponding average sale, and average sale per contact made can only be accurately compared to a subsequent year when the figures are converted to *equivalent dollars in sales volume*. Sales volume figures are converted to equivalent dollars by adding or subtracting price increase percentages from one year to the next, to 100%, then applying that percentage factor to the figures of the earlier of the two years.

The *success ratio* is the percentage of contacts made by a salesperson to whom sales are made.

The *activity ratio* is the percentage derived by comparing the total contacts made within a given territory during a single year, with the average number of contacts the salesperson has made per year for each previous year in the same territory. It serves as an indicator of the salesperson's efforts.

A landscape designer's efforts can best be assessed by completing a *time and wages study*, which reveals the costs for producing landscape plans, along with sales generated by such plans, and the percentage cost of sales resulting from landscape plans.

The ability to listen can be more of an asset to the salesperson than the ability to speak persuasively or eloquently. A salesperson should not necessarily make a sale at each opportunity, but should, instead, do that which ultimately serves his customer best.

SUMMARY QUESTIONS

1. Name two types of products normally sold on the basis of consumer's needs.
2. Name two types of products normally sold on the basis of consumer's desires.
3. Name four general types of advertising.
4. Why should a salesman not wear flashy clothes?
5. Why is *prospecting* done?
6. Describe a *soft sell* approach to prospecting.
7. Why is it important for a salesperson to carefully measure a lawn before estimating the cost for a customer?
8. Why is a sales presentation more aptly called a sales education?
9. Why are the customer's objections to making a purchase considered favorable for the salesperson?
10. During an argument between a couple who are deciding upon a purchase, what should the salesperson do?
11. Who is the committee anchor? What does this person do? Is the anchor always the same person?
12. If a salesperson sold a total volume of $200,000 last year and prices increased by 7% this year, how much must he sell this year in equivalent dollars of sales volume to equal last year's sales?
13. Salesman A made 540 contacts during the year and sold to 276 of them. Saleswoman B made sales to 300 out of 800 contacts. Which one had the highest success ratio?
14. A salesman averaged 500 contacts per year in a given territory. This year he moved to a new territory where he made 400 contacts. What is his activity ratio for the year?

15. Why is the percentage of cost of sales from a landscape plan the most important figure on the landscape designer's time and wages study?

16. What three sources of information are necessary to complete the time and wages study for the landscape designer?

17. Why is it desirable that a salesperson be a good listener?

CHAPTER 8

Hiring, Training, and Retaining Employees

A business is only as good as those people hired to represent it. Employees are the living, breathing force behind what would otherwise be a lifeless entity. Therefore, the hiring, training, and retaining of good employees is one of the major concerns of management.

Hiring, training, and retaining employees are often considered to be three different tasks, when, in fact, they should be incorporated into one continuous process. At the moment an employee is hired, the training and retention process should already be underway.

Hiring is a process by which an employer secures the services of an individual for periods of time in return for compensation.

Training is a process by which the employee is taught to perform duties for the employer in a prescribed manner.

Retaining describes the action of the employer toward the employee that are designed to enable the employer to continue receiving the services of that employee for extended periods of time.

Hiring Employees

The Two-Way Job Interview

Hiring help is often done on a completely one-sided basis. The employer assumes that he is doing the applicant a favor by considering him for employment. Nothing could be further from the truth! In fact, each applicant offers the firm a unique set of talents and skills. While it may not be possible for a business to take advantage of those particular talents and skills at the time of application, the wise employer will find out what they are in the hopes of being able to utilize them later. The employer with a one-sided approach to hiring will miss many opportunities if an applicant is considered for only one specific job. An open-minded employer, who takes time and effort to find out as much as possible about each applicant, will hire employees with larger capabilities.

A good job interview is of mutual benefit, with both the interviewer

Figure 8-1. Employees are the lifeblood of a business. Here, an employee rakes soil over grass seed using a fork.

and the applicant discovering facts about each other. A good company interviewer is also an educator, telling the applicant about each phase of the business and allowing plenty of time for the applicant to ask questions. Four important things are accomplished during such a two-way interview:

1. The applicant is made to feel that the company is interested in him personally.
2. As the interviewer discusses each segment of the business, the applicant is more apt to disclose his specific talents and skills as they might relate to that segment.
3. The image of the company can be enhanced as the applicant is told about the operation of the business.

4. Limitations of applicants are more likely to be discovered during a two-way discussion.

At the conclusion of such an interview, both parties should have enough information to know whether the employment of the applicant would be mutually beneficial. The result of such an interview will often be that the applicant will be hired for a totally different type of job than the one for which he applied. The following example will illustrate:

> A landscape nursery once hired a young woman, primarily to work as a clerk in the firm's retail garden store. The company had been reluctant to consider women for other types of work within the business because they felt that women had too many physical limitations. During the interview and subsequent hiring procedure, this young lady indicated that she liked outdoor work and had many interests and talents along with the ability to meet people well. Her interests as expressed verbally or on the application form included journalism, creative writing, biology, and sports. She also demonstrated, as time passed, a flair for sketching, good mathmatical ability, and the ability to learn new tasks very quickly.
>
> When the need arose for additional help with the firm's daily bookkeeping, this woman was given that responsibility. She undertook many physical tasks in the nursery that were heretofore considered "man's" work. She eventually took the entire advertising budget for the business in hand. She scheduled, arranged, and accounted for all advertising, and many of her illustrations were used in the firm's advertisements. She demonstrated a good sales ability, to the point that she was further trained for landscape designing and sales work.

This employee made valuable contributions to the business, primarily because the interviewer made the effort to find out about her many talents, and the management followed up by testing her abilities and making use of them.

Selling Employment

A good interviewer will also be a good salesperson. A strong, educational sales pitch will sell applicants the idea that this is a good place to work. The retention process is well underway when the interviewer has impressed each potential employee with belief in the value of working for the firm. Even the training process is begun by the interviewer when he sells the job, because a large part of doing any job well is believing that it needs to be done well. The interviewer should also allow the applicant plenty of opportunity to sell himself as a good potential employee.

Regardless of whether an applicant is hired, if he goes away from an interview with strong, positive feelings about the business, he might influence acquaintances to apply later. Most employers cannot have too many applicants from which to choose.

An interviewer should never assume that an applicant who is not hired at the time of application will not be interested later. If a solid impression has been made by the interviewer, it is possible the applicant might be available later, even if he has temporarily taken another job. Once again, an example will illustrate:

> I once advertised a position for a foreman trainee. I received a letter of inquiry from a young man working for a state agency, and I replied immediately, giving him some general information and asking that he come in for an interview. We talked at length, and, although he had no experience in the field or related work, I felt that he possessed certain personality traits that would eventually make him an excellent supervisor. We discussed the operation of my business, the pay, advancement opportunities, fringe benefits, and all other job conditions. I offered him the job.
>
> After a week or two had passed, I received a letter from this man declining the job offer because he would be forced to take a cut in pay and benefits should he change jobs. I was disappointed, but I hired another man who worked out well.
>
> The following year, I needed to hire another man for the same type of position, so I advertised again. I also wrote a letter to the man who had originally turned the job down, stating that the position was again available and that I would still like to hire him. He responded, and I hired him this time, with the same cut in pay and benefits as before. That man went on to become the most stable of our employees, took on each new responsibility given him, and was an excellent career supervisor. He advanced rapidly, regaining all of the loss in pay and benefits, and more.

In this example the business was able to hire a man who eventually became their top employee, just because the interviewer took the time to thoroughly explain the job and sell the company to him. Even though the company did not hire this man after the first interview, they kept his application on file, and it paid-off when they called to offer him the job a second time, a year later. He was so sold on the job that he even took a cut in pay! The retention process was well underway before the company even hired this man.

Employment Application Forms

Most businesses use an application form, which is filled out by each prospective employee. This form provides helpful information when a decision must be made to hire or not to hire an individual. Additionally, the application form supplies information that will be needed if the applicant is hired, such as his social security number, birthdate, address, and name.

A carefully conceived application form can provide much more information for the interviewer, as well. The firm might ask specific questions about various skills needed within its operation; for example: Can you do any carpentry work? Can you weld? Can you operate small tractors? Are you licensed to operate motor vehicles in this state? Of course, each business must devise the questions to suit its own needs.

While an application form can ask the applicant for a listing of previous work experiences and references of various types, there are many questions that cannot be asked because of laws devised to protect human rights. The law does not allow questions about an applicant's race, sex, religion, or anything else that could lead to discrimination.

An astute interviewer can learn a lot about an applicant by watching him fill out the application form. Reading speed and comprehension are important considerations for certain jobs, and the interviewer can observe the qualifications of the applicant in those areas as he or she reads and fills out the application form. If a prospective employee fills out the application form in a neat and orderly fashion, he or she will most likely handle company records in a similar fashion. Even if the employer is hiring laborers, the interviewer can usually tell whether the applicant has done manual labor recently, just by looking at the condition of his or her hands.

Each applicant should be asked what prompted him or her to seek employment with the company. By asking this question, the company can find out which type of advertising is most effective for attracting job applicants, and how much word-of-mouth recommendation they receive from other employees and applicants. The employer should review these applications occasionally because this one question serves as a good gauge of the firm's hiring practices.

A sample employment application form for a landscape nursery is shown in Tables 8–1 and 8–2.

The upper section of the application form contains all of the necessary biographical data about the applicant. This section is the most likely place for questions to be asked that are not legal, so it is very important to determine the legality of questions before the form is printed. Most of the information in this section is vital for the preparation of paychecks, W-2 forms reporting income for the year, social security withholding, and federal and state income tax withholding.

The second section of the application form contains questions about the applicant's previous work experiences. The questions on the sample form are specifically suited to one landscaping operation and should be varied to suit each individual business. Note that all questions that can

TABLE 8-1. Employment Application Form—Front Side

Name _____   Social Security No. _____
       last   first   middle

Address _____   Phone _____

Previous Address _____   Birthdate ____/ ____/ ____

Person to Notify _____   Phone _____
(in case of accident)

Spouse Name _____   No. Dependents _____

Address where you can always be reached _____

List any previous work experience at nurseries

List other work experiences

Can you do the following?

Yes	No		Yes	No	
—	—	Carpentry work	—	—	Operate small tractors
—	—	Welding	—	—	Operate 4-speed trucks
—	—	Landscape desiging	—	—	Operate loader tractor
—	—	Store clerking	—	—	Manual labor

Do you have a valid driver's license in this state? _____

List other talents or skills that might benefit this company

Names of previous employers that we might contact as references

Name	Address	Phone

What prompted you to apply for work with this company?

TABLE 8-2. Employment Application Form—Back Side

Fill in the blocks of time you are able to work below

	Monday	Tuesday	Wednesday	Thursday	Friday	Saturday
AM						
PM						

Because we are concerned for your welfare and safety, we ask that you read the following safety rules. If you are hired, you must obey them.

1. Wear substantial shoes or boots to protect your feet—no sneakers.
2. Bring leather gloves with you each day—wear them as needed.
3. Certain jobs require hard hats. We will provide them, but you must wear them.
4. Observe all no smoking signs in and around building.
5. Do not ride on tractors unless you are driving.
6. Observe all other safety related signs.
7. First-aid kits are located in each truck and each office. If you or a coworker are injured on the job, seek medical aid as needed immediately. Later, report to office for paper work.

The following rules also apply

1. Please be considerate of our customers. They provide your wages.
2. Please be here during the times you say you will. If you can't come, call at least ½ hour before you are to report.
3. Your supervisors are trained to lead you. Your cooperation with them will be returned to you.
4. Fill out all company records with extreme care and neatness.
5. We do all of our work with a great deal of pride. Will you share in that pride of workmanship with us?

Thank you for considering our company for employment!

THIS SECTION FOR COMPANY USE ONLY

Date Hired ____/ ____/ ____   Payrate _____ Date Started _____

Date Terminated ____/ ____/ ____   Reason _____

Reason for not Hiring _____

_____

be answered with a yes or no have boxes for that purpose. This conserves space and saves the applicant time. Where a written answer is required, adequate space is provided.

The application form provides space for the applicant to list former employers as references, complete with their addresses and phone numbers, and to indicate why he or she sought employment with the company.

The small chart on the form enables the applicant to indicate the hours he or she is free to work. This type of chart is particularly convenient if the same application form is used for both full- and part-time employees.

The next section of the application form contains safety rules and some general guidelines. These rules are included to give the employee a chance to decide beforehand whether or not he or she is willing to obey them. Also the applicant's understanding of company rules is a first step in the training process should he or she be hired.

The last section of the work application is marked "for office use only." This section provides the permanent work record of the employee. Management should frequently review the "reason for termination" question to determine why people leave their employ. The "reason for not hiring" can be important and also should be reviewed because under different circumstances the applicant might be highly employable.

Training

First impressions are important. The work habits that are initially formed by a new employee are likely to stay with him, so it is very important that these be good habits. Even the simplest procedure, such as raking soil to prepare a seedbed, must be thoroughly explained and demonstrated to an employee before he is asked to perform the task himself. Training employees, not just to perform tasks, but to perform them in a prescribed manner, should not be underestimated. Such training provides the backbone for a company's style and quality of work.

Good training programs are continuous. From the time a new employee is hired, he should receive some type of training every day he works. Training programs will also contribute to an employee's desire to stay with the company because a person who is well trained for a job will develop a sense of pride and well-being.

People learn and progress at different rates of speed and are affected more by direct experiences than by teaching. For these reasons, it is inadvisable for a business to set a time limit on an initial training period, because of the inherent implication that the employee should be completely trained at the end of that period. An initial training period to teach the rudiments of a job is fine, but it should be clearly labeled, so the employee does not become discouraged when he finds out that the initial training did not render him an expert.

Training Guidelines

The type of job for which an employee is being trained will dictate much about the type of training required. A laborer will not normally require the extensive training given a salesman or management trainee, for example. The laborer is often considered a temporary employee, so extensive training without production is prohibitive from a cost standpoint. A laborer should always learn by doing, but only after careful explanation and demonstration by a capable supervisor. A management trainee or salesman trainee initially should be trained to do the physical work, just as a laborer would, but then their training must go beyond that into more classroom-type training. Even though the training for various types of work differs, there are guidelines for training any person to perform any task. These are specified in the following list.

1. Explain the task thoroughly. Tell the employee what is to be accomplished, how to accomplish it, and the results to be expected.
2. Demonstrate the proper way to perform the task. Commonly used, but improper, methods should be pointed out as well, so he will not be tempted to try these on his own initiative.
3. Have the employee perform the task. Evaluate his performance, always making sure that criticism is constructive.
4. Have the employee perform the task again.
5. Evaluate again. Be sure to offer at least as much praise as correction.
6. Continue steps 4 and 5 as necessary, until the employee continually performs the task correctly.

Normally, the word *criticism* seems to have a negative connotation. Good constructive criticism, however, includes both praise for work well done and suggestions for improvement. Corrective suggestions sting less when preceded by praise for those tasks done well. The trainer who browbeats his employees is a sad case. He spends all of that time and effort training people who are looking for a way out before the training is even completed. The golden rule, "Do unto others as you would have them do unto you," really applies to the training of employees. It should always be remembered that an employee who is taught improperly or incompletely is unlikely to perform tasks as desired, so training must be thorough. A trainer must never criticize an employee for mistakes caused by a lack of information.

Who Does the Training?

In a new or small business, the manager ordinarily does most of the employee training. As the business grows, however, it becomes impossible for the manager to personally train each new person, and, as a result, part of the task must be delegated. Since one of the major reasons a business becomes successful is that its employees have become knowledgeable and skillful, there should be no reluctance on the part of the manager to delegate responsibility for training new employees. In fact, the manager's delegation of such responsibility is one of the ways he spreads his talents and skills among a larger work force. Such delegation of authority to supervisors is highly complimentary to them. The manager again successfully combines the training and retaining processes by saying, in effect, "You have learned your job so well that I now want you to teach others." This recognition will have a great effect on the supervisor's desire to stay with the firm.

Some employees become proficient in areas beyond the knowledge and skills of the employer. A wise manager will recognize the opportunity to take advantage of this proficiency by allowing the employee to train him in these areas. Foolish, vain managers refuse to recognize the possibility that an employee can know more about anything than they. The manager's acknowledgement of his employees' skills and expertise and his willingness to be taught by them is another successful combination of the training and retaining processes.

Ideally, each employee in a business is constantly helping train someone on a lower level to do his or her job properly. The net result is that each individual moves up the ladder of responsibility. As the business grows, the people at the top of management develop new responsibilities also, so everyone benefits.

Since more and more people are involved with the training of new employees, it is important to review training procedures frequently. The original training methods and styles of work should be changed only when something better is suggested. Honest evaluation of each change is important, so new ideas prove their value.

Retaining Employees

Many of the requirements for retaining good employees have already been mentioned because they take place during the hiring and training processes. Retention becomes more of a factor, however, when the employee has been well trained to do specific jobs and becomes more valuable to the employer. The retention of employees, while easily defined, is very diffcult to accomplish.

Simply stated, *the retention of good employees is accomplished by fulfilling more of the needs of each employee than could any other prospective employer*. Now comes the hard part. It is very difficult to identify employee needs and desires. Furthermore many employees expect much more than they will ever achieve. For the majority of people, the achievement of a goal leads to the establishment of new goals and escalating desires and needs. It is unlikely that a business can ever provide exactly what the employees desire, so the successful employer merely comes closer to that goal than competing businesses.

The needs and desires of employees are as variable as the employees themselves. Some are very concerned with job security, insurance, retirement plans, and the like, while for others the future is now, and today's payrate is the major concern. Still other employees are more concerned with job titles and prestige, and some might be more concerned with working conditions. Since any number of combinations of these desires and needs might exist within a given work force, their identification is a major task for management. Those responsible for the retention of good employees must be very observant, always maintaining open communications between the work force and management.

Salary levels are probably the single most important factor in the retention of employees. Management must be aware of the salaries being paid by other firms that compete for the same work force. Failure to stay abreast might be signaled by the exodus of good employees, too late for any adjustments.

The subject of pay raises tends to make people nervous. Managers are nervous about pay raises because they are usually charged with the decisions about the timing and amounts of such raises; certainly not easy decisions. Employees desire pay raises, but are often reluctant to talk about them, feeling they lack any control over the matter. Correctly handled, pay increases are probably the best retention tool at management's disposal, but if handled poorly, pay raises only serve to increase the amount of compensation paid.

There are three basic reasons for pay increases to employees: long service, increased proficiency, and cost-of-living adjustments. All three are excellent reasons at times for raising the compensation of employees, but often the effects of such raises are detrimental, because of the manner in which they are given.

Longevity should be rewarded. Certainly any employee who remains faithful to a company for a number of years has a value beyond his production. Others view his continued association with the business as an endorsement of company policies toward employees. Care must be exercised though, or soon the pay increases for a long-time employee might constitute compensation that can no longer be justified in terms of profit. It is no favor to an employee to establish a payrate that his production cannot possibly justify. Many fine workers of long standing have lost jobs simply because their salaries became too high from years of nonproduction-related pay increases.

Raises given for improved performance are easily justified because increased proficiency results in larger production, which is always profitable for the company. These raises should be made at a separate time, if possible, so that their purpose is not confused with compensation for long service or cost-of-living increases. It is a shame to waste the valuable effect of telling a person that his work has improved so much that a pay raise is warranted. The retentive value of such a raise is tremendous, and the acknowledgement of a worker's efforts by increasing his compensation provides much incentive for further improvement.

During inflationary times, cost-of-living raises are frequently given. These should probably not really be considered raises, since their purpose is to maintain the purchasing power of wages. If the average cost of purchasing goods and services increases by 7% during a year, for example, a cost-of-living pay raise for that period would equal 7% of the worker's salary, in order that the worker might continue to possess the same buying power with his earnings. There exists a danger that a cost-of-living increase annually might become expected on the part of the employee, even during the times of a stable, or deflationary economy, or that the employee might think he is receiving a merit raise, when he knows, in fact, that his performance was mediocre. If the value of merit raises is diminished by other raises, incentive for better performance is lost. The expectation of a pay increase each year at a specified time, regardless of economic circumstances, can result in disharmony between employees and management. Therefore, the reasoning for any pay increase should always be explained clearly to the employees.

To Raise or Not to Raise

The initiation of a pay increase is normally the result of management's recognition of the need for one. At times, however, employees request raises on their own initiative. Often, such a request completely surprises the manager, who is not prepared to properly deal with the problem. Decisions might be too quickly rendered in such cases, before proper deliberation.

From his viewpoint, the employee obviously feels he deserves a pay increase. Therefore, the manager must carefully consider the situation before rendering a decision or risk alienation should he decline. For that matter, the pay increase might very well be justified, and a hasty decision might not allow the manager to see the justification.

The manager's reaction to an employee's request for a pay increase should be one of noncommittal interest, initially. He must listen carefully to the reasons for the request, then carefully weigh the pros and cons of such a move carefully. If warranted, the increase should be given, but to automatically grant the increase to a nondeserving employee, even a good worker who will eventually earn the raise, might lead to a never-ending stream of opportunistic employees with the same motivation.

Outright refusal of a pay increase could be construed by the employee as a vote of no confidence, so the manager must exercise caution. If the employee is a good worker, the manager has the opportunity to challenge him further at the same time the request for a raise is denied. A statement might be made like, "John, you are a fine employee, and we expect even greater things of you in the future. The fact is though, that your present level of performance, while it is improving, does not warrant a pay increase at this time. Perhaps working a little more overtime during the coming fall season and a little more attention to detail on your jobs will achieve the increase for you. I'm sure you can do these things and much more in the future. I'll keep a close watch on your work and will issue the raise just as soon as it is justified."

This type of statement will be disappointing to the employee, but the challenge issued and the confidence expressed in the statement will usually outweigh the disappointment.

If an employee is able to logically recognize his value to the business and requests a rational pay increase based upon his contributions, he should be granted the raise, with congratulations for a job well done. Management might do well to keep a close eye on him in the future as well, because the recognition of such value is a trait that might lead him to higher supervisory positions within the company.

Increases in Compensation—How Much?

The amount of each pay raise is a question that must be resolved according to certain guidelines that are unique to each business. The manager must have a thorough knowledge of his own business as well as other businesses competing for the same labor force. One factor that is more important than any other in determining the amount of a pay increase is profit. The only reasons for offering pay raises are to increase or maintain profit levels and to retain good employees. The guidelines for establishing the amounts of raises that the company profit goals will allow are given in Chapter 12, "Labor Analysis." These guidelines, along with the manager's knowledge of competing payrates are used to determine feasible increases. However, there is one other consideration. The year of the labor analysis being used must be judged. Was the year typical? Were profits during the past year exceptionally high, or low? Pay raises are very permanent in nature. Once an increase is given, the amount of that increase will continue for the entire work history of that employee. For this reason, the temptation to give exceptionally large increases in a profitable year should be studied thoroughly for its far-reaching consequences before action is taken. By the same token, not offering pay raises in an unprofitable year might be a mistake if that year is judged atypical.

How does an employer reward his employees for an exceptional year without continually paying the amount of a large pay raise indefinitely? One method might be the payment of surprise bonuses. The combination of surprise along with reward is a great tool for the retention of employees. A bonus payment allows the employer to reward workers for an exceptional year without any cost carry-over into subsequent years when profits are not as good.

If bonuses are given each year with regularity, the surprise element is lost, as is the distinction between a bonus and a raise. Employees soon learn to expect a yearly bonus, just as they do a yearly pay increase, so bonuses must be based upon performance, profits, and irregular timing in order to maintain the surprise element.

Surprises do not have to be bonus payments to be effective. An unexpected half-day off or a special treat for coffee break will serve to stimulate employees at times and add a little spice to their work life. An imaginative employer can devise methods of surprise that will benefit his employees and influence their decision to stay with the company at a much lower cost than permanent pay increases.

Fringe Benefits

A fringe benefit is any financial benefit provided, at least in part, by an employer for an employee, which is not salary. For example paid vacation, paid holidays, sick leave, health and disability insurance, life insurance, retirement programs, or other such programs are fringe benefits.

Most employers feel that providing for a paid vacation and paid holidays is worthwhile, because the break in work is refreshing for an employee and renews his interest in his work. Also, paid sick leave, health and disability insurance, life insurance, and retirement programs offer security to the employee and his family that he might not otherwise provide for himself.

Fringe benefits are costly to a business. The firm should educate the work force regarding the value of such benefits and the reasons for providing them. The danger exists that some of the work force may not realize the value of such programs to them or that they may not know how to use the program properly. Regardless of the origin of the benefit, management should arrange educational periods to explain each program, the reasons for its implementation, the cost of the program, its benefits, and the methods of using the program. The company should leave no doubt about the value of such programs to employees as extra compensation for their work.

When a new program is being explained, this is a good time to reinforce the value of existing programs as well. For example, if a new disability insurance program is being implemented, management can discuss the coverages of a complementary nature that are already in effect; for example, workman's compensation insurance, unemployment compensation, and social security. This allows the company to make sure the employees know how to use these various programs, and the respective coverages they afford.

Because some of the programs instituted offer income tax advantages to the businessman, there is a tendency for employees to discount the value of such programs to themself. In such cases, the employer is wise to advise the workers that the same income tax advantages exist for them as well and that the value of such programs, primarily retirement, are no less valuable because of those tax advantages.

Other Employee Benefits. Many times, federal regulations require employers to spend large amounts of money on behalf of their employees to provide safety standards or improve working conditions. Wise managers take advantage of this opportunity to let workers know that these improvements are being made, at great expense, on behalf of the employees. Even if the company would not choose to do these things without the federal regulations, they can be used to advantage for the retention of employees.

SUMMARY

Hiring, training, and retaining good employees is one of the foremost management functions of a business. Good employees are the lifeblood of a business because they set the tone for production and quality. These functions can be combined to a large extent by setting up careful interviewing and hiring procedures.

The interview of each applicant for work should be a two-way exchange, rather than an interrogation by the interviewer. This will enable the interviewer to discover more about the specific set of talents and skills possessed by each applicant, while selling the applicant on the idea that the business is a good place to work. If the applicant is thoroughly sold on the company, the retention process is well underway before he is even hired.

Application forms should be devised with care, so maximum information can be gathered about each applicant. Listing important employee rules on the application form is one method of initiating the training process. Files of work application forms should be maintained. A person who is not hired immediately may be well suited for some other job at a later date. These files also serve to let management know which types of advertising for help are most effective and why workers leave their employ. Much care must be exercised in the selection of information requested by the work application form. Any information gathered that could lead to discrimination against an applicant because of race, sex, age, or religion is prohibited by law.

Employee training should be an ongoing process. Ideally, each employee should train one who is below him in responsibility to eventually take his place. A business' growth and its ability to retain the services and loyalty of good employees is closely related to the success of its training program.

Initial training periods of a set duration should be carefully labeled to ensure that employees will not be disappointed when such training fails to make them expert at every task.

The delegation of training responsibilities to well-qualified supervisors is a good combination of the training and retaining processes, as well as being a good way for management to spread itself over a larger work force.

A business retains a good work force by allowing them more of those things they want in their lives than any other competing employer could give them. The challenge to management is to recognize employee desires and needs and to be keenly aware of competing salaries.

Pay raises are given for longevity, merit, and cost-of-living adjustments. The reasons for giving a raise should be carefully spelled out. Raises should always be given with a profit motive in mind and should not become too predictable in either amount or frequency.

Surprises are valuable in various ways as an aid in retaining employees. Bonus payments are valuable as a reward for a profitable year, because, unlike raises, the amount of a bonus does not carry over into subsequent years' compensation.

Fringe benefits are good retentive aids for employees, but they should always be carefully explained so the employees will realize their value and necessity.

SUMMARY QUESTIONS

1. What is the definition of *hiring?*
2. Explain the meaning and significance of a two-way interview.
3. Why is it important to "sell" the company to prospective employees?
4. Why can no questions be asked on a work application form about religion?
5. How can a work application form help begin the training process?
6. Why should applicants be asked the reason for applying to a particular company?
7. Why is the proper training of employees important?
8. List the six steps for training anyone to do anything.
9. What is *constructive criticism?*
10. Why is the delegation of training responsibility important to management?
11. Why is it difficult for a company to provide all that an employee desires?
12. Name the three basic types of pay raises.
13. What is the primary factor guiding the amount given in a pay increase?
14. Why are bonus payments a good alternative reward for an exceptional year?
15. What two dangers are inherent in providing fringe benefits for employees?

CHAPTER 9

Supervising Employees

"Good supervisors are hard to find." Businessmen utter this statement frequently. The fact, though, is that supervisors are not unavailable, they are simply difficult to identify and more difficult to train.

Incisive application forms and extensive interviewing procedures allow a business the first opportunity to evaluate each applicant for characteristics, talents, and skills that eventually might make him capable of supervising the work of others. A second opportunity occurs during the initial training period, and a third opportunity exists during the entire span of an employee's work for a company. By predetermining the criteria necessary for supervisors and carefully observing each employee during his training period and subsequent years of employment, management can usually find supervisory material they ordinarily would not have known existed.

What is a supervisor? *A good supervisor is an individual who can combine materials, machinery, and manpower for the successful completion of a job(s).*

Identification of Potential Supervisors

Although supervisors differ greatly in personality, there are certain traits that must be present in any individual who will be expected to lead others. Following is the list of these traits.

1. The ability to follow instructions accurately.
2. The ability to communicate with others and the patience to listen.
3. The ability to learn tasks and ideas quickly.
4. The ability to read and comprehend material.
5. Self-discipline and the ability to organize activities efficiently.
6. The ability to write neatly and orderly.
7. Possession of a fairly even temperament.

During each potential employee's interview, several observations can be made about his or her possible leadership abilities. Self-confidence, general attitude, and the applicant's ability to express himself or herself can be readily discerned by a capable interviewer. The applicant's reading speed, comprehension, and the neatness and thoroughness with which he or she fills out the application can also be observed. The employee's past history, revealed on the application form, might indicate past leadership roles. None of these observations will allow an interviewer to be certain of an applicant's ability to supervise, but they are indicators that the potential might be present.

The initial training period will reveal whether or not the new employee has the ability to learn new tasks quickly and to follow instructions accurately. Much can also be learned about the employee's self-discipline and organization, as well as his temperament. Those employees who are easily and quickly trained might well be watched in the future as new supervisors are needed.

After the initial training period, as each new employee settles into the routine of his job, other facts become apparent, particularly about his work habits and his temperament. Most employees try hard to make a good impression the first few days on a new job, but eventually they settle into their more usual patterns of behavior. During this time, it also becomes apparent whether the employee has actually learned to perform the work proficiently.

Since people learn and progress at different rates of speed, no time limit should be set on a prospective supervisor to "prove himself." It might take months or even years to discover the potential for leadership, particularly in a young person who is still maturing.

Training Supervisors

After the successful identification of an employee's leadership potential he or she must receive further training to become a supervisor. Initially, this training must ensure that the employee has a good knowledge of the technical and mechanical aspects of the work. If the employee has been identified from among the laboring force, at least part of this training has already been accomplished. If not, the initial training will most likely include some work with the laboring force; that is, simply learning how the jobs are done.

As much as possible, the potential supervisor should work under the auspices of the firm's most competent foremen, so that he might learn from their examples. He should be allowed to participate in the planning processes involved with each job and should be instructed in the record-keeping procedures. He should also be involved in all contacts

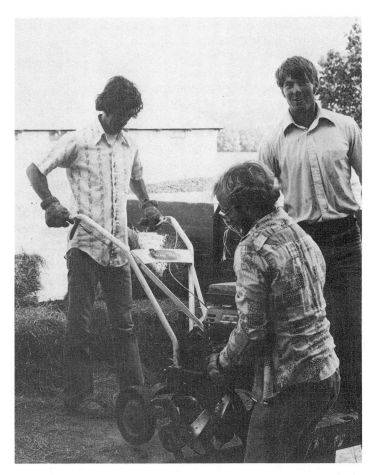

Figure 9-1. A foreman watches his crew members unload at the end of the day.

the foreman has with the customer and with management, concerning the job.

Steps of Supervision

1. Study the job thoroughly, analyze the best way to attack the job.
2. Preparation of materials and tools.
3. Explanation of tasks to crew.
4. Disposition of men and machines to most efficient use.
5. Observation, correction, and suggestions to crew.
6. Final check of job quality.

7. Customer contact.
8. Return to base and cleanup.
9. Completion of job records.
10. Reflection.

The training of a supervisor includes making him completely familiar with the following ten steps. They are essential to the supervision of any job.

1. *Study the job thoroughly and analyze the best way to attack the job.* A foreman must have access to any pertinent drawings, specifications, and instructions in advance of beginning work on the job. The length of time he will need to study will depend on the difficulty of the job and his previous experience. He needs to be able to thoroughly understand the goals of the job and plan the best way to accomplish these goals. He determines the starting point and outlines the steps by which to accomplish the tasks with the least amount of effort and in the shortest amount of time. He must decide which of the tasks is most difficult and least difficult, so he can assign the proper workers when the time comes. For most jobs, the time required for an experienced foreman to complete this analysis will be minimal.

2. *Preparation of materials and tools.* The foreman should study in advance the lists of materials and tools to be used in the completion of a job to make sure of their availability. This results in less confusion among crew members and higher efficiency levels during the loading. Normally, such lists of materials and tools are provided along with drawings, specifications, and instructions. These are usually prepared by a salesman, who is already familiar with the job, and are checked by the foreman.

3. *Explanation of tasks to crew.* This is the foreman's first on-the-job contact with the crew of laborers. This explanation of tasks can be very brief, often accomplished in the truck on the way to the jobsite. The crew members need to be told in general terms about the job, how it will be accomplished, and the type of results they can expect. Specific instructions for doing individual jobs can wait until the job actually begins. Initial instruction of this type serves mainly to make the laborers feel they are involved in the success or failure of the job on a personal basis. Time goals can be set for completion of the job or certain phases of it. A crew will accomplish more if they are given high, but realistic, goals for which to strive.

4. *The disposition of men and machines.* As soon as a crew is assigned to a foreman, he should begin planning their disposition. Individual crew members should be matched to specific jobs according to their abilities. Those experienced at the operation of machinery should be assigned to that machinery, while those with little or no experience

should be assigned the simplest tasks. Several things are accomplished by this type of disposition.

a. Greater initial efficiency on the job. The foreman can only be in one place at one time, and the utilization of experience at certain tasks allows that task to be started with instruction only, not training at the same time.

b. The supervisor can concentrate his efforts and time on those who are less experienced, which results in better training and subsequent improved production from the inexperienced.

c. The customer sees efficiency, because the work begins immediately when the crew arrives at the jobsite.

d. The crew forms good work habits, develops more confidence in their supervisor, and they learn to recognize the cost of "stand around" time.

It is always possible, of course, that the foreman might be assigned an entirely inexperienced crew. In such a case, the foreman should pick out the simplest task to be done and quickly show one man how to perform it. The others can unload tools and equipment and place them near the area in which they will be used. He might choose, instead, to train all personnel to do the task at one time. Either way, all workers will be occupied productively upon arrival at the jobsite. As soon as one or more crew members are able to perform the simplest task, the foreman moves on to the next simplest task, and so forth, until all crew members are occupied productively.

5. *Observation, suggestion, and correction.* As soon as all crew members are busy, the foreman begins to circulate. He returns to those crew members first occupied to make sure they are performing their work in the prescribed manner. If not, he corrects any defects immediately, so incorrect procedures do not become habits. He also suggests any changes in work habits that might make the labor easier or increase production.

This phase of supervision is very important because it regulates the quality of the work as well as the training of employees. It is a difficult task for supervisors of small crews, since they often perform physical work as well as supervise. It is hard for them to leave the work they are doing often enough to observe other crew members. However, a good supervisor always realizes that the production of his crew as a unit, not his individual production, is his primary responsibility. Two or more people, properly supervised, can usually produce more work than one experienced person, so proper leadership is always the priority. Observation, suggestion, and correction continues throughout the duration of each job.

6. *The final check.* As a job is being finished, the foreman should check each phase of the work to make certain the plans, specifications, and instructions have all been fulfilled. This should be done while the

crew members are finishing the work, so they are not standing around waiting for him.

7. *Customer contact.* Before the supervisor contacts the customer, he should issue instructions to crew members to begin the cleanup and loading procedure. This customer contact is very important because it gives the customer a chance to discover flaws in the work while the crew is still there to correct them. This also serves as an expression of confidence in the crew's work. It is much more difficult for a customer to complain about the work later, if he or she is invited to do so immediately. Customer contact by the job foreman, followed by a contact from the salesman involved with the job, leaves the customer with the unmistakable impression that the company is striving to please.

8. *Cleanup and return to base.* The cleanup of tools, equipment, and debris on a job should not be considered unimportant. Much time can be lost if trash and equipment are haphazardly loaded together and must be sorted out later. Each item to be loaded should be designated for a particular spot on the truck, so it can be unloaded quickly, without resorting. All tools and equipment should be cleaned as they are loaded to facilitate easy unloading, and also to make it easier to charge the time of these operations to the customer, as rightfully they should be.

   The return trip should not be wasted in idle chatter. This is a good time for the foreman to critique the job, with suggestions for improved performance on future jobs of a similar nature. It is also a good time to issue instructions for each crew member's duties upon arrival at the home base. Any questions crew members might have about the job just finished can be answered at this time also.

9. *Completion of job records.* The foreman is responsible for the completion of job records. But this task should actually be initiated earlier, when the crew arrives at the jobsite. The foreman should write down the time of arrival and make notations about the types of work being performed by each crew member. He should make notations each time a crew member finishes a machine operation or a specific type of labor. The labor record and all other job records should then be finished and checked for accuracy and neatness before being turned in to management. The foreman is usually also responsible for the individual records of his crew members. He must make sure they fill out any timecards, time-use records or other forms properly.

10. *Reflection.* We all learn from experience, if we pause to reflect on that experience. If new and better methods were discovered during the progress of the job, some quiet reflection on the foreman's part will better help him to remember that method in the future. He should also reflect upon the performance of crew members, increasing his knowledge of their individual strengths and weaknesses. The next time each crew member is assigned to him, he will be able to

exploit the strengths and improve on the weak areas. The foreman should always ask himself these questions upon completion of a job.

a. Did we meet the company's standards for quality?

b. Did I realize maximum performance from crew members?

c. Was the customer satisfied with both our performance and our demeanor?

d. Could I have used more efficient methods?

Any observations the foreman might make about the job that could be helpful to either the sales staff or management should be brought to their attention. Management relies heavily upon the observations of a good supervisor regarding new ideas, better methods, and laborers' performance. By the same token, the supervisor should always be prepared to accept criticism from management or the salesman of a particular job and to remain flexible enough to make changes.

Once a potential supervisor has been trained to follow these ten rules of supervision, he is ready for the simplest form of supervision; that is, the supervision of a single crew.

Types of Supervision

There are four basic types, or degrees, of supervision:

- Single-crew supervision
- Multiple-crew supervision
- Supervision of supervisors
- Supervision of managers

Although the ten basic rules of supervision still apply in all cases, there are special factors to be considered at each supervisory level. We shall discuss the differences as we study each category.

Single-crew Supervision

The criteria for single-crew supervision are found in the ten basic rules of supervision discussed earlier. Since the foreman works with only one crew of workers at a time, this is the most elemental type of supervision. The difficulty of leading a crew should not ever be underestimated, however, nor should the importance of this type of supervision. The success or failure of many business ventures depends upon single-crew supervisors. The decisions they make and the strategy they employ are often the most decisive moves made within a business. Taken singly, those decisions may not affect large volumes of work, but collectively they represent a great deal of responsibility.

Multiple-crew Supervision

One of the measurements of the value of a supervisor is the number of workers over which he is able to spread his talents and skills. Many supervisors who have demonstrated a thorough understanding of the ten basic rules of supervision and complete mastery of single-crew supervision are capable of spreading their value further by leading multiple crews simultaneously. Instead of using his skills to lead three to five men on a single crew, the foreman is able to lead six, ten, or more men. Some additional abilities are required, however, so demonstrated proficiency at single-crew supervision does not automatically mean that a foreman can proceed to multiple crews.

The steps for supervising multiple crews, while similar to those for single crew, differ from the standpoint that the foreman can only be present on one jobsite at a time, and yet he must guide the performance at all jobsites for which he has responsibility. When the foreman analyzes his attack, he must consider each job separately, but also consider them together. He must plan to be at one jobsite first, so other jobs must start without him. Equipment and tools must be planned for each crew, and sometimes equipment must be planned for more than one job, requiring much coordination. Generally, more preparation time must be allowed for multiple-crew supervision.

The disposition of men is crucial to the success of multiple-crew supervision. The foreman must select a crew leader for each crew, usually the most experienced laborer who has demonstrated some leadership qualities and a strong ability to follow directions. This is an excellent use of those workers who are being trained to become foremen. The foreman than determines which job he will spend the most time on personally and places the least effective crew leader on that crew. In like manner, he also places the most experienced crew leader on the crew with which he will spend the least amount of time. He assigns the best laborers to this crew also, leaving the most inexperienced laborers, who will require the most supervision, more directly under his control.

Thorough instructions, including a list of materials, tools, and machinery needed for each job, are given to the crew leaders, under whose direction the loading begins. Initial instructions for beginning each job are given to the respective crew leaders during the loading. The foreman must give each crew leader the minimum instruction necessary to keep the crews well organized until he can get to the job himself. Too much instruction may only confuse the crew leaders, who are probably much less capable than he is. Each crew leader should be asked to repeat his instructions in case any clarification is necessary.

The supervisor proceeds first to the jobsite of the least experienced crew to organize the work. When the work is satisfactorily underway and crew members are occupied with tasks of sufficient duration, the foreman can then proceed to the site of his second least experienced crew. He carefully observes the work to see if his instructions are being carried out. If so, he does not interfere with the work of the crew members, but merely issues further instructions to the crew leader and leaves for a third jobsite, or back to the first one. By not interfering with the operation of the crew, the foreman shows confidence in the authority of the crew leader. Of course, if operations are not as they should be, he makes corrections and suggestions, but he should always go through the crew leader. The crew members should be left with no doubts about the authority of the crew leader.

The foreman must return to the jobsites regularly; observing, suggesting, and correcting. Necessarily, the jobsites must not be miles apart.

The foreman who supervises more than one crew must make the final checks and contact the customers, but because of time limits, it may be necessary to do some of this work after working hours or later in the week. The foreman may have to rely upon the judgment of the crew leader as to the quality of the job, at least until he can check it personally.

At the end of the day, the multiple-crew supervisor has much to reflect upon. The progress of each crew must be reviewed, along with the performance of each crew leader. Crew leaders should be constantly evaluated as possible supervisors. The foreman must communicate with his crew leaders, causing them to reflect on the job just finished, and obtain their impressions of the performance of individual crew members.

Supervision of multiple crews requires a greater degree of organizational ability than single-crew supervision. The supervisor must be able to organize the men as a unit as well as for the individual jobs. He must be able to allocate tools and machinery. He must be a diligent recordkeeper, disciplined enough to check each job record for accuracy. He must be highly cooperative, able to work closely with management, salespeople, and crew leaders.

Supervision of Supervisors

In most businesses, some controls are exercised over foremen by either management or salespeople, or both. These controls constitute the supervision of supervisors. This type of supervision differs from crew supervision in several ways. The people being supervised are much more knowledgeable and well trained than crew members. Since the management people who supply this supervision are more concerned with overall efficiency than with the details of individual jobs, those job details are largely left to the foreman.

There is a different set of criteria for the supervision of supervisors. These are listed as follows:

1. The recognition of each foreman's abilities, and the application of those abilities for maximum use.
2. The disposition of jobs to the entire work force.
3. The disposition of laborers to jobs.
4. The preparation of initial instructions, drawings, and specifications.
5. Mid-way critiques of larger jobs.
6. Quality checks.
7. Record checks.
8. Job critiques.
9. Job appreciation followup.

A closer look at each of these is warranted.

The recognition of each foreman's abilities, and the application of those abilities for maximum use. As mentioned earlier, all foremen have different capabilities. While some are capable of supervising only one crew at a time, others can manage two, three, or more crews. Management must recognize the extent of each foreman's abilities and utilize them to the maximum. Those foremen who are particularly adept at a certain type of job should be assigned where their skill can be used to advantage.

Management should also frequently analyze the abilities of the work force in general in order to select crew leaders who might be trained for further supervision. They must constantly glean information from the foremen concerning the abilities of those on the labor force.

The disposition of jobs to the entire work force is the responsibility of management. As jobs are dispatched, the recognition of the capabilities of individual foremen again becomes an important consideration. The geographic proximity of jobs must be such that it is possible for the foreman in charge of two or more jobs to move to all locations. Multiple jobs assigned to one foreman should not be of the same degree of difficulty either, since the foreman cannot spend equal amounts of time on each jobsite. Since most businesses have a limited number of machines and tools for specific jobs, it is necessary that the disposition of jobs be so made as to ensure that the equipment will be available where needed. Readiness of materials to be used on jobs must be considered by management before such jobs are dispatched. Before jobs are started, management must know that all materials are available and assembled, and that the foreman knows the whereabouts of these materials.

The salesperson often promises a delivery or performance date on a particular job to the customer. Management must consider these promises in the disposition of work to avoid customer disappointment or irritation. Frequent communications between the sales force and the dispatcher is imperative.

The disposition of laborers to jobs again relies upon the management's knowledge of the abilities of various foremen. Ideally, the most inexperienced or most difficult laborers will be assigned to the crews of the most capable supervisors. The best foreman should be able to increase the production from these employees. The most experienced workers, except those chosen as crew leaders, should be assigned to the least effective foremen. There are exceptions to this rule, however, since a job might require special technical skills or particularly adept machine operators. Then the more experienced help could work with the best foremen.

In order to determine the proper number of crew members for each crew, the dispatcher must be very familar with the types of jobs being done. Once again, the communications between the dispatcher and the salesperson must be maintained. Input from the foreman who will be in charge of the job is important too, but the ultimate decision must belong to that person who has to fit an entire work force to several jobs. The ideal number of workers is seldom available.

The proper preparation of instructions, drawings, and specifications for a job is a responsibility of those who supervise the supervisors. Usually, this task is done by the salesperson for each job, since he or she is the one most familiar with the job initially and is ultimately responsible for the success of the job. These documents serve to educate and prepare the foreman for the actual performance of the job, so their completeness and accuracy is critical. Situations often occur in which a job may be started with no verbal communication of instructions from the salesperson to the foreman, so the written instructions need to be quite complete.

Management and the job foreman should meet for a mid-way critique on any job of substantial duration (one day or more). The progress of the job can be reviewed, particularly from a labor standpoint, and management, in this case possibly the salesperson can make suggestions for efficient completion of the job. The foreman may not otherwise be aware of how his job progress compared with the progress that was estimated. In the event of slow progress, there may be no solution available, but at least the situation can be discussed during a mid-way critique. The foreman might be able to point out reasons for the slow progress, which will lead to more accurate bids or estimates in the future.

Periodic quality checks are necessary to be sure that the standards for quality previously set are being met consistently. Because of the time consumed, it is not necessary to make quality checks on each job, especially for experienced foremen. Each foreman will maintain his own standards of quality, but the periodic quality checks will ensure a consistent set of standards for the entire business.

Record checks need to be accomplished daily. Written records are the basis for all income for the business, so accuracy is a must. Management must make a daily check of job sheets, timecards, time-use records, and any other record filled out by employees because, as time passes, memories dim and accuracy is lost.

A *job critique* must be performed with the foreman upon completion of the job. This evaluation of efficiency, quality, and profitability on a job serves as part of the foreman's training and serves also to keep management abreast of problems encountered, customer reactions, and the progress of employees. Praise should be given at this time to the foreman of a well-done job, but suggestions for improvement are also in order.

Employees should not be allowed to forget the jobs they have done. They should be encouraged to return to the jobsites frequently to view the progress of their work. A well-done landscaping job will grow in value and beauty as time passes, and management should take advantage of this to increase their workers' pride. Any compliments received from customers should be quickly relayed to the job foreman, and, in turn, to the laborers. The return of employees to the jobsite occasionally can be important to the customer. He or she will realize that these people are pleased by their work.

Supervision of Management

The owners of a business are often the entire management in a small firm. As a business grows larger, however, other people might become involved in management. These management-level people must be supervised also. Even an owner-manager should set goals and rules by which to supervise his own activities. Otherwise a business quickly becomes a disorganized hodgepodge.

The supervision of management personnel might better be labeled *umpiring*. People capable of management duties need little day-to-day supervision, so it becomes more a matter of setting goals and standards, establishing limits of authority, and periodically checking to see that the goals and standards are being upheld.

Good managers operate best when they have a "free hand" to manage as they see fit. The establishment of standards for return on equity invested, customer relations policies, and quality of work is usually sufficient guidance. As long as these standards are being met or surpassed, the owner should not interfere. Frequent inspections and critiques, however, are of value in apprising management personnel of the owners' views on their progress.

The value of praise for a job well done is just as important to management personnel as to other workers. Very few people can operate without recognition of their work, and managers, who are often completely alone with their thoughts, decisions, and responsibilities, might even require more praise than others.

Management personnel generally require little supervision because in most cases they have ascended the ladder of supervision from crew leaders to foremen, then from single-crew supervisors to multiple-crew supervisors, and finally to supervisors of supervisors. In order to have progressed to that point, management personnel must have had a thorough indoctrination in the day-to-day activities of business operation.

SUMMARY

A good supervisor is an individual who can combine materials, machinery, and manpower for the successful completion of a job(s).

Good supervisors do not just happen. Normally, they are trained by management after being identified as having leadership potential. A person must possess certain qualities to become a supervisor. For example, he or she must be able to follow instructions accurately, communicate well with others, learn tasks and ideas quickly, and so forth.

Management can assess an individual worker's leadership qualities during the original job interview, the initial training period, and the remaining time the employee works for the company. Each of these periods affords the opportunity to observe certain traits more than others.

There are ten basic steps of supervision that must be mastered by any potential supervisor. For example, he or she must analyze the job thoroughly;

prepare materials and tools; explain all tasks to crew members; make the most efficient use of the work force; and so forth.

Multiple-crew supervision differs from single-crew supervision, primarily because the foreman must be absent from the jobsite for periods of time, during which a designated crew leader must provide the on-the-job supervision. Consequently, the foreman must plan much more thoroughly and must be more explicit with instructions. A well-organized mind is a prerequisite for multiple-crew supervision.

The supervision of supervisors is different from crew supervision in that those performing this service are more concerned with overall efficiency than with job details.

Supervision of management personnel involves the establishment of goals, standards of quality, and limitations of authority. Periodic checks are required to make sure that goals and standards are being met, but otherwise little interference is necessary or desirable.

Good supervision is vital to any business, since two well-supervised workers can usually produce more work than one industrious and experienced person.

SUMMARY QUESTIONS

1. What three elements does a supervisor combine for the successful completion of a job?
2. When does management get the first opportunity to discover an individual's leadership potential?
3. When is an employee's true personality and temperament likely to surface?
4. In what capacity is an employee usually trained for supervision, initially?
5. Why is it important for a foreman to reflect upon a job just finished?
6. Why is it important to briefly explain the tasks ahead to a crew before they start working on a job?
7. Why must a foreman place priority on his supervisory duties instead of on the physical work he does on a job?
8. What makes customer contact by the foreman, while still on the job, so important?
9. Name the four basic types of supervision.
10. How does multiple-crew supervision increase a foreman's value?
11. Why should a foreman, in charge of more than one crew, always issue instructions through the crew leaders?
12. What is the primary requirement for multiple-crew supervision?
13. Who is normally responsible for the instructions, drawings, and specifications given to a foreman prior to starting a job?
14. Why is job appreciation and followup important?

CHAPTER 10
Work Scheduling

Earlier it was stated that "All business activity *begins* with sales." For the business cycle to be complete, however, the sale must be consummated: the work completed, the customer billed, and the amount due collected. A very important part of this cycle is the scheduling of the work.

Work scheduling involves the timing of all activities from the date of the sale until the work is complete and the customer billed. Considerations include the ordering and assembly of all necessary materials, the coordination of the needed manpower with adequate supervision, and the preparation and distribution of the proper tools and machinery. Attention must be directed also to a number of other important factors such as the weather, the changing seasons, the relationship between the sales season and the work season, and the customer's life style.

Many people may be involved in making decisions about work scheduling, even if there is one person responsible for the final dispatchment of the work. The salesperson must be involved because of his or her contact with and commitment to the customer. Those responsible for assembling materials orders (e.g., the nursery digging crew) must certainly be involved. The landscape designer, responsible for plans and specifications, must be included in the process, as must the dispatcher. Finally, the manager of the business must be at least aware of the scheduling to make sure that work planned for a period of time will mesh well with other scheduled company activities. Subcontractors, if used, will also affect the timing of a job.

Factors Influencing Scheduling

As previously mentioned, many factors must be considered before work can be scheduled. Each of these factors warrants discussion.

Sales

The sales season often precedes the work season by at least three or four weeks. Many landscaping sales must be made in advance of the work season, in order to have the necessary time for ordering materials and coordinating other activities. Thus, the progress of the sales season will have a direct effect on the work scheduling; if the sales season is running slow, the work scheduling will also be delayed. The weather and other seasonal considerations can also affect the progress of sales. One major reason for a delayed sales season in the spring might be a long winter. Potential customers might not think about landscaping at the time they would normally. Similarly, a long hot summer might cause customers to delay making preparations for fall purchases.

The types of sales being made will also affect the work scheduling. Although a business might attempt to do similar types of work each year, the jobs will vary to a degree, particularly if multiple services are offered. A firm primarily in business to landscape new buildings might need to adjust its sales in the event of a decline in new construction, while a business that combines maintenance work with new landscaping might find it desirable to eliminate or reduce some of its maintenance work in order to take advantage of a housing boom. The types of materials available can affect the types and amounts of sales made, which also affects the scheduling.

Figure 10-1. After others have gone, or before they arrive, the work dispatcher works at the lonely task of preparing a day's work schedule.

Just as the work done by a landscape nursery is seasonal, so is the sales season. As one season is completed, preparations for the following season will already have been started. Failure to start these preparations early enough will result in a lag in the work scheduling as the seasons change. During the season for selling landscaping jobs involving the installation of plant material, the sales staff must look ahead to summer or winter months and prepare to make sales for those seasons. If this preparation is not made, the work season, which follows the sales season, will arrive without any work having been sold long enough in advance for adequate preparation to have been made to do the job.

The requirements for doing each job will also affect the scheduling. The sale of three jobs, each of which requires a backhoe for completion, might preclude simultaneous completion of those jobs. In such a case, the sale of other, more diverse jobs might be required to keep crews busy. Similarly, the sale of several landscaping jobs, each requiring plants to be dug, might cause a slowdown if the digging crew is unable to keep up. It is the job of the sales staff to try to avoid such conflicts, while the dispatcher must foresee such conflicts and be prepared for them when they occur.

In the interest of smooth work scheduling, maximum work performance, and resulting profits, the sales staff should be constantly on the alert for possible sales of work to be done during the off-seasons. Many landscaping firms do construction-type jobs because they occupy laborers and supervisors during times of the year when they would not otherwise be productive. Often, these jobs are difficult to sell, particularly on short notice. The sales staff might have to make such sales well in advance of actual performance, when the opportunity presents itself. If the sales staff does not do this, chances are that at least part of the crew will be laid-off during the slow period.

Seasonal Considerations

All landscaping operations are seasonal to a degree. Even in the more temperate climates, seasons exist, and, even though the conditions may be suitable for planting year-round, the landscapers in those areas experience a slowdown in activity during the off-seasons. Three approaches have been taken by landscapers who wish to extend the busy seasons. They are educating their customers to the fact that planting can now be accomplished over a longer season, thanks to better handling methods and the advent of container growing. They are also accomplishing more planting activity during the season because of increased efficiency and larger work crews. And finally, they are adding other types of services. For example, many types of landscape construction work including swimming pool installation, sprinkler system installation, decks, patios, fences, retaining walls, and so forth, are undertaken by landscapers primarily to lengthen their work seasons. (The length of the planting season, however, is not affected.) The addition of such services can also serve as a hedge against bad weather. Many of these construction services can be performed regardless of the weather, while planting, seeding, or other earth-moving operations might have to cease. These services contribute greatly to smooth work scheduling, provided some work in these areas can be held in reserve to be done during periods when other work must be stopped.

Weather

It is impossible to visit with a group of nurseryowners for more than five minutes without at least one comment being made about the weather. Usually, such comments are unfavorable. Weather affects the progress of every single phase of the landscaping business and is a primary consideration for work scheduling.

Although both weather and the seasonal cycle are often considered to be enemies of the landscaper, in reality, they are old friends. Without the changing seasons, the beautiful flowers, colorful foilage, and other manifestations of nature's beauty would not exist. Without the spring rains, grass would not green, flowers would not bloom, and customers would have no impetus to buy the landscapers' goods and services. Most retail store owners, when quizzed about the best time of the year for them to make sales, will answer quickly, "Christmas." Customers are more than willing to buy then. The store owner must only convince them to buy from him. The changing seasons and weather provide the same type of stimulus for landscaping customers, only at different times of the year. The wise landscaper will take advantage of this phenomenon, instead of complaining about it.

There are other advantages afforded by changing weather and seasons. Employees tend to produce best when they have too much to do. The bulk of the year's production in a landscape nursery might be done in a fairly short period of time during the busy season. This is because the employees are under pressure to "make hay while the sun shines." Additionally, employees tend to be happiest when they are busiest. The heavy work load during these busy times also stimulates better concentration on the part of employees, which results in higher efficiency levels.

Weather and seasonal influences create variety for a work force. Since the types of services offered must change from one season to another, the employees' tasks must necessarily change also. Such changes generally have a positive effect on employees because they decrease boredom. Employees' interest is revived and they approach each season with a renewed vigor. Large factories, where repetition is a byword, often spend thousands of dollars each year trying to negate the effects of boredom on their employees.

Seasonal and weather-related changes are good for management personnel too, because they pose a greater challenge. In businesses where the work is essentially the same day after day, management can be lulled into a sense of well-being. Since the management of a landscape nursery must be constantly aware of the new season approaching or a weather front entering the area, they must be constantly prepared for change.

A work-disrupting rain need not be a big problem, if work is properly scheduled. Pruning, trimming, tree surgery, and fertilizing are some examples of work that can be done shortly after a rain, along with the construction activities mentioned earlier. Some of this work can be stockpiled in anticipation of rainy weather, which is sure to come later.

There are times that weather does substantially disrupt the work schedules for extended periods. When this occurs, there is a strong temptation for the landscaper to resume work even though he knows conditions are not good for planting. Three weeks of steady rain will make any landscaper nervous. But if the landscaper is too impatient, he might have to pay the consequences later by replacing plants that die or by suffering a loss in reputation. Each business operator must know the soils in his area well, so he can determine whether planting under adverse conditions is worth the risk.

Winter weather eliminates all customer-related work done by landscapers in some areas, except for snow removal. Work scheduling does not cease during the winter, however. Most landscape nurseries use this time of the year for major equipment overhauls, building projects on their own grounds, and repair and maintenance of existing buildings. These projects must be scheduled just as efficiently as the other work done by the firm. Other projects usually take place at this time also, including the potting of bare-root plants for the coming season and the stockpiling of fertilizer and other materials that will be used later. Many businesses utilize this time of the year for employee vacations, training schools, or other employee educational programs, which are designed to cause the work to progress more smoothly later, when the busy season encroaches.

Crew size

Since the amount of work scheduled for a period of time is directly related to the number of men available for work, crew size is an important factor in work scheduling. Many businesses keep only a skeleton crew in the winter and summer off-seasons and hire additional help during the spring and fall busy times.

In order to maximize work efforts during good, seasonal weather, part-time employees must often be hired in advance of the need for them. It takes time to advertise, interview, hire, and train new employees. When the good weather hits, the landscaper wants to have a crew to work with immediately. Hiring ahead of time is difficult, because the business can ill-afford nonproducing personnel. Consequently, newly hired employees are often told not to report until they are called. While this procedure results in the loss of some employees before they ever work, it does provide a ready work force at the right time.

The crew hired must suit the supervisory capacities of the business. Unsupervised novice workers are unlikely to relieve the work load of a business, in most instances. In fact, the employment of untrained and unskilled labor, doing unsupervised tasks, can compound the work scheduling problems because their poorly done work often must be redone.

When the work sold exceeds the crew-size capacity of a business, there are only two viable alternatives, other than subcontracting. One is to turn down some of the potential sales, and the other is to hire and train more supervisors in preparation for a larger crew size.

Season-ending layoff of some part-time workers presents a difficult problem for those involved in work scheduling. It is difficult to release a good worker just because of a work slowdown. Still, such practices are necessary to make a profit, since the company is unlikely to sell as much labor during the off-season, regardless of the services they offer. Naturally, crew reduction should begin with the least productive workers, but some thought should always be given to who needs the job the most.

Individual crew size is a daily problem encountered by those involved in work scheduling. The number of crew members on each job can easily determine the job's profitability. When tasks must be accomplished in a particular order on a job, the addition of one or two extra workers can be disastrous to profit, regardless of the supervisor's capabilities. A business normally has one individual in charge of the disposition of men, machinery, and tools. This person is called the *dispatcher*. Decisions about crew size are the result of good communications between the dispatcher and the salesperson and foreman for each job. The dispatcher must be familiar with each type of work done, so he can more accurately determine the proper crew size. Familiarity with the individual foremen is necessary also. Each foreman has the capability of supervising a limited number of laborers, and the assignment of more will reduce his efficiency.

The location of a jobsite is a consideration for determining crew composition. Remote locations require full-time workers so the crew is not forced to return to headquarters during the day. Part-time workers must usually be dispatched locally.

Other factors must be considered when scheduling individual crew members to particular jobs. Which crew members are licensed and capable of driving vehicles? Which ones can operate specialized equipment? Which are trained to do special jobs? As discussed in Chapter 9, the most inexperienced crew members are normally assigned to the most experienced foremen, and the most experienced crew members are normally assigned to the least experienced foremen. Exceptions occur when special skills are involved or when crew members are used as crew leaders for foremen involved in multiple-crew supervision.

Services Offered

The number of services offered by a business will affect the work scheduling to a large extent. When more services are offered, they are likely to be more seasonal. For example, powerraking, leaf cleanup, fertilizing, mowing, and spraying are all services that must be performed on a timely basis. Lawn mowing cannot be delayed more than a day or two, or the service loses its value to the customer. The scheduling of these services becomes primary in importance, causing other, sometimes more profitable, work to be delayed. Even so, these services are usually offered because they afford steady business and, once established, do not require much sales work. Such services carry through the otherwise slow summer months and often provide work that can be done with very little supervision.

Maintenance services are often considered "friend-makers." A maintenance customer might purchase and landscape a new home or relandscape his old one. Excellent advertising benefits result from people seeing crew members, trucks, and equipment working in yards as they pass by. Maintenance serves this purpose well, since crews normally work at several locations each day. Clean, well-painted trucks, with highly visible signs displaying the company's name, address, and phone number aid in the realization of these advertising benefits.

Customer Considerations

Customer considerations must always rank high in the factors affecting work scheduling. A customer orders from a particular business because he feels it will supply goods and services of the quality desired, at the appropriate time. The salesperson on a job normally is required to indicate at least an approximate delivery date or time of performance. These delivery or performance dates must be met in order to maintain the customer's good will.

Keeping promises made to customers involves efforts on the part of both the salesperson and the dispatcher. If salespeople are well informed about the work load of the business and the time required for each type of job, impractical promises can be avoided. This is difficult, since weather or other unexpected problems can wreak havoc with the most carefully made schedules. Salespeople should always make it clear to their customers that they cannot foresee such interruptions and that delivery or performance times are realistic forecasts based on usual circumstances. The dispatcher should inform the sales staff whenever there is an interruption in the progress of work. This allows the sales staff to keep customers posted in the event their work will be done either sooner or later than anticipated. Informed customers are usually understanding, but they often will not tolerate unexplained delays.

Whenever possible, work should be scheduled so it will not interrupt the daily life of the customer. For example, if a lawn mowing customer is known to work at a job from four o'clock in the afternoon until midnight, it is likely that he will sleep late in the morning. Scheduling his mowing for eight o'clock in the morning might disrupt his sleep, which will do nothing positive for his opinion of the company. Similarly, the scheduling of a new lawn seeding on the day a customer is leaving town for a week might cause him to be anxious about the well-being of the seedbed during the entire week.

Most customers are not concerned about all of the other work a business has lined up. Instead, they are primarily concerned, and rightfully so, only with their own order. A business should always recognize this fact, and once work is begun on a customer's property, the entire job should be finished as quickly as possible. Leaving a job already started, in order to satisfy another customer, is usually not a good idea. The result will be two unhappy customers, each with an unfinished job and no knowledge of when the job will be completed.

Finally, customers order goods and services sometimes in preparation for a special occasion. Perhaps they might wish to have some landscaping installed prior to a son's or daughter's graduation, or their daughter's wedding. When such is the case, the business must be sure the work is completed prior to that special occasion. Otherwise, the business had no right to accept the job in the first place. Failure to meet such a deadline might result in cancellation of the job or the loss of reputation that accompanies a customer's dissatisfaction.

Principles of Disposition

A dispatcher begins each day's planning the day before. That day's production must be assessed, including those tasks remaining to be completed. He analyzes the tools, equipment, and manpower that will be needed for completion of unfinished work and plans those tasks first on the following day's schedule.

Maintenance or other jobs that must be done on a timely basis are scheduled next, for to delay them might negate their effectiveness. The proper amount of help, machinery, and tools for completion of these jobs is entered into the schedule, which can be made on a calendar pad, a daily work form, or a piece of paper. The labor selected for these jobs in some cases might involve those with special qualifications or skills. Normally, the same supervisor is used on an uncompleted job.

Next, the dispatcher makes a listing of the remaining supervisors available for the next day, along with the remaining labor force. The jobs to be started next have already been determined as a result of constant consultation with the sales staff, with the digging crew, and with others in charge of materials readiness. The availability of tools and equipment is determined to make sure the jobs can be done properly, without conflicting needs for limited pieces of such tools and equipment.

When all this has checked out, the dispatcher can then assign crew members to the various jobs. A foreman is chosen first for each job. Selection is on the individual's skills and knowledge, on the crew size to be supervised, and on the difficulty of the tasks. Much thought and care is taken in assigning jobs to multiple-crew supervisors. The jobs must be of varied degrees of difficulty and movement between jobs must be geographically feasible. Crew leaders are then selected for those jobs to be supervised on a migratory basis. Tasks on various jobs involving special skills from the labor force are analyzed, and workers are assigned appropriately. The remaining laborers are then assigned in accordance with their own talents and with those of the supervisors.

Although an ideal number of crew members has been determined for each job, it is not always possible to assign that number. If 11 laborers are available on a given day and three jobs are scheduled, for which the ideal number of laborers would be 10, there are three possible options for resolving this conflict. The most obvious solution is to send one laborer home for the day, but this practice can soon dilute a labor force as discouraged workers quit. An alternative is to substitute another job that requires the correct number of workers. The third option is to operate one crew with an additional laborer. If this alternative is chosen, the dispatcher must do so with care, so as not to sacrifice efficiency and profit. The types of jobs and the capabilities of the supervisors warrant close attention to ensure that the extra man is productive to the effort.

After all crews are assigned, the dispatcher must then plan for contingencies. The possibility of inclement weather must always be considered. The dispatcher should take inventory of those types of work available in case it should rain or some other weather-related delay is encountered. The jobs that can be done for customers in bad weather should be considered first, then those jobs around the business grounds not affected by bad weather.

The expected labor force might be depleted by illness or other absences. If several workers do not show up, it might be necessary to either delete one of the planned jobs for that day or plan another one with a lower personnel requirement. Absenteeism is hard to plan for. The dispatcher can help prepare himself by becoming familiar with general patterns of absenteeism. On Mondays and Fridays, for example, or on days preceding and following holidays, absenteeism might be higher. To a degree, the dispatcher can also familiarize himself with the eccentricities of individual crew members.

Contributions of Work Scheduling to Profitability

Since one of the primary goals of any business is the realization of a profit, the scheduling of work should always be done with that goal in mind. Profit goals for a business are normally long standing, reaching far into the future. Scheduling a job during the wrong time of the year or in inclement weather, while it might result in a higher monthly profit, will often not be in keeping with the long-range goals. Since a business is judged by its past performance, the results of such actions might contribute to a declining reputation. Potential customers, who see crews working under conditions they believe to be unfavorable to high-quality results, are likely to look elsewhere when they have a need for similar products and services. The results of one poorly planned and executed job can influence the loss of many potentially profitable jobs in the future.

The profitability of a service-type business depends, to a large extent, on the labor force that represents it. The well-being and enthusiasm of that work force are influenced by the work-scheduling procedures. Repeated scheduling of one type of work for a foreman or other worker might result in boredom. Dissatisfaction or disinterest of crew members will be manifested in work of a lower quality and, perhaps, even frequent resignations. Even though it is wise to schedule employees to fit their qualifications and skills, the dispatcher must mix in enough other work to keep employees stimulated. Enthusiastic and interested employees produce profitable work of the highest quality.

Any extension of the working season is bound to increase the profitability of a firm, provided the pricing is correct and costs are controlled. The proper scheduling of work can cause the labor force to operate at maximum strength longer than normal at the end of a season.

Choices always exist concerning the types of work to emphasize at any one time. Early in the spring, a landscape nursery might be able to choose between adding more maintenance-type operations, such as the powerraking of lawns, or pushing right into landscaping jobs. Judgments are made at that time. If the sales staff believes that an abundance of landscaping jobs are available to the business, and these jobs are judged to be more profitable to the business, the choice might be made to limit the maintenance jobs. If, on the other hand, limited landscaping jobs are judged to be available, then the undertaking of additional maintenance work at the beginning of the season, when it is available, might prolong the landscaping at the end of the season. In either case, the choice is designed to increase the sales volume for the season, make more efficient use of personnel, and increase profits.

Poor judgments have an equal impact. If the judgment is made to push into the landscaping season and eliminate powerraking, and the result is the completion of all landscape jobs prior to the end of the season, the business might be forced to end the season early. Patience and good judgment, which can only be developed over a period of time with the proper experience, must rule.

Scheduling Work That Is Not Sold

Although the work around the buildings and grounds of the business is considerable, it seems that there is always adequate off-season time to do it. Because of its seasonal nature, all nonessential work of this type should be postponed as long as profit-making work can be done. However, essential maintenance and repair work must be attended to. Equipment must work properly. The failure to make repairs to essential equipment will result in job delays, with a resulting profit loss.

The timing of nonessential work is important too. Painting, concrete finishing, and other temperature-related items should be scheduled at the times during the off-season when the temperatures are suitable. Indoor repairs, maintenance, and construction can be scheduled during the winter or during inclement weather.

SUMMARY

The scheduling of work for a landscape nursery involves the coordination of all materials, men, machinery, and tools for the successful and profitable completion of jobs. Such scheduling is done by a dispatcher, with cooperation from the landscape designer, sales personnel, foremen, digging crew, subcontractors, and the manager of the business.

Factors that affect work scheduling include: sales, the seasons, weather, crew size, number of services offered, and the customer's life style.

The sales made in advance of a new season will control work scheduling. Types of jobs sold also affect scheduling, since equipment, tool, and materials availability preclude the completion of some jobs simultaneously.

Landscapers have successfully extended their work seasons by educating customers to expect planting later in the season, increasing the work force for more intensive effort during the normal season, and adding more services.

Seasonal changes and the weather, often considered the enemy, are important to the landscaper because they provide variety, stimulate employee activity, and generate sales. The effect of bad weather can be minimized by stockpiling jobs that can be done regardless of weather conditions.

Part-time labor must be hired in advance of the need for it, so no delay is experienced when the busy season begins. Crew size is dependent upon the number and quality of supervisors, as well as the amount of sales made. Season-ending layoffs, though difficult, are necessary for adequate profit.

Crew size is determined by the job requirements and the capabilities of the foreman. Location of the jobsite and individual skills of the crew members are also factors for consideration.

The larger the number of services offered, the more seasonal they are likely to be. Maintenance-type services are usually more critical from the standpoint of timing.

A business must always strive to schedule work in accordance with promises made to its customers. Additionally, scheduling should take into account the customer's daily life, when possible.

The disposition of work for a day begins the day before. All work in progress is first planned, followed by the jobs that involve critical timing. After the supervisors are picked for new jobs, the remaining crew members are selected. Work plans involve the placement of tools and equipment and consideration of location.

Dispatchers must prepare adequately for all contingencies, primarily employee absences and weather interference. Essential repair and maintenance work must be done during the busy seasons, but all other work not sold should be planned for dead periods.

Decisions about work scheduling have far-reaching effects on the profitability of a business.

SUMMARY QUESTIONS

1. Why do landscape sales usually precede the actual work by at least three to four weeks?
2. How do unusually long winters or summers affect work scheduling?
3. Why are planting seasons longer than they used to be?
4. How do the changing seasons affect the sale of landscaping?
5. How should the intensity of a busy season stimulate an increase in efficiency of landscaping employees?
6. Why is part-time help sometimes hired in advance of a busy season?
7. What does a *dispatcher* do?
8. When more services are added, why are they likely to be of a seasonal nature?
9. What is meant by fitting the work schedule to the daily schedule of the client?
10. How are foremen assigned to various jobs?
11. Why is it inadvisable to continually send excess help home for the day?

CHAPTER 11
Planning for Profit

Businesses are started for many reasons. Many people start a business because it allows them to make a living doing what they want to do. Some start a business simply to be their own boss. Others may believe that a potential for higher than average income is to be gained from owning a business.

Regardless of the reasons for business ownership, one motivation must be present for success. That motive is profit. Without profit, no business can survive for any length of time.

This chapter is concerned with the profitability of a business and the business papers that indicate profitability: the *Balance Sheet* and the *Profit and Loss Statement*. The interpretation of information presented on these two forms tells the story of a business's success or failure.

The Balance Sheet

A *balance sheet* is simply a listing of the business's assets and liabilities, with the difference between the two representing the capital, or equity of ownership. This financial paper is extremely important to a businessman because it tells him how his funds are invested, the debts he owes, and the amount left over, which is the net worth of the business. The balance sheet, though changing often, continues throughout the life of the business.

Table 11–1 shows a sample balance sheet for a fictitious nursery called Green Tree Nursery. The first section of the balance sheet is a listing of all current assets. A current asset is anything owned by the business that is in the form of cash or can be converted into cash in a relatively short period of time. Another name for current assets is *liquid assets*, indicating the assets can be liquidated into cash easily. Green Tree Nursery considers any asset that can be liquidated into cash within one year to be current.

All cash held by the nursery on the day the balance sheet is prepared is included in the current assets. *Cash in bank* represents the balance of the firm's checking account. *Cash on hand* is the amount of cash kept in the cash register for making change. *Petty cash* is a fund maintained to pay for small cash expenses for which a check is impractical. Petty cash is reimbursed periodically by writing a check to cover the amount of cash used from the fund, so the $200.00 balance is maintained constantly.

Accounts receivable are considered current assets because it is expected that the customers who owe Green Tree Nursery will pay those accounts within a short period of time. These accounts receivable represent all credit sales made by Green Tree Nursery to its clients.

The *inventory* of goods already paid for by Green Tree Nursery to later be sold to customers is also considered a current asset. It is expected that these goods will be sold within a relatively short period of time and thus converted into cash.

There are many other assets a business could have which would be considered current, such as negotiable bonds, savings accounts, and stocks in other businesses, just to name a few.

Fixed assets represent those assets owned by the company which are not so easily converted to cash as the current assets. These include the land, buildings, and equipment owned by the firm, minus the accumulated depreciation on these assets. Since depreciation is an expense allotted for wear and tear and decreasing value through aging, the amount of depreciation as it accumulates is subtracted from the value of the assets.

Some other examples of fixed assets that might appear on a business balance sheet are: long-term savings certificates, long-term bonds, or organizational costs for a corporation, which are to be expensed over several years by amortization.

Figure 11-1. The balance sheet—always balanced.

TABLE 11-1. The Balance Sheet

GREEN TREE NURSERY
BALANCE SHEET
DEC. 31, 1976

Assets
  Current Assets
    Cash in bank $10,500
    Cash on hand   400
    Petty cash   200
    Accounts receivable   42,500
    Inventory   37,600

        Total current assets $91,200

  Fixed Assets
    Land $68,900
    Garden store building   22,600
    Shop building   26,700
    Warehouse   16,900
    Greenhouse   5,000
    Equipment   110,640
      Less: depreciation   −64,917

        Total fixed assets $185,823

            Total assets $277,023

Liabilities
  Current Liabilities
    Accounts payable $ 0
    FICA payable   1,612
    Withholding payable   2,976

        Total current liabilities $ 4,588

  Long-Term Liabilities
    Notes payable $26,700

        Total long-term liabilities $26,700

            Total liabilities $31,288

Capital
  Green Tree Nursery, capital $245,735

        Total liabilities and capital $277,023

The third section of the balance sheet is for liabilities. A *liability* is any debt owed by the business to someone else. Liabilities can be either *current*, in which case they are to be paid in a fairly short period of time, or *long-term*, if the balance is owed over a period of years.

All bills received by Green Tree Nursery for expenses of conducting business are considered *current liabilities* until they are paid. The *FICA taxes payable* and *withholding taxes payable* are also current liabilities, since Green Tree Nursery's management considers anything payable within one year to be a current liability.

Long-term liabilities usually involve money borrowed over a period of years for capital improvements. A mortgage on a building would be considered a long-term liability, as would a long-term note to buy land. A three-year note to buy a new piece of equipment would also be considered a long-term liability.

The difference between the total assets of a business and its total liabilities is the *net worth* of the business. This is often referred to as the *owner's equity*, or the *owner's capital*. Simply stated, the owner's capital account represents that part of the total value of the assets of a business that are unencumbered by debt.

The word *balance* in balance sheet indicates that something must balance for accuracy. *In order for a balance sheet to be correct, the total assets must equal the total liabilities plus the capital.* Double lines are drawn under those two figures on the balance sheet to indicate that they are balanced.

The balance sheet continues to be updated throughout the life of a business. It may be made out once a year, once a month, or at any other interval desired by the management. The balance sheet helps management properly balance the assets owned, with liabilities owed, for proper cash flow. It acts as a barometer for the growth of a business.

The balance sheet, by itself, does not reveal anything about the profitability of a business. It merely compares the total assets owned by the business to the total liabilities owed by the business by establishing the capital, or net worth of the business.

The Profit and Loss Statement

The *profit and loss statement* is a financial paper that gives an accounting of the total sales, the cost of goods sold, the expenses incurred in business, and the resultant net profit or loss for any given period of time within a business year. Sometimes called an *income and expense statement*, the profit and loss statement can be prepared as often as the management feels necessary, but at least one such statement at the end of the business year is essential for income-tax reporting. The figures on the profit and loss statement, unlike the balance sheet, do not continue beyond the end of the business year, when a new profit and loss statement begins.

A sample profit and loss statement for the fictitious Green Tree Nursery is shown in Table 11–2.

TABLE 11-2. The Profit and Loss Statement

GREEN TREE NURSERY
PROFIT AND LOSS STATEMENT
DEC. 31, 1976

Sales		
Hardgoods	$120,670	
Labor	92,162	
Plant materials	114,968	
Total sales		$327,800
Cost of Goods Sold		
Cost of goods sold—hardgoods		$ 78,435
Gross profit		$249,365
Expenses		
Wages	$112,600	
Payroll taxes	9,234	
Seeds and plants purchased	57,606	
Gas and oil	6,200	
Telephone	3,880	
Utilities	2,400	
Postage	1,200	
Office supplies	970	
Machine hire	6,230	
Interest	1,600	
Taxes	1,100	
Repairs and maintenance	6,100	
Legal and accounting	2,200	
Advertising	6,100	
Total expenses		$217,420
Net profit		$ 31,945

Figures are representative, but are not average. Cost of plants sold is included in the expense category, "seeds and plants purchased," since many of the plant purchases are lined-out, not to be sold for several years. Firms growing some of their own material often account for plant purchases in this manner.

The profit and loss statement is broken into three sections: *sales, cost of goods sold,* and *expenses.* Sales on the sample are broken into three categories: *hardgoods, labor,* and *plant materials.* All sales made by Green Tree Nursery during the business year are recorded in this section.

The cost of goods sold section is a listing of the wholesale cost for goods that are purchased for resale. It does not include freight, handling, or other related costs, since those costs are expenses. The total cost of goods sold is subtracted from the total sales to leave the gross profit.

Any and all costs of doing business are recorded in the expenses section. Wages, gas and oil, advertising, etc., are all necessary costs that enable the nursery to complete the sales transactions. The total expenses subtracted from the gross profit leaves a figure called *net profit,* or *net loss.* Net profit is the amount of money taken in that is in excess of the amount paid out as a cost of doing business for the year. If the total expenses are greater than the gross profit, the resulting difference is a net loss.

Rate of Return on Equity

The only valid determination of the profitability of a business, or comparison of the profitability of different businesses, is the *Rate of Return on Equity.* The rate of return on equity is the percentage of an owner's equity invested in a business, which is returned to the owner as net profit during a given business year.

The *equity* an owner has invested in a business is the amount of the assets owned by the business that is unencumbered by debt. Therefore, the total investment in a business may be considerably higher than the equity in the business, if money has been borrowed to secure assets. A distinction should be made between the rate of return on total investment in a business and the rate of return on equity, because often they are quite different, if the total investment includes borrowed money.

Two figures must be known to calculate the rate of return on equity. The net profit for the year's business can be found at the bottom of the year-ending profit and loss statement, and the net worth, or equity, of ownership can be found as owner's capital on the year-ending balance sheet for the business. From the sample balance sheet for Green Tree Nursery, we find the total equity to be $245,735, as of the last day of the business year. The net profit for Green Tree Nursery for that particular year is $31,945, as shown on the profit and loss statement for Green Tree Nursery in Table 11–2. These two figures can now be used to calculate the rate of return on equity for the year.

The rate of return on equity is calculated by use of the following formula:

$$\frac{\text{Net profit}}{\text{Owner's equity}} = \% \text{ Return on equity}$$

Using the figures gathered earlier for Green Tree Nursery, the calculations would be as follows:

$$\frac{\text{Net profit } \$31,945}{\text{Owner's equity } \$245,735} = 13\% \text{ Rate of return on equity}$$

This means that 13% of the owner's cash investment is being returned to him in net profits this particular year. If the same rate continues each year, in eight years the owner will have recovered his entire cash investment.

There are several reasons why the rate of return on equity is so important.

1. It is the only true means of determining the profitability of a business. Net profit means nothing unless the amount of profit relates favorably with the amount of cash investment necessary to achieve that profit.
2. It is the only accurate means of comparing the investment in a business with other investments the owner could choose to make with the same funds. He could invest in a savings account and earn a percentage of return on equity with a much lower risk involved, for example.
3. The rate of return on equity is the only stable means of comparison of the profitability of a business from year to year, since the amount of equity invested can change.
4. The rate of return on equity provides a basis for determining the feasibility of any further cash investment the owner might consider making in his business.

Let us examine each of these reasons more closely. If two businesses both have a net profit of $10,000 at the end of a given year, but the owner of business A has a total of $110,000 equity, while the owner of business B has $91,000 equity, which business is most profitable? Using the formula for determining the rate of return on equity, we find that:

$$\text{Business A} \quad \frac{\$10,000 \text{ Profit}}{\$110,000 \text{ Equity}} = 9.1\% \text{ Return on equity}$$

$$\text{Business B} \quad \frac{\$10,000 \text{ Profit}}{\$91,000 \text{ Equity}} = 11.0\% \text{ Return on equity}$$

Business B is more profitable than business A during this particular year. It will take over one year longer for the owner of business A to recover his investment than it will for the owner of business B, if the same rate of return continues. Therefore, although the two businesses produced the same amount of net profit, the rate of return on equity calculation was able to show a marked difference in the profitability of these businesses.

Each investment should be compared often with other investments the owner could choose to make with the same money. If the owner of business A has the choice between investing his $110,000 in bonds that yield a 9% return and there is little risk involved, he might decide that a 9.1% return from his business investment, which does involve a considerable risk, is not too favorable. This does not mean that it would be possible for him to sell his business and reinvest quickly; to do that might require considerable time. Probably, it just means that he will strive for a more favorable return on his equity in the future, either by making higher net profits or by finding a way to reduce his equity in the business so the money removed can be put to work earning interest elsewhere.

Successful businesses will show a progressively larger net profit throughout the years, as they grow. Many businessmen are satisfied if the current year's net profit exceeds those of the previous year. Sometimes, comparisons are made between the net profit and the total sales, and if the percentage of profits to sales stays the same or increases, this is considered to be a good sign. But the only real test of profitability within a business from year to year is the rate of return on equity. Higher profits can cost the businessman dearly if he made too much additional investment in order to achieve these profits. Let us use business A again as an example.

Last year, business A had a net profit of $8,000. This year, the net profit was $10,000, an increase of $2,000. Upon completion of the year-end balance sheet, the owner of business A found out that his equity in the business had increased from $85,000 to $110,000 in one year's time. Small investments for trucks, machinery, and additional inventory, made to enable the firm to do a larger volume of business, had increased the owner's equity by $25,000. The owner of business A then calculated his rate of return on equity for both years:

Year 1 $\dfrac{\text{\$8,000 Profit}}{\text{\$85,000 Equity}}$ = 9.4% Rate of return on equity

Year 2 $\dfrac{\text{\$10,000 Profit}}{\text{\$110,000 Equity}}$ = 9.1% Rate of return on equity

Thus, it was found that by increasing the total net profits from $8,000 to $10,000 the business actually became less profitable, because of the amount of additional investment required to produce that extra profit. Three-tenths of one percent may not seem like much to worry about, but based on a $110,000 investment, three-tenths of one percent equals $330. Moreover, if the trend toward a lower return on equity goes unchecked, it will become magnified as the firm grows.

Each year of a business's existence, the rate of return on equity should be calculated, not only as a check against the loss of profitability by increased investment, but to enable management to strive for a higher return each year.

The rate of return on equity can also be used to help determine the feasibility of an investment in equipment, land, buildings, or anything else that might be purchased for a business. First, it is necessary to determine the rate of return on equity desired from the business. Common sense must enter the picture because, while a 40% return would be very nice, there are not many businesses that can demonstrate that kind of profitability. Competition usually dictates the rate of return possibilities. Using 15% as a desired rate of return on equity, let us look at the possible construction of a garden store as an example:

The estimated cost of construction for the prospective garden store is $30,000, complete with shelves, plumbing, and office furniture. The average inventory needed to stock the store is estimated to be $12,000. The average increase in operating capital to operate the store is estimated to be $3,000. This is the amount needed for cash on hand, additional accounts receivable, and increased current liabilities, which tie up capital. The total estimated investment in the store will be $45,000.

Sales in the projected garden store are estimated (conservatively) at an average of $115,000 per year for 10 years. The net profit is estimated to average 5.5% of sales, which would yield an average net profit per year of $6,325. The formula for determining the rate of return on equity can be used to project the profitability of this proposed venture:

$$\frac{\$6,325 \text{ Aver. projected yearly profit}}{\$45,000 \text{ Aver. projected equity invested}} = \begin{array}{l} 14.1\% \text{ Projected rate of} \\ \text{return on equity.} \end{array}$$

The decision in this case would probably be to proceed with building the garden store, because the averages were figured for 10 years, when in reality the store should operate several years more, doing increasing business each year. The 14.1% projected return is close enough to the 15% rate of return desired, considering the conservatism of the estimates of costs and sales.

This same procedure can be used to evaluate any other investment under consideration by a business. In most cases, the most difficult consideration is the estimation of how much extra sales revenue can be generated by the additional investment.

Like almost any other formula for business analysis, the rate of return on equity can be influenced by other factors. It is always necessary to remember that the business's total assets and its equity, or capital, are only the same figure if the business has no liabilities, which is seldom the case. The amount of debts owed by a business, including all borrowed money, has a large effect on the amount of equity.

Effect of Borrowed Money on the Rate of Return on Equity

If a business borrows money to purchase anything that would be considered an asset, it does so with the idea that the increased assets will in some way increase the amount of profit the business can realize. Borrowing money to increase the assets of a business does not increase the owner's equity in the business, because the amount of money borrowed is a liability, which balances the amount of increase in assets. (Assets minus liabilities equals capital). If properly planned, borrowing money for part of an investment should result in as high or higher a proportionate increase in profit as the resulting increase in equity as the loan is paid off. In other words, the borrowing of money to increase assets should result in the same or higher rate of return on equity for the amount of equity created by the transaction. When a business borrows money, it follows that the targeted rate of return on that money must be higher than the interest being paid on the loan, in order to make a profit.

Let us again refer to the example of the proposed garden store used earlier. If only $10,000 of the required $45,000 investment is made in cash, and the remaining $35,000 is borrowed at a 9% annual interest

rate, the following calculation of return on total investment would result.

Investment	$10,000	Cash equity
	35,000	Borrowed money
	$45,000	Total investment
Projected sales	$115,000	
Projected profits	$ 6,325	
Minus: interest on	−3,150	9% Annual interest on $35,000
borrowed money	$ 3,175	Remaining net profit

$$\frac{\$3,175 \quad \text{Net profit}}{\$45,000 \quad \text{Total investment}} = 7.1\% \text{ Return on total investment}$$

So, using the total investment to determine a rate of return, the result
would be a 7.1% return on investment. However, since $35,000 of that
investment is borrowed money, only $10,000 is equity, so the following
calculation shows the rate of return on equity:

$$\frac{\$3,175 \quad \text{Net profit}}{\$10,000 \quad \text{Equity}} = 31.75\% \text{ Rate of return on equity}$$

Borrowed capital, in this case, could be used to dramatically increase
the rate of return on equity actually invested in a business. It should be
pointed out that the borrowing of money to finance the purchase of
assets also increases the risk involved in making the investment. The
rate of return on the total investment must be compared with the
amount of interest being paid on borrowed money when deciding
whether or not the investment is a good one. If the proposed garden
store does not make the net profit that was projected as an average, what
happens to the return on investment? Let us look at a calculation of the
rate of return on both the total investment and on equity, when the
profits are less than expected.

Example #1   Entire $45,000 investment cash equity—no borrowed
money. Total net profits realized—$3,900.

$$\frac{\$3,900 \quad \text{Net profit}}{\$45,000 \quad \text{Equity invested}} = 8.7\% \text{ Rate of return on equity}$$

Example #2 $10,000 cash equity invested, $35,000 borrowed at 9%
annual interest. $3,900 total net profit realized, before interest.

$$\frac{\$750 \text{ Net profit } (\$3,900 - \$3,150 \text{ interest})}{\$45,000 \text{ Total investment}} = \begin{array}{l} 1.7\% \text{ Rate of return on} \\ \text{total inv.} \end{array}$$

$$\frac{\$750 \text{ Net profit}}{\$10,000 \text{ Equity investment}} = 7.5\% \text{ Rate of return on equity}$$

The situation appears to have reversed now, with the total cash investment being superior to the investment involving borrowed money. The total cash investment still projects an 8.7% rate of return on equity, even when projected profits drop from $6,325 to $3,900. The investment made using borrowed capital is able to show only a 1.7% return on the total investment and a 7.5% return on equity, when the profits drop.

The reason for this dramatic change is that the rate of interest charged on borrowed capital is not flexible. It remains constant, in this case at 9%, regardless of the profits realized. This illustrates the primary risk of borrowing money to complete an investment.

The possible benefits of using borrowed capital are many. Businessmen are able to borrow money to make purchases to advance their business earlier than they would be able to if they waited for cash to accumulate. Higher rates of return on equity are achieved when profits are good. The businessman's own cash can be spread much further by adding borrowed money to it. A successful history of borrowing money and subsequently meeting all obligations of the loan will create a good credit rating for the businessman, which is always important to creditors with whom he does business.

The disadvantages of using borrowed money primarily stem from the increased risk. Other factors that might be considered disadvantages include having assets tied up as loan security, or collateral. Most loans involve a lien against assets by the lending institution, as a means of recovery in case the borrower defaults. A *lien* is a legal device that gives the holder of the lien first rights to the value of the property covered by the lien. An asset that has a lien against it cannot usually be sold unless the debt is satisfied and the lien removed. As long as the conditions of the loan are properly met, liens against assets are usually no problem to the businessman.

Changes in the Balance Sheet

The balance sheet serves as the pulse of the business. All transactions involving changes in the owner's total assets, liabilities, or capital have an effect on the balance sheet, which carries forward from the beginning to the end of the business. All of these changes are important to management, because the stabilitiy and liquidity of the business are measured by the balance sheet.

Remember that any financial transaction that increases or decreases an asset or a liability of a business will change the composition of the balance sheet. Because of the need for the balance sheet to balance (assets must equal the liabilities plus the capital), each time an asset is increased, there must be a corresponding decrease in another asset or an increase in either a liability or owner's capital, or both, in amounts equal to the total increase in the asset. Similarly, a decrease in an asset must be equalized by a corresponding increase in another asset, or decreases in liabilities, and/or owner's capital.

If a business purchases a new truck, there are basically three possible ways to make the transaction. The owner can purchase the truck entirely from cash that is already in the business, he can put new cash of his own in the business, increasing his equity investment, or he can borrow the money from a lending institution. Table 11–3 is a listing of the various balance sheet accounts that might be affected by these transactions, and the effects on each.

TABLE 11-3. Truck Purchase—Effects on Balance Sheet

Account	Using cash from within the business	New cash put in by owner	Cash borrowed entirely for purchase
Cash	Reduced	Unchanged	Unchanged
Total current assets	Reduced	Unchanged	Unchanged
Equipment	Increased	Increased	Increased
Total fixed assets	Increased	Increased	Increased
Liabilities	Unchanged	Unchanged	Increased
Owner's capital	Unchanged	Increased	Unchanged

In the first method, where cash is used from within the business, the increase in one asset is offset by a reduction in another asset, and there are no changes in the liabilities or owner's capital accounts. When new cash is put into the business by the owner, however, one asset is increased, but the owner's capital account is increased correspondingly, with no changes in liabilities. The third method, where cash is borrowed to make the purchase, involves the increase of an asset, with an increase in liabilities to balance, and no change in the owner's capital account. Only the second method increases the owner's equity invested in the business.

Sources and Uses of Funds

Sometimes it helps to think of all transactions that affect the balance sheet in terms of *sources* and *uses* of funds. Each time a transaction is made involving the assets, liabilities, or capital of a business, there must be corresponding sources and uses of funds.

Following are lists of sources and uses of funds by classifications on the balance sheet:

Sources	Uses
Equity increases	Asset increases
Liability increases	Liability decreases
Asset decreases	Equity decreases

Let us now take another look at the truck purchase discussed earlier and classify the sources and uses of funds in making the transaction by each of the three methods.

1. Using cash from within the business to make the purchase.
   a. Source of cash—cash account—asset decrease.
   b. Use of cash—equipment account—asset increase.
2. New cash put into business by owner.
   a. Source of cash—new equity—capital account increases.
   b. Use of cash—equipment account—asset increases.
3. Cash borrowed entirely for purchase.
   a. Source of cash—notes payable account—liability increase.
   b. Use of cash—equipment account—asset increase.

The truck purchase results in the same use of cash regardless of the method of the transaction, but the source of the cash is different in each method; the source in the first method results from a decrease in assets, in the second method from an increase in owner's equity, and in the third method from an increase in liabilities.

Sources and uses of funds are important because one of the management responsibilities of any business is to maintain a proper level of liquidity for maximum profits, while still being able to meet all obligations properly. It is possible, for example, for a firm to experience such a large volume of business during a period of time that all of its cash would have been "used" for increased inventory and increased accounts receivable. These accounts receivable would be paid in time, but the immediate result is a cash shortage and a resulting inability to pay bills without a "source" of funds. In such a case, one source might be a short-term bank loan. Then the source would be an increase in liabilities. If it were possible to collect enough accounts receivable to pay the bills, the source would be a decrease in assets. Other possibilities include the owner permanently infusing more of his own cash into the business, in which case the source would be increased equity, or the sale of a fixed asset (not usually a good idea), which would result in reduced assets being the source.

Most businessmen concern themselves with the problem of liquidity in advance of its occurrence by planning an adequate cash flow. *Cash flow* is a term which simply means the business is prepared to have enough cash on hand to handle its obligations in a timely manner and still conduct the maximum amount of business.

As sales are made, inventory is used that must be replaced and expenses are incurred that must be paid. If some, or all of these sales are credit sales, that amount will reside in accounts receivable for a period of time before it is paid by the customers, becoming cash. Normally, many of the firm's obligations must be met before the corresponding accounts receivable are collected, so plans must be made for cash to be available to pay those obligations. A cash-flow plan can be generated by simply anticipating all cash payments that must be made during each month and all cash receipts to be received during each month. The difference betweeen the two will result in either a positive cash flow or a negative cash flow. If the result is a positive cash flow, the business will receive more cash during the month than it will need to handle its obligations, replenish inventory, and so forth. A negative cash flow indicates that sources must be developed for additional cash during the month to enable the firm to meet its obligations.

Sources and uses of funds become very important to a businessman who is planning the cash flow for his business. He must first make a listing of these normal sources and uses as follows:

Sources of Cash	Uses of Cash
Cash sales	Inventory replenishment
Receipt of accts. receivable	Payment of accts. payable
Liability increases	Removal of profits
Equity increases	Payroll
Sale of fixed assets	

Next, the businessman must chart the cash influx and outflow for each month of the year, allowing for unexpected circumstances, such as unusually high credit sales during a given month, which would drive the cash flow toward the negative; that is, more expenses would be incurred because of the increased business, and more inventory would need to be replenished, but the additional accounts receivable would not be collected until later. To properly chart cash influx and outflow, the businessman must know the due date of all of his obligations and the average collection time for his accounts receivable.

The landscape nursery business, being highly seasonal, is fraught with surges in both income and disbursements of cash during certain times of the year. Early spring is a time, for example, when expenses are usually fairly high because work is being done. Also, inventory is high because many goods are purchased in advance of the season. Yet cash income is low because the sales that have been made are tied up in accounts receivable, and the businessman will not receive the cash for these sales for 30 to 90 days. It is a time of negative cash flow, and plans must be made for cash to be available to meet obligations. At the other extreme, late fall might be a time of very positive cash flow for a landscaping business. This is due to the fact that the accounts receivable have been liquidating into cash regularly during the summer and fall, and expenses are winding down as the fall season closes. Also, there is very little inventory replenishment at that time of the year.

Many businesses, especially new ones, have been forced to close simply because they did not plan for a large negative cash flow at the beginning of a year and were unable to find the cash to survive. Many adjustments can be made to a business that will result in a more favorable cash flow. The amount of inventory carried can be a factor. Obviously, a business must have goods to sell, but if the inventory is overloaded, it will contribute to a negative cash flow. If accounts receivable are normally being collected in 60 days, and that time can be reduced to 30 days, this change will have a very positive effect on the cash flow. Also, the rate of inventory turnover will have a great impact on the cash flow. If the inventory can be completely turned over in 60 days instead of 120 days, cash will be realized from that inventory twice as fast. Buying inventory items that have a 30 to 90 day "dating," will also have a positive effect on the cash flow. This means that the business owners have 30 to 90 days in which to sell the items and collect cash for them before they must pay their supplier. Owning unnecessary assets, such as a truck that the business does not need, will have a negative effect on the cash flow because that money could have been used to better advantage as operating capital.

By preparing a cash-flow chart for each month of operation, management can anticipate the needs for cash at all times during the year. Table 11–4 shows a cash-flow chart for Green Tree Nursery. The chart simply gives a listing of the cash to be received by the business during each month and the cash that must be paid out. This differs from the profit and loss statement in that it deals only in cash; not total sales, cost of goods sold, and expenses. Only the cash received and expended during that month is considered.

TABLE 11-4. Cash-flow Chart

GREEN TREE NURSERY
CASH FLOW
April 1976

Cash Influx

Cash sales (less returns)	$ 2,800	
Accounts receivables (aver. 30 days old)	9,700	
Interest-savings cert.		
(4 mo. cert. due 4/2/76)	1,540	
Total cash influx		$14,040

Cash Outflow

Wages	$10,600	
Other accts. payable	6,200	
Inventory due		
Smith Bros.	2,300	
Bill's Nursery	4,300	
United Chemical	7,890	
Capital expenditure (new tractor)	6,800	
Total cash outflow		$38,090
Negative cash flow		($24,050)

For the month of April, 1976, the management of Green Tree Nursery realizes that they are going to need approximately $24,000 more cash than they will receive during the month, so they must plan to find a "source" for that cash. The money that has been in a savings certificate, which contributed $1,540 of the cash influx for April, would be one possible source. They might secure a short-term bank loan to carry them through the period until a positive cash flow will allow them to pay back the loan. Since they are buying a new tractor with part of the cash outflow, possibly they would sell the one they are replacing as a source of some of the needed cash. The important thing is that they know in advance the cash requirements for each month and the cash available each month, so they can plan accordingly. Cash-flow plans should be made at least three months in advance at all times.

SUMMARY

The only accurate measurement of the profitability of a business is the rate of return on equity invested, as compared to other investments the owner could choose to make. The amount of risk involved in the investment and the liquidity of the investment are factors the owner must consider in determining a satisfactory rate of return on equity.

Two financial forms are necessary in order to calculate the rate of return on equity for a business—the balance sheet, and the profit and loss statement.

The *balance sheet* is a listing of all assets, which are all items of value owned by the business; liabilities, which are all debts owed by the firm; and owner's capital, which is the net worth of the business. To be accurate, the balance sheet must always balance; that is, the total assets must equal the liabilities plus the owner's capital. The balance sheet changes with each transaction involving assets, liabilities, or owner's capital, but continues throughout the existence of the business.

Each transaction involving the balance sheet must have a double effect. If an asset is reduced, either another asset must be increased, a liability must be decreased, or owner's capital must decrease proportionately. It helps to think of the transactions involving the balance sheet as being *sources* and *uses* of funds. Sources are decreases in assets, increases in liabilities, or increases in owner's capital. Uses are increases in assets, decreases in liabilities, or decreases in owner's capital. All transactions involving the balance sheet must have one or more sources of funds and one or more uses of funds. The balance sheet may be prepared as often as desired, always for the close of business on the day for which it is dated.

The *profit and loss statement* is an account of all sales made by a business during a period and the resulting costs of producing these sales (the cost of goods sold and expenses). The sales minus the cost of goods sold equals the gross profits, from which the expenses are deducted. The result is a net profit or loss. *Net profit* is the amount of money "made" by a business. A *net loss* is any money "lost" during the period.

A profit and loss statement can be made out for any period of the year. A final profit and loss statement at the end of the year must show sales, cost of goods, expenses, and profit or loss for the entire year. The profit and loss statement does not continue beyond the end of the year. A new set of figures begins the new year.

The *rate of return on equity* is the percentage of the total cash equity invested in a business that is being returned by profits to the owner in a given year. The calculation formula for rate of return on equity is as follows:

$$\frac{\text{Net profit}}{\text{Owner's equity}} = \% \text{ Return on equity}$$

This rate of return on equity is the only true means of comparing the profitability of a business from year to year or comparing various investment possibilities. It serves as a tool for determining the feasibility of additional investment in equipment, buildings, or land. The rate of return on equity is the only means of judging the profitability of a business after additional investment has been made.

Cash flow is a term used to describe the movement of cash into and out of a business. Many businesses fail simply because they do not anticipate the need for cash at certain times of the year and, therefore, are not able to meet their obligations. Wise businessmen prepare monthly cash-flow schedules in advance, so the need for cash to operate soundly can be anticipated.

SUMMARY QUESTIONS

1. For what length of time is the balance sheet valid?
2. Distinguish between a current asset and a fixed asset.
3. What is the difference between a cost of goods sold and an expense?
4. What must be balanced in order for the balance sheet to be correct?
5. What final figure does the profit and loss statement ultimately reveal?
6. Does the profit and loss statement carry over into subsequent years?
7. How does the rate of return on equity differ from the rate of return on total investment?
8. A business, with a total cash equity of $300,000, realizes a $45,000 net profit for the year. Calculate the rate of return on equity for that business for that year.
9. Why does the net profit of a business tell us nothing about the profitability of that business?
10. Why is it necessary to calculate the rate of return on equity each year, instead of just comparing profits?
11. What are some of the advantages to be gained by borrowing some of the money to invest in a business?
12. Name three examples of "sources" of funds for a business.
13. Why is the cash flow especially important to a seasonal business?

CHAPTER 12
Labor Analysis and Pricing

Labor sales are a major part of a landscape nursery's revenue. The pricing of that labor is responsible in large part for the profitability of a business. Obviously, the labor sold must be priced higher than its cost in order for the business make a profit, but identifying these labor costs can be difficult. The successful nursery owner must be able to analyze labor costs and price labor profitably.

A *Labor Analysis* is a process by which management can accumulate labor costs, categorize labor purchased, and allocate amounts and costs of labor to various functions of business operations.

Hopefully, most of the labor purchased by a landscape nursery will be resold to customers. However, sales, management, bookkeeping, landscape designing, equipment repair, building and grounds maintenance, care of plants in storage, garden store operation, and nursery field production and harvesting are all examples of types of labor that might be purchased by a landscape nursery but not resold directly to a customer. Still, these labor costs must be passed on to customers in some manner.

Considering all labor purchased to be a cost of labor sold is a mistake. Some of the types of labor just mentioned should rightfully be considered a cost of materials sales. Since situations often arise in which a firm's labor prices are compared to those of a competing business, those prices should only reflect actual labor costs. A good labor analysis will help management separate the labor purchased into costs of labor sales and material sales.

A labor analysis will allow management to view the progress of the business from an efficiency standpoint, as will be demonstrated later on in this chapter, but in order to do so, the analysis must be done in a very consistent manner each year. Any changes in procedure will distort the results.

There are two types of labor pricing in the landscape nursery industry, the *Retail Price* method and the *Cost-Plus Profit Percentage* method, hereafter referred to simply as *Cost-Plus*.

The retail price method involves the accumulation and analysis by management of all labor information for a period of time, in order to forecast the same information for the coming period of time and to set hourly retail labor prices. Usually, these prices are set for one year. Most landscape nurseries that perform a wide variety of jobs, ranging from small maintenance or planting jobs to larger landscaping installations, should use this method.

All variables facing the business, such as job size, job difficulty, machine costs, and labor distribution, are considered as a unit for the entire period labor prices are used. Of course, should conditions change drastically during that period, a new labor analysis can be done, and prices can be reset at that time.

Cost-plus pricing requires all costs to be assembled for each job, during the course of the job; then a percentage of the total cost or a flat dollar amount is added on for profit on the job. Each job is considered to be a separate entity, instead of being part of the entire costs for a period, as in the retail price method.

The cost-plus pricing method is used mostly by those landscape contractors who perform large landscaping jobs acquired by bidding. Since these jobs are usually bid and since the conditions, specifications, and labor markets can vary, the costs for labor on each job can be considerably different. To price the labor exactly the same on each of these jobs would not be a fair assessment of costs and would probably result in the loss of contracts, should the prices be too high, or the loss of profits, if prices were too low.

There are businesses that use both the retail price method and the cost-plus method of pricing labor. The cost-plus method is used for large jobs, and retail prices are used for all other work. The cost-plus method, while more accurate on larger jobs, is not practical on smaller jobs because it requires more intense bookkeeping procedures and costs are much harder to identify.

Both the retail price method and the cost-plus method of labor pricing require careful analysis of labor costs for accuracy. The approach to the analysis differs somewhat in each case, as we shall see in the remainder of this chapter.

Preliminaries to a Labor Analysis–the Retail Price Method

The first step in any labor analysis is to gather information. A listing of the information required follows:

1. The direct cost of labor purchased during the period of analysis.
   a. Wages paid (commissions and bonuses included).

    b. Direct payroll taxes and payroll-related insurance premiums.

    c. Retirement funds.

2. The number of hours of labor purchased.
3. A breakdown of how the hours of labor purchased were used, by categories.
4. Proportionate amounts of sales volume.

    a. Labor sales percentage of total sales.

    b. Materials sales percentage of total sales.

5. A definition of the categories in which labor is sold.
6. The total expenses other than wages, payroll taxes and direct insurance, and retirement funds, plus expenses directly related to materials.

Sources for Required Information

Every business must make out at least one profit and loss statement during the business year for income-tax reporting purposes. This financial paper, discussed earlier in Chapter 11, will supply much of the information necessary for a labor analysis. Wages (including commissions and bonuses) appear in the expenses section of the profit and loss statement, as do the payroll taxes and direct insurance premiums, hereafter referred to as payroll taxes and insurance, collectively. These costs are FICA (or social security) taxes, unemployment compensation insurance, workman's compensation insurance, and other payroll-related insurance provided by the company, such as life, health, or disability insurance premiums. These taxes and insurance premiums may not be listed as separate items on the profit and loss statement, in which case they must be obtained from cancelled checks or receipts.

Retirement funds are normally itemized on the profit and loss statement, but if these funds are invested in insurance, they may be included in an all-encompassing insurance account. If so, it will be necessary to refer to the cancelled checks or receipts again.

Because of federal wage-and-hour labor laws, most businesses use some type of a timecard system to record the number of hours worked by employees. These cards are the source for the number of hours of labor purchased. If no timecard is used, the hours can be estimated, based upon the number of hours worked, on average, in each pay period. Multiplying the average number of hours worked by an employee in a pay period by the number of pay periods he worked will provide a close estimate of his total hours.

Some type of a recording system will be required to supply a breakdown of uses of labor by categories. Unless each employee is hired to perform only very specific tasks, it will be necessary to record the various uses of his time. Most businesses find it more efficient to have employees perform in several areas of labor use, rather than in one specific area. For example, an employee might work on a jobsite for a customer during part of a day, then spend the remainder of the day unloading and stocking plants.

The various uses of labor can be recorded effectively on a *Time-Use Record* as in Table 12–1. The hours an employee works are broken into the categories of use that a company feels are most important to recognize. This form can be filled out by each employee daily or by his supervisor.

This particular time-use record has six spaces for one work week. It could have been designed, however, for two weeks, one month, or any time span desired.

TABLE 12-1. Time–Use Record

Date	Total Time	Hours Charged	Productive Nursery	Equipment Repair	Building Maintenance	Lost Time
Totals						

Employee Name_____

The time-use record is divided into seven vertical columns. The left-hand column is for the date of each work day recorded, and the second column is for the total number of hours worked by the employee on that date, usually recorded to the nearest quarter hour. The third column is for hours of the employee's time that were charged to business customers on each day. Any work done by the employee in the nursery's growing fields or plant-holding areas, which has to do with the growing, harvesting, or maintenance of plant material, is recorded in column four, titled productive nursery work. Column five is for time spent repairing equipment, and column six for hours worked on building and grounds maintenance. The last column is for lost time, which is the remaining total time not recorded in one of the other time-use columns.

Space is provided at the bottom of the columns for totals, and there is a place for the employee's name. The time-use record can be made any size desirable. If the employee is to fill out the record himself, perhaps it is best to make the time-use record the same size as the timecard, so it may be attached to the timecard and filled out at the same time.

Management can take totals of each category on the time-use record at any time, but totals must be taken prior to performance of a labor analysis, to provide the breakdown of how labor hours purchased were used.

The time-uses shown in this example are by no means the only ones that might be recorded. Each business must decide its own major uses of time. Other possible time-uses include sales, garden store, stocking, landscape design, and inventory, just to name a few.

As mentioned earlier, the profit and loss statement is the source for information about the percentage of total sales represented by labor and materials. Normally, sales are broken into categories in the sales section of this financial statement. If not, this information will probably be available on the sales invoices used for billing customers for work.

Landscape nurseries usually sell labor and machine work by categories. Different levels of technical skill, tools, machinery, training, licensing, and insurance costs are encountered in the diverse types of labor performed. There are three classes of labor sold to customers, which are broken down further into categories.

1. *Labor that requires special training or skills.* Crew supervisors are often charged for at a special rate because they are more experienced, more highly trained, and paid higher salaries. Special skills, such as pruning, tree work, consultation, landscape designing, and so forth, are all possible categories in this class of labor.
2. *Machine work.* Any labor category that includes the cost of machine operation must reflect that cost. All machines have a unique set of operating costs.
3. *Higher licensing or insurance costs.* Spraying and tree climbing are examples of labor categories that are charged to customers at a higher rate, because higher training, licensing, and insurance costs to the business require it.

Because labor is usually sold in categories, it is necessary to know the number of hours sold at each rate in order to perform a labor analysis.

The use of another form, called a *Job Sheet,* is recommended for recording all materials and labor used on a job. This job sheet can be used as a source for hours of labor sold by categories. It has many other uses as well.

A sample job sheet is shown in Table 12–2. The example is divided into four sections. The top section contains information about the customer and the work instructions. The customer's name, work address, billing address, and phone number appear at the top of the sheet. The next spaces are for written instructions for completion of the individual parts of the total job, with boxes to be checked as each job is completed.

TABLE 12-2. Sample Job Sheet

BROWN'S NURSERY
JOB SHEET

Customer Name _____ Address _____ Phone _____

Billing Address _____

Instructions

Check box below
when each instruction
completed

1. _____ ☐

2. _____ ☐

3. _____ ☐

Special Tools and Equipment Required
1. _____   3. _____
2. _____   4. _____

LABOR RECORD

Date	Labor Category	Crew	Time In	Time Out	Total Time	Rate	Total

Total labor _____

MATERIALS

Item	Size	Quan.	Unit Price	Total	Item	Size	Unit Price	Unit	Total

Date completed ___/___/___   Date billed ___/___/___   Total hardgoods _____
Employee in chg. _____   Inv. No. _____   Total plants _____
Total labor _____
Sales tax _____
Total charge _____

Any specialized tools or equipment required to complete the job can be written in the spaces that follow, but normally anticipated tools and equipment, such as rakes or shovels would not be written in. This part of the job sheet, like the written instructions, aids in the smooth completion of the job.

The second section of the job sheet provides for a labor record. Labor is recorded by categories as it is performed. The date is entered on the left, the labor category in the second column, and initials of those working in the third column. This provides a check on the total time recorded and helps management answer questions should they later occur. Time-in and time-out columns are provided to record the exact times the crew begins and ends work. The total time column records the combined total time of all individuals working on the job. This particular job sheet was devised for a business that uses a retail price method of pricing labor, so columns are provided for the retail rates charged for each category and the total charge resulting from multiplying the retail rate by the total time.

The third section of the job sheet is used for recording all materials used on a job, with spaces for sizes, unit prices, and total prices of those materials.

The final section of the job sheet is used to record data for billing. At the right-hand side of the sheet, totals of all materials, labor, and sales tax are compiled. The name of the supervisor in charge of the job is provided for at the lower left-hand side of the sheet, along with the date of completion. In the middle of the sheet, in this fourth section, are spaces for the date of billing and the invoice number to be entered.

As is the case with any form, each business should analyze its needs and create a job sheet that will suit its purposes. In the interest of conserving space and paper, the labor section can be printed on the reverse side of the job sheet, for example, allowing more days of labor to be entered on a single sheet and more materials and other information on the front side. Some firms prefer to use a job sheet for only one day's activities, issuing a new job sheet the following day, so there is less chance of the records of an entire job being lost.

Since the job sheet will normally accompany a landscaping crew to the jobsite, it must be fade-proof, smudge-proof, and printed on sturdy paper stock to take the abuse it will receive.

The total hours of labor sold by categories can be removed periodically from job sheets as they are billed or summed later as a preliminary to the labor analysis.

The final item of information required for a labor analysis, the total expenses not already included in any of the other information collected, can be obtained from the profit and loss statement. The total expenses, found at the bottom of the expenses section of the profit and loss statement, minus the payroll taxes, direct payroll insurance, retirement funds, and direct materials expenses leaves the other expenses as a remainder. (Freight is an example of an expense that is directly related to materials sales.)

The Labor Analysis–Retail Price Method

The information for a labor analysis having been gathered, it is then necessary to provide a means of assembling that information into a meaningful form, which will tie all of the bits and pieces together. This information can best be assembled on a form called the *Labor and Machine Work Table*. Completion of this table reveals the total amount of labor purchased, the total cost of producing the labor for sale, the average cost of such labor per hour, the specific revenue produced by each labor category sold, the specific costs for labor and machines in each category, and finally, the net gain or loss on labor sales.

Table 12–3 is a sample labor and machine work table. The table is divided into eight vertical columns. In the far left column, each labor category sold by the nursery is listed separately, followed by a listing of each labor use category not sold. All hours of labor for each of the categories are listed in column 2. Column 3 lists the retail prices or rates charged for each labor category sold. Column 4 is for total charges made by categories. Machine charges are itemized in column 5, labor charges in 6, labor costs in 7, and gross gain or loss in column 8.

It is necessary to prepare a labor and machine work table in a systematic fashion. The following list outlines the steps to be followed, in order. If you get lost, do not worry. Later we will go through each step again more slowly.

1. Calculate the hours of labor purchased from timecards for the total period to be analyzed, and enter as total of column 2.
2. Total hours charged by categories of labor sold from job sheets. Enter category names in column 1 and hours for each in column 2.
3. Total the time-use records.
   a. Synchronize totals from time-use record to totals of job sheets.
   b. Synchronize lost-time total to total hours from timecards.

c. Enter synchronized totals for time-use categories not charged to customers.

4. Retail labor prices, which have been used during the period being analyzed, are entered into column 3. These are multiplied by the total hours for the same category in column 2, to provide the total charges, which are entered in column 4, for each category of labor charged.

5. Machine charges, which should have been established at the starting point of the period being analyzed, are entered in column 5, at the actual amounts of cost, calculated from records kept during the period.

6. Machine charges are subtracted from the total charges in each category, with the remainder entered in the column titled "Net Labor Charge."

7. The actual labor cost is calculated, as it applies to labor sales.

   a. Direct labor expenses, including payroll taxes and insurance, and retirement funds are added to the wages to arrive at the gross labor cost.

   b. Overhead labor, which is that portion of the total labor that applies to the sale of materials, is calculated.

   (1) Salaries of those involved in the sale or administration of materials sales are identified.

   (2) Respective percentages of total sales are calculated for materials and labor.

   (3) The percentage of material sales (of total sales) is multiplied by the total cost of the personnel involved in the sale or administration of material sales, to arrive at the overhead labor figure.

   c. Overhead labor is subtracted from the gross labor cost to leave the net labor cost, or actual labor cost.

   d. The net labor cost is divided by the total number of hours purchased during the period, found at the bottom of column 2, to arrive at the net cost per hour of labor.

   e. The net cost per hour of labor is multiplied by the number of hours of labor in each category to arrive at the labor cost, which is entered into column 7.

8. Gross gain or loss on labor is calculated by subtracting the labor cost from the net labor charge. Enter totals from each category in column 8.

9. Total all columns on the labor and machine work table.

10. Calculate other expenses and enter the total in the space for that purpose beneath the total of column 8.

11. Subtract other expenses from the gross gain or loss on labor to arrive at net gain or loss on labor.

Sample Labor Analysis–Retail Price Method

In order to examine the calculations and procedures for filling out the labor and machine work table more closely, a fictitious nursery called "Brown's Nursery" has been used. The sample labor and machine work table (Table 12–3) has been filled out for this firm. Since much of the information required for a labor analysis is provided by the profit and loss statement, that financial paper has been provided in Table 12–4. All figures used in the examples are contrived, and although representative, are not to be considered average.

TABLE 12-3. Brown's Nursery—Labor and Machine Work Table

1	2	3	4	5	6	7	8
						Labor	Gross Gain
Labor	*Total*	*Retail*	*Total*	*Machine*	*Net Labor*	*Cost*	*or Loss*
Category	*Hours*	*Rate*	*Charge*	*Charge*	*Charge*	*@$5.63/hr*	*on Labor*
Labor	6,700	$12.00	$ 80,400	0	$ 80,400	$ 37,721	$42,679
Supervision	2,500	15.00	37,500	0	37,500	14,075	23,425
Tractor	420	19.00	7,980	$2,940	5,040	2,365	2,675
Pruning	260	15.00	3,900	0	3,900	1,464	2,436
Spraying	135	17.00	2,295	405	1,890	760	1,130
Powerrake	110	18.00	1,980	330	1,650	619	1,031
Rototiller	95	18.00	1,710	285	1,425	535	890
Lost time	6,031	0	0	0	0	33,954	−33,954
Equipment Repair	600	0	0	0	0	3,378	−3,378
Building Maintenance	900	0	0	0	0	5,067	−5,067
Totals	17,751			$135,765	$3,960	$131,805	$99,938* (99,940)†	$31,865

Total hours charged: 10,220   Minus other expenses: −$16,097
Overhead labor: $22,260   Net gain on labor: 15,768

*Total sum of categories at $5.63/hour.
†Difference between two figures caused by rounding-off hourly cost to nearest whole cents.

Assume that Brown's Nursery is a business engaged only in landscaping work, including some spraying, powerraking, and lawn seeding. The firm has no garden store and no growing fields. All the labor purchased by Brown's is for the purpose of retail sales. The firm uses the retail price method of pricing labor, which is sold in seven categories of labor and machine work. All employees are salaried by the hour and record their time on a mechanical time clock with timecards. Each employee

TABLE 12-4

BROWN'S NURSERY
PROFIT AND LOSS STATEMENT

Sales
Materials	$153,096	
Labor	135,765	
	$288,861	
Total sales		$288,861

Cost of Goods Sold
Cost of goods	$ 97,981	
Total cost of goods sold		$ 97,981
Gross profit		$190,880

Expenses
Freight	2,000	
Wages	$110,090	
Payroll taxes	8,047	
Retirement funds	1,651	
Workman's compensation insurance	1,400	
Group health insurance	1,012	
Other insurance	2,346	
Utilities	1,765	
Telephone	1,745	
Interest	4,197	
Advertising	4,378	
Depreciation	9,432	
Gas and oil	5,004	
Office supplies	1,256	
Repairs and maintenance	4,126	
	$158,449	
Total expenses		$158,449
Net profit		$ 32,431

fills out a time-use record (see Table 12–1), and supervisors record employee labor on job sheets (see Table 12–2). Three employees are involved in the sale and administration of both materials and labor.

Given this information the labor analysis can begin for Brown's Nursery. First, the labor and machine work table is filled out according to the order established earlier.

1. The total hours of labor purchased are added from the timecards and found to be 17,751. This total is entered at the bottom of column 2.
2. The total of labor charged in each labor category is provided by adding the figures taken off of the job sheets. These totals are found to be: labor—6,700 hours, supervision—2,500 hours, tractor—420 hours, pruning—260 hours, spraying—135 hours, powerrake—110 hours, and rototiller—95 hours. These seven labor categories are listed in column 1, and the hours of each are written in column 2.
3. The time-use records are totaled.
   a. Since the time-use records are filled out by each employee, while the job sheets are filled out only by supervisors, the job sheets are judged more accurate. Since the two records contain different totals of hours charged to customers, it is necessary to synchronize the totals. According to the job sheets, a total of 10,220 hours were charged customers, but the time-use records are found to total 10,645 hours charged to customers. The following calculation is made so the other categories of labor use can be adjusted.

$$\frac{\text{Total hrs. charged—job sheets } 10,220}{\text{Total hrs. charged—time use } 10,645} = 96\%$$

   The other categories of time-use are then multiplied by 96%, and the totals are entered in the spaces for equipment repair and building and grounds maintenance in column 2. Lost time figures must be further synchronized before they are entered.
   b. The total hours of labor purchased, at the bottom of column 2, is the total hours purchased obtained from the timecards. Since the synchronization just discussed is between the time-use record and the job sheets, further synchronization is necessary so all of the hourly totals by category will equal the total from the timecards, which has to be accurate. This simple calculation involves subtracting the total hours of all other categories except lost time from the total hours. That remainder is then entered in column 2 as lost time.
4. Retail prices for labor, which have been used during the year, are entered in column 3 and multiplied by the hourly totals for each category of labor sold. The total charges that result are entered in column 4.
5. Machine charges are calculated. Each machine used by the nursery has a unique set of costs for operation. Brown's nursery maintains a record of repairs and maintenance performed on each machine during the year. Job sheet forms are used for this purpose to eliminate the need for another form. Depreciation schedules are maintained for income tax records. Following is an example of the calculation of machine charges for two tractors owned by the nursery, which were used exclusively to produce the 420 hours of tractor time sold to

customers. The two tractors were purchased for a combined value of $7,000. They each are being depreciated on a straight-line method over a seven-year period. Each tractor burns about three gallons of gasoline per hour.

Yearly depreciation	$1,000
Gasoline, 3 gal/hr. × 420 × $.60/gal.	756
Oil and lubrication	
(from maintenance records)	380
Repairs and maintenance	
from maintenance records)	800
Total cost of operation	
(both tractors)	$2,936

$2,936 ÷ 240 hours = $7.00/hour

All other machine costs are calculated in the same way, and the totals are entered in column 5.

6. Machine charges are subtracted from total charges, and the resultant net labor charge is entered in column 6. At this point, the tractor category for the labor and machine work table would appear as follows:

TABLE 12-5

	2	3	4	5	6	7	8
Tractor	$420	$19.00	$7,980	$2,940	$5,040		

7. Net labor cost is calculated.
   a. Gross labor cost is figured. From the profit and loss statement for Brown's Nursery (see Table 12–4), wages are listed in the expenses section as $110,090 for the year. Direct payroll expenses are added to these wages to obtain the gross labor cost. Payroll taxes, which includes the FICA taxes and unemployment taxes, workman's compensation insurance, retirement funds, and health insurance, which is provided by the company, are those expenses that are deemed directly applicable to labor sales. The total of these expenses, $12,110, is added to the $110,090 wages to equal $122,200 total gross labor cost. These direct payroll expenses are noted to be 11% of the wages ($12,110 ÷ $110,090).
   b. As indicated earlier, three persons are involved in sales and administration work that produces materials sales as well as labor sales. The timecards for these people show that they were paid a total of $37,838. Since the business is involved strictly with a landscaping operation, 100% of their salaries is involved with landscape sales. Direct payroll expenses, in the amount of 11%, are added to these salaries, for a total gross cost of $42,000 ($37,838 × 1.11).

Percentages of total sales are calculated for materials and labor. The profit and loss statement shows that of the total sales of $288,861, $135,765 were labor sales and $153,096 were material sales. The following calculation is made to arrive at percentages of each.

$$\frac{\text{Total labor sales } \$135,765}{\text{Total sales} \quad \$288,861} = 47\% \text{ Labor sales}$$

$$100\% - 47\% = 53\% \text{ materials sales}$$

Overhead labor is calculated by determining the amount of gross labor cost that must be removed from labor cost as a cost of materials sales. This is accomplished by multiplying the gross cost of the three persons involved in both types of sales by the percentage of material sales:

$$\$42,000 \times 53\% = \$22,260 \text{ overhead labor}$$

c. Overhead labor of $22,260 is then subtracted from the gross labor cost of $122,200, leaving $99,940, which is the net labor cost for Brown's Nursery, for the year being analyzed.

d. The net labor cost of $99,940 is divided by the total number of hours purchased (17,751) to yield a cost of $5.63/hour purchased, as an average.

e. The hourly cost of $5.63 is multiplied by each of the hourly totals of both the labor sold and labor used categories, and these totals are entered in column 7. Because of a fractional remainder in dividing the cost into an hourly figure, the column totals $99,938, after each category is multiplied by the hourly cost.

8. Each category's labor cost is subtracted from any net labor charges made for that category, and the difference is posted in column 8 as a gross gain or loss on labor.

9. All columns are totaled on the labor and machine work table, indicating a total gross gain on labor of $31,865.

10. *Other expenses* are those which are not considered to be directly related to either wages or materials. The profit and loss statement for Brown's Nursery shows that the total expenses were $158,449 (see Table 12–4). Total wages are $110,090, direct payroll expenses were earlier calculated to be $12,110, and direct materials expense (freight) is $2,000. The sum of these ($124,200) is then subtracted from the total expenses ($158,449) leaving a total of $34,249, which is other expenses for both labor and materials. Labor's share is calculated by multiplying $34,249 by 47%, which yields $16,097 other expenses related to labor sales only.

11. This figure ($16,097) is subtracted from the gross gain on labor of $31,865, leaving $15,768 as the net gain on labor.

The calculation of a net gain or loss on labor results in the opportunity to reveal the net gain or loss on materials also. This is done by subtracting the net gain or loss on labor from the total net profit for the period, which is found on the year-ending profit and loss statement. From the profit and loss statement for Brown's Nursery in Table 12–4, the net profit for the year is found to be $32,431.

Total net profit ($32,431) minus net gain on labor ($15,768) equals the net gain on materials ($16,663).

The labor and machine work table has now been completed. The table can be maintained in company files and compared with subsequent years. Labor and machine work tables from several years of operation, if done in a consistent manner, will be invaluable to management. The value of the table not only affords an opportunity to study the past year's performance, but also allows management to forecast the next year's activities.

Forecasting and Pricing–Retail Price Method

There is always some guesswork involved in forecasting the next year's business. No one can know exactly how much labor a business will sell in the future or exactly what the labor will cost. Proper use of the labor and machine work table can at least give management an overview of the possibilities.

Forecasting labor revenues and costs is done by reversing somewhat the procedures for filling out the labor and machine work table. The steps in the process are as follows:

1. Determine the changes in labor cost that will occur as a result of pay raises, increases in federal minimum wage requirements, increased or decreased numbers of personnel, or any other known change in hours purchased or the cost of these hours.
   a. Calculate changes in the amounts paid full-time employees, plus respective direct labor expenses (payroll taxes, insurance, retirement).
   b. Calculate the changes in labor cost for those involved with overhead labor.
   c. Calculate the changes anticipated for the remainder of the laboring force.
2. Anticipate the number of hours of labor that will be purchased by the business during the coming year and how these hours will be used and sold. Project these estimated hours sold and used onto the proper spaces in columns 1 and 2 of the labor and machine work table.

3. Adjust the gross labor cost anticipated above by any projected increase or decrease in hours purchased.

4. Remove adjusted overhead labor from the anticipated gross labor cost to arrive at the forecasted net labor cost. Divide the net labor cost anticipated by the estimated hours purchased, to arrive at the labor cost per hour. Multiply all hours projected by categories by the labor cost per hour and fill in the amounts for each labor category in column 7.

5. Update other expenses.
   a. Estimate the total expenses, other than direct payroll and materials costs, for the coming year by economic forecasts and past history.
   b. Estimate percentages of total sales that will be materials sales and labor sales.
   c. Multiply total other expenses by the anticipated labor sales percentage, to arrive at other expenses as they relate to labor sales. Fill in this figure in the space for other expenses below column 8 on the labor and machine work table.

6. Determine the desired net gain on labor for the coming year and fill in the amount in the proper spot below other expenses.

7. Add the desired net gain on labor to the anticipated other expenses to arrive at the gross gain on labor, which is entered as the total of column 8. This figure is the margin that management wishes to achieve between the labor sold and labor bought, by pricing.

8. Add the anticipated net labor cost total entered earlier in column 7 to the gross gain on labor total of column 8, to arrive at the necessary net labor charge total for column 6.

9. Calculate machine charges for the coming year and enter in proper categories in column 5. Total column.

10. Add total machine charges to total net labor charges to arrive at the total charge that will be necessary. Enter this figure as a total of column 4.

11. Set labor prices to produce the total charges desired.

We can use Brown's Nursery again as an example of this forecasting procedure.

Assume that Brown's Nursery has used the labor and machine work table for several years, so they have a consistent record by which to base estimations. The management knows that they have some opportunity for growth during the coming year, but they believe that growth will occur in only one category—labor. They will operate with the same people making sales and handling the administrative work. It is estimated that they will be able to sell 10% more labor hours, or 670 hours, and that 100 more hours of lost time will result. All other labor categories will be forecast at the same number sold and used as last year.

Brown's Nursery's employees are all to be given a 10% pay raise, regardless of position, primarily to account for cost-of-living increases. It is expected that all expenses other than payroll and direct payroll taxes, insurance, and retirement funds will increase by 10%, because of an inflation rate forecast by economists. Payroll taxes and insurance are expected to increase from 11% to 12% of wages, mostly due to an increase in FICA (social security) rates.

Because of some increased investment in facilities and an increase in the amount of capital that will be necessary to operate during the year, the management of Brown's Nursery determines that the net gain on labor should be targeted to increase to $18,000 from the $15,768 realized the previous year. This increase of $2,232, along with an increase of $2,517 in net gain on materials, for a total net profit increase of $4,749, is desired to return 15% on $31,660 increased equity investment. (See Chapter 11.)

Records over the years show that the 47% labor sales and 53% materials sales experienced the previous year were reasonably average, so those percentages are to be used for forecasting the coming year's activities.

1. Since all employees are to receive a 10% increase in pay, the total wages from the profit and loss statement from last year are increased by 10%. Payroll taxes and insurance are then calculated at 12% and added to the anticipated cost of wages. The following calculations are used:

   $110,090 (previous year's wages) × 1.10 = $121,099

   $121,099 × 1.12 = $135,631 (cost for same labor bought last year)

   The same three persons were involved in overhead labor at increases of 10% in wages and 1% more payroll taxes and insurance. Materials sales cost of 53% is used to determine the amount of their cost to be removed as overhead labor.

   Last year's salaries ($37,838) × payroll taxes and insurance (1.11) equals total cost ($42,000) × 53% equals overhead labor ($22,260) for previous year.

   Anticipated salaries ($41,621) × payroll taxes and insurance (1.12) equals total cost ($46,616) × 53% equals overhead labor ($24,706) for coming year.

2. The number of hours of labor purchased and sold have already been anticipated by management. Increases of 670 hours of labor and 100 hours of lost time make the projected total hours purchased 18,521 for the coming year (17,751 plus 670 plus 100). These projected hours

of labor sold and labor used are entered into column 2 of the projected labor and machine work table. (See Table 12–9)

3. Since a total of 770 hours more labor are projected to be purchased, the cost of these hours must be added to the cost of the hours from last year, which were previously adjusted to the coming year's cost. These additional hours are anticipated to be of the lowest on the pay scale, so management estimates that they will average $3.00/hr.

$$770 \text{ hours} \times \$3.00/\text{hr.} = \$2310 \times 1.12 \text{ (payroll taxes and insurance)} = \$2,587$$

$$\$2,587 + \$135,631 = \$138,218 \text{ gross labor cost}$$

4. Overhead labor, previously calculated to be $24,706, is removed from gross labor cost of $138,218 to leave $113,512 as net labor cost. The net labor cost is divided by 18,521 projected hours, indicating an average cost of $6.13/hr. ($6.1288267 actual). All of the hours of labor are multiplied by $6.13, and the total costs are entered into column 7 of the labor and machine work table. Because of a fractional difference in the cost/hour, the total of the column is $113,534 when $6.13 is multiplied by the hours in each category.

5. All expenses except those considered directly applicable to payroll (payroll taxes, workman's compensation, health insurance, and retirement funds), are then adjusted for the coming year by a 10% increase. The profit and loss statement from last year reveals that these expenses were $34,249; therefore, a 10% increase means they are projected to be $37,673 the coming year ($34,249 × 1.10).

   Other expenses as they relate to labor sales are then calculated by multiplying the $37,673 by 47% (labor sales percentage) to obtain $17,706, which is entered into the other expenses space below column 8. At this point in the forecast, the bottom of the labor and machine work table would appear as shown in Table 12–6.

TABLE 12-6

1	2	3	4	5	6	7	8
Totals	18,521					$113,534 *	
						($113,512)†	

Total hours charged:_____	Minus other expenses:	$(17,706)
Overhead labor: $24,706	Net gain on labor:	(18,000)

*Total of categories at $6.13/hour.
†Difference between two figures caused by rounding-off hourly cost to nearest whole cents.

Note that in the total space for column 7, there are two figures, the estimated figure and the actual total of the various categories priced at $6.13. When a projected labor and machine work table is made out, the projected figures should be enclosed in parentheses, with the actual figure immediately above.

6. The net gain on labor is determined by management, and this figure ($18,000) is entered into the table. This is the amount of net gain on labor desired by the firm during the coming year.

7. The desired net gain on labor ($18,000) is then added to the other expenses ($17,706), resulting in $35,706, which is the necessary gross gain on labor that will be the total of column 8. This represents the margin that must be achieved, by pricing labor, between the labor sold and the labor bought.

8. The gross gain on labor is now added to the anticipated net labor cost, which is the total of column 7, to provide the net labor charge, which is targeted for the total of column 6.

The totals columns on the labor and machine work table would now appear as shown in Table 12–7.

TABLE 12-7

1	2	3	4	5	6	7	8
Totals	18,521				($149,218)	$113,534	
						($113,512)	($35,706)
Total hours charged:_____					Minus other expenses:		($17,706)
Overhead labor: $24,706					Net gain on labor		($18,000)

9. Machine charges had to be recalculated because it was anticipated that gasoline would average $.65/gallon, instead of $.60/gallon, as in the previous year, and oil, lubrication, repairs, and maintenance were expected to increase by 10%. Depreciation was expected to remain the same since no new machinery was purchased and none had been completely depreciated. New machine charges were filled in for each category, and column 5 was totaled at $4,261.

10. Machine charges of $4,261 were then added to the net labor charge total of $149,218 in column 6 to get total charges of $153,479, which were entered as the total of column 4.

11. The remaining task of forecasting labor prices and costs is to find the hourly rates necessary to produce the total charges that will ultimately produce the gross gain on labor desired. The totals column of the labor and machine work table now appears as shown in Table 12–8.

TABLE 12-8

1	2	3	4	5	6	7	8
Totals	18,521		($153,479)	($4,261)	($149,218)	$113,534	($35,706)
						($113,512)	
Total hours charged:_____					Minus other expenses:		($17,706)
Overhead labor: $24,706					Net gain on labor:		($18,000)

Setting Prices

Some experimentation is involved in setting the retail prices so the total labor charges in column 4 will be closely approximated. By figuring the desired difference between the total labor charges and those of last year, management can derive an average increased charge per hour to use as a starting point.

$$\$153,479 \text{ (total charges next year)} - \$135,765 \text{ (last year)} = \$17,714$$

$$\frac{\$17,714 \text{ (increase)}}{10,890 \text{ (hr. sold)}} = \$1.63/\text{hour average increase in charges}$$

Management's first decision about setting prices regards the pricing of the categories for the past year. Were any categories priced too low or too high? Scrutiny of the past year's labor and machine work table (Table 12–3) tells management that each category showed a net margin on labor in healthy proportions. Had one or more of the categories showed a net loss in column 8, every attempt would be made during the coming year to price that labor category for a net gain.

Competition will have an effect on the pricing of various labor categories, so management must decide which areas to increase the most. Brown's Nursery feels that they can most easily raise their tractor rates and remain competitive; therefore, these rates are raised by $3.00/hour, to $22.00/hour. More competition is developing for powerraking and rototilling services, so these rates are raised only $1.00/hour to a total of $19.00/hour. Spraying and pruning are both technical services, which restricts competition, so these rates are raised by $2.00/hour each, to $19.00/hour and $17.00/hour respectively.

Calculations of total charges are now made for each of these labor categories, and these revenues are added to see how much revenue must be produced by the two largest categories of labor sold, labor and supervision. Total charges for these categories for which prices have been set is found to be $20,120, leaving $133,359 as the targeted total charge to be produced by the labor and supervision categories.

By trial and error, it is found that an increase of $1.00/hour of labor to $13.00/hour, and $1.50/hour for supervision to $16.50/hour will produce a total charge of $157,180, which is $3,701 more than the targeted amount ($153,479).

Now the management must make decisions about the competitiveness of the prices set. Much of the increased revenue is being produced by the additional 670 hours of labor they hope to sell ($8,710). Therefore, management decides to leave the prices set as they are, with the extra $3,701 providing a cushion against the failure to produce enough labor sales to meet the goal of 670 additional hours. The remaining calculations on the labor and machine work table are now completed and these forecasted figures may be compared with the actual results at the end of the year. (See Table 12–9.)

TABLE 12-9. Brown's Nursery Labor and Machine Work Table—Projected

1	2	3	4	5	6	7	8
Labor Category	Total Hours	Retail Rate	Total Charge	Machine Charge	Net Labor Charge	Labor Cost @$6.13/hr.	Gross Gain or Loss on Labor
Labor	7,370	$13.00	$ 95,810	$ 0	$ 95,810	$ 45,178	$50,632
Supervision	2,500	16.50	41,250	0	41,250	15,325	25,925
Tractor	420	22.00	9,240	3,117	6,123	2,575	3,548
Pruning	260	17.00	4,420	0	4,420	1,594	2,826
Spraying	135	19.00	2,565	454	2,111	828	1,283
Powerrake	110	19.00	2,090	370	1,720	674	1,046
Rototiller	95	19.00	1,805	320	1,485	582	903
Lost time	6,131	0	0	0	0	37,583	−37,583
Equipment Repair	600	0	0	0	0	3,678	−3,678
Building Maintenance	900	0	0	0	0	5,517	−5,517
			$157,180	$4,261	$152,919	$113,534	$39,385
Totals	18,521		($153,479)	($4,261)	($149,218)	($113,512)	($35,706)

Total hours charged	$10,890		Minus: other expenses	$17,706
				$21,679
Overhead labor	$24,706		Net gain on labor	($18,000)

Notice, in the space for net gain on labor, the net gain will be $21,679, if Brown's Nursery is able to sell exactly the number of hours of each category and all other criteria is exactly as pictured in the labor and machine work table. However, that is virtually never the case. The purpose of this forecast is to prepare for the coming year as closely as possible, but predictions are never 100% accurate. For that reason, it is wise to forecast two or three different possibilities ranging from pessimistic to optimistic, so all probable results of the prices set can be viewed.

Competition for business eliminates the possibility of always pricing labor exactly as management would like. Thus, retail prices are often a compromise between the ideal and the practical. It is important to remember though, that no business can realize a profit on labor if a satisfactory margin is not maintained between net labor cost and net labor charge, regardless of the number of sales made.

Cost-Plus Analysis and Pricing

Analysis of costs and pricing of labor is accomplished differently in a cost-plus pricing situation because all costs are applied on each job.

There are two general types of expenses recognized by those who use a cost-plus pricing system: Fixed Costs and Job-Related Costs.

Fixed costs are those expenses that occur to a business, regardless of the number or size of jobs completed. Salaries of permanent supervisory or administrative personnel, plus the accompanying payroll taxes and insurance, are examples of fixed costs, since these people are not directly involved with any one job. Other fixed costs might include insurance, licensing, organizational memberships, depreciation, accounting, telephone, utilities, and office supplies.

Job-related costs are those expenses that can be directly related to a specific job; they would not have occurred if that job had not been done. Wages paid to employees who work on specific jobs are job-related costs that apply directly to those jobs. Other typical job-related costs include special liability insurance for a job, machine hire, interest, jobsite offices, portable toilets, or consultant fees.

Fixed costs must normally be totaled at the end of each year, because some of these payments are only made at one time of the year. These costs can be obtained from the profit and loss statement and from calculations made where only part of an expense is fixed and the remainder is job related. For example, if Brown's Nursery, the fictitious firm used in the study of a labor analysis by the retail price method, used the cost-plus method of pricing instead, the overhead labor of persons involved in the sale of labor would become a fixed cost of labor. The remaining cost of these persons' labor would be a fixed cost of materials. All of the remaining labor costs for Brown's Nursery would be job related and, therefore, applied to individual jobs. If an expense cannot be readily identified and designated to a specific job, it should be considered a fixed cost.

Fixed costs are usually apportioned to individual jobs according to the proportionate volume of sales the job accounts for. Brown's Nursery had a total sales volume of $288,861 for the year used as an example, as shown on the profit and loss statement (see Table 12–4). If they had a contract for a job with a total value of $34,000, that job would account for 11.77% of their total sales volume for the year. The fixed labor cost ($22,260) is then multiplied by 11.77% to find that $2,620 of that cost should be applied to that particular job. All other fixed costs are apportioned in the same fashion.

Job records are important in a cost-plus pricing scheme to ensure accurate assimilation of costs. Three collection forms are recommended for daily use, the Daily Labor Report, Daily Expense Report, and Daily Materials-Use Report. Each day, the labor, expenses, and materials are recorded on these forms as they occur. The totals from these daily forms are then logged into a journal with each day's totals for a total job record. Examples of these three forms are found in Tables 12–10, 12–11, and 12–12.

TABLE 12-10. Daily Labor Report

DAILY LABOR REPORT		
Job No. _____ Date _____		
Employee's name _____		
Time in		XXXXXXX
Time out		XXXXXXX
Regular time		XXXXXXX
Overtime		XXXXXXX
Payrate		XXXXXXX
Wages		
Payroll taxes and Insurance		
Retirement funds		
Total cost		

TABLE 12-11. Daily Expense Report

DAILY EXPENSE REPORT				
Job No. _____ Date _____/_____/_____				
P.O. No.	Expense	Vendor	Amount of Invoice	Explanation
Total Daily Expenses $_____				

Each of the three forms shown in the examples serves as a collection device. The total amounts from each daily form are then entered into a permanent record for the entire job. In these examples, the fixed expenses have not been accounted for. These are, instead, added to the totals of accumulated labor, expenses, and materials on the totals sheets

TABLE 12-12. Daily Materials Report

Daily Materials Report

Job No. _____   Date _____/_____/_____

P.O. No.	Material	Size	Quan.	Unit cost	Total Freight	Total cost	Vendor
				Total daily materials used			

at the end of the job. This is because it is difficult to apportion those fixed expenses on a daily basis. To do so would involve calculating the percentage of the total job done that day.

The *daily labor report* can also be used as an employee timecard, if desired. If so, it is necessary to print some more information on the card, usually on the back, for payroll deductions, check number for payment, and other deductions. Usually, employees are not paid daily, so another timecard is used that will encompass the entire pay period.

The daily labor report contains all of the information about each individual's work day. Time-in and time-out sections are provided to enable the calculation of the employee's total time on the job that day. This is further broken down into regular time and overtime. There are spaces for the direct payroll expenses (payroll taxes and insurance) and retirement funds. The total cost of the employee's labor, except for fixed expenses, which will be added at the end of the job, is shown in the last space on the form. The form also contains a space for the employee's name, the job number, or name of job, and the date the information is compiled.

The *daily expense report* contains five vertical columns. The left-hand column is for the purchase order number, if used. The name of the expense, as it would appear in the profit and loss statement, is written in column 2, and the name of the vendor from which the expense was incurred is written in column 3. These three columns provide a check during the job's progress on the validity of the vendor's bid for the services offered. Column 4 is for the amount of the expense, and column 5 allows space for an explanation of the expense.

Total daily expenses, minus the fixed expenses that are to be added at the end of the job, are shown at the bottom of the form. This figure is then logged into the journal of all daily expenses. Spaces are provided for the date and the job number or name.

The *daily materials-use report* is discussed here because it is a part of the daily reporting done on a cost-plus pricing job. This report, shown in Table 12–12, contains the purchase order number, if any, in the left-hand column and the name of the material used in column 2. The size of the material, if applicable, is recorded in column 3 and the quantity used in column 4. The cost per unit in column 5 is the wholesale price paid for the material. Freight is a direct cost in column 6, with total cost recorded in column 7, again minus the fixed costs. Column 8 provides space for the name of the vendor of each material, again for later reference regarding the status of a bid given for materials. The date and the job number, or name, are also provided for.

Sometimes, different daily material-use report forms are used for hardgoods and plant materials.

Let us again use the fictitious Brown's Nursery for an example of a year-end analysis by the cost-plus method.

Brown's Nursery completed a job during the past year that had a total value of $34,000. The job had been bid by management, using a target of 12% ($4,080) of the total price as profit. At years-end, it is now necessary to analyze the job to determine whether that goal was reached, so bids for the coming year can be made wisely.

Job-related labor, other expenses, and materials were recorded during the progress of the job on daily labor reports, daily expense reports, and daily materials-use reports, then recorded in journals for job totals. It was found that the total of all amounts gathered from these forms was $22,146, of which $11,713 was the cost of goods sold, or wholesale prices paid for materials, and $10,433 was job-related expenses.

The fixed expenses were determined by consulting the profit and loss statement prepared for the firm's activities for the entire year (see Table 12–4). Those fixed expenses that could not be directly applied to any one job were found to be: salaries of personnel involved in general sales or administration, or overhead labor, other insurance, utilities, telephone, advertising, depreciation, and office supplies. The total amount of these fixed expenses was found to be $68,284 for the year. Since this particular job totaled $34,000 and the total sales for the year were $288,861, the following calculation was made to find out how much of the these total fixed costs should be applied to this one job:

$$\frac{\text{Job total } \$34,000}{\text{Tot. sales } \$288,861} = 11.77\% \qquad \$68,284 \times 11.77\% = \$8,037 \text{ total fixed costs that apply to this job}$$

These fixed costs ($8,037) are then added to the $22,146, which is the cost of goods sold and job-related costs combined, to arrive at a total actual cost of doing the job of $30,183. When this figure is subtracted from the total revenue of the job, the resulting net profit is $3,817 instead of the $4,080 (12%) that was targeted. The actual profit percentage realized is calculated as follows:

$$\frac{\text{Profit from job \$3,817}}{\text{Tot. value job \$34,000}} = 11.22\%$$

This information will be valuable during the coming year as other bids are calculated.

Profit Amount

The profit percentage added to the total costs for an individual job will vary for a number of reasons. Some of the reasons are listed as follows:

1. *The size and scope of the job.* It usually is more efficient for crews to work on one large job than several smaller ones of equal total volume. Profit percentage can be slightly lower on a large job for this reason, and usually must be lower, because of competition for the job.
2. *Job difficulty.* Specifications on jobs vary greatly. The degree of difficulty involved in performing a contract will affect the profit percentage required, because more highly skilled supervision is required, possibly more highly skilled labor, and more management time. If highly skilled employees are tied up at the more difficult jobsite, other jobs may suffer from a lack of efficiency and may result in lesser profits as well.
3. *Job location.* The more remote a job site is, the more likelihood there is for problems to arise. It is necessary to increase the profit percentage on jobs further from the home base to allow for extra cost to solve these problems.
4. *Guarantees and warranties.* The amount and extent of a contractor's liability will affect the amount of risk he is taking when he bids on a job. Consequently, the profit percentage must reflect the amount of that risk.

The ultimate goal of a cost-plus contractor should be to produce enough net profit from a combined total of the jobs done during the year to realize a satisfactory return on his equity investment.

The Foreman's Time and Wages Study

Each type of labor purchased by a landscape nursery must be managed individually, as well as collectively. Management needs a tool at its disposal that will indicate the relative costs and values of each labor class. The labor and machine work table accomplishes much of this because overhead labor is separated out, and the relative cost of the work force is then compared to the revenue it produces. The work force, however, is made up of two classes of labor: the supervisors and the laborers.

Since the supervisors are more permanent and more costly to a business than the laborers, it is necessary to study their time more closely as part of the labor analysis. This can be accomplished by means of a *Foreman's Time and Wages Study*, as shown in Table 12–13.

The foreman's time and wages study is divided into three sections. The uppermost section gives a breakdown of hours worked and wages paid. Payroll taxes and direct insurance costs, along with retirement funds, are added into the total cost to show what each employee actually costs the business. The hours paid for the service of the employee are broken into regular hours, overtime hours, holidays, vacation, and sick pay hours.

The total cost is then divided by the hours the employee actually worked to arrive at the cost per hour. Note, in the examples, the difference between the hourly payrates and their actual cost per hour to the business, for hours actually worked. Nonworking hours for which the employee is paid, such as holidays, vacation, sick time, and overtime, and such benefits as retirement funds and direct payroll expenses all serve to increase the average hourly cost. Management should always be cognizant of these costs and, perhaps, should show them to each employee, so he might be more aware of his total cost to the business.

Not only does the top section of the foreman's time and wages study make everyone aware of the actual costs, but it also serves to forecast the impact of possible wage increases. Management can use this form to project the raises desired for foremen and determine the total increased cost to the business by giving these raises.

The middle section of the foreman's time and wages study consists of the information contained on the time-use records for these individuals. This information allows the management to study the relative effectiveness of each foreman and the effects of additional duties given to specific foremen, as far as the number of hours he charges to customers.

The last section of the foreman's time and wages study is an account-

TABLE 12-13. Green Tree Nursery—Foreman's Time and Wages Study

	Foreman A	Foreman B	Foreman C	Foreman D
Regular hours worked	1,900	1,894	2,040	1,850
Overtime	180	160	50	180
Total hours worked	2,080	2,054	2,090	2,030
Holiday, vacation				
Sick pay	140	140	80	140
Total hours paid	2,220	2,194	2,170	2,170
Payrate	$7.00	$6.50	$5.00	$5.00
Total wage	$16,170	$14,871	$10,975	$11,300
Payroll taxes and				
insurance	$ 1,940	$ 1,664	$ 1,317	$ 1,356
Retirement	$ 808	$ 694	$ 549	$ 565
Total cost	$18,918	$17,139	$12,841	$13,221
Average cost/hr. worked	$9.10/hr.	$8.34/hr.	$6.14/hr.	$6.51/hr.
Total hours charged	1,040	1,150	1,420	1,300
Building and grounds				
maintenance	200	150	50	80
Equipment repair	300	260	60	30
Lost time	680	634	640	760
Tractor time charged				
@ $18.00	$1,800	$5,400	$9,000	$1,800
Supervision @ $13.00	7,800	6,500	3,900	5,200
Pruning @ $13.00	1,300	1,560	1,040	520
Labor @ $12.00	2,880	2,760	6,480	9,120
Total revenue from				
charges	$13,780	$16,220	$20,420	$16,640
Minus machine charge				
@ $6.00/hr. tractor	−600	−1,800	−3,000	−600
Net gain (or loss)	($ 5,738)	($ 919)	$4,579	$2,819

Total hours paid—all foreman: <u>8,754 hours</u> Total net charge—all foreman: <u>$61,060</u>
Total cost—all foremen: <u>$62,119</u> Total net gain—all foremen: <u>$741</u>

ing of the hours charged to customers by each foreman. This information can be obtained from the job sheets. Net gains or losses are calculated at the bottom of the form. A business may not expect to make a profit on its supervisors solely on the strength of charges made for their time. Their real value lies in their ability to supervise others in a lower pay scale, thus enabling them to spread their skills and expertise over several other workers. Nevertheless, the total net gain or net loss on the foremen as a group should not be allowed to fluctuate wildly from year to year, or profits will be affected.

The total hours of the remaining labor force can be deduced by subtracting the total hours of the foremen, as totaled on the foreman's time and wages study, from the total hours purchased during the year for the entire business. Likewise, the total cost of foremen can be calculated, subtracted from the cost of all labor, to leave the cost of the laboring force.

Laborer to Foreman Ratio

The *laborer to foreman ratio* is the number of laborers supervised by each foreman, on average, during the whole year. The higher this ratio is, the lower the average cost per hour will be for the business. The following calculation is for a business that paid for 15,000 hours of laborers' time during a year and 10,000 hours of supervisors' time:

$$\frac{\text{Laborers}}{\text{Foremen}} \quad \frac{15,000 \text{ hours}}{10,000 \text{ hours}} = 1.5{:}\ 1.0 \text{ Laborers to foremen ratio}$$

This ratio, while not intended to be average, might seem quite low. Remember though, that foremen often work on a year-round basis, while labor is hired seasonally. Thus, if the seasonal labor only worked during six months of the year, the ratio during that period would be three laborers to each supervisor. The goal of management should be to maintain as high a laborer-to-foreman ratio as is possible without sacrificing quality or work efficiency.

Specialized time and wages study forms can be devised to study special employees, such as landscape designers. (See Chapter 7.)

Labor Efficiency Percentage

The *labor efficiency percentage* is that percentage of the total hours purchased by a business in a given year, which are sold to customers. The calculation of this percentage completes the labor analysis. Following is a sample calculation of the labor efficiency percentage for a firm exclusively engaged in landscaping operations, which bought a total of 26,000 hours of labor and sold 14,000 of those hours to customers.

$$\frac{\text{Hours sold}}{\text{Hours bought}} \quad \frac{14,000}{26,000} = 53.8\% \text{ Labor efficiency}$$

Outside influences, such as bad weather, throughout a given year can influence this percentage, but management should watch the trend closely. Increasing the percentage would be desirable because that would mean the business was charging more of the hours it buys directly to customers, with less resulting lost time. A trend toward lower percentages might mean that the business has too many supervisors on a year-round employment basis, poor job sheet reporting procedures resulting in the failure to charge enough hours, or otherwise is reducing efficiency and losing profits.

SUMMARY

Since labor sales are a large portion of the revenue of a landscape nursery, it is necessary to price that labor properly in order to realize a desirable net profit.

A *labor analysis* is a process by which management can accumulate labor costs, categorize labor purchased, and allocate amounts and costs of labor to various functions of business operations.

Two different types of labor pricing are done by landscape nurseries.

1. *Retail price* method is done by accumulating all labor information for a period of time, analyzing that information, then forecasting the same type of information for the coming year, in order to set retail labor rates to be charged to customers.
2. The *cost-plus profit percentage* method involves the collection of all costs of doing a job, during the progress of the job, and adding a percentage of the total cost, for profit.

The first step of a labor analysis is information collection. Several business forms are used to collect the information, including the following:

- The year-ending profit and loss statement
- Job sheets
- Timecards
- Time-use records
- Cancelled checks
- Receipts for bills paid

The *labor and machine work table* is used to analyze labor that is to be priced by the retail price method. Completion of this table reveals the total amount of labor purchased, the total cost of producing labor for sale, the average cost of such labor per hour, the specific costs for labor and machines in each category sold and used, and the net gain or loss on labor sales.

The net gain or loss on materials sales can be determined by subtracting the net gain or loss on labor from the total net profit or net loss as found on the year-ending profit and loss statement, after the labor and machine work table has been completed for the previous year's activities.

The labor and machine work table can effectively be used to forecast the labor activities of the coming year, thus enabling management to set new retail labor rates.

There are two distinct types of costs recognized in *cost-plus* labor pricing: fixed costs and job-related costs.

1. *Fixed costs* are those expenses that occur to a business, regardless of the number or size of jobs completed.
2. *Job-related costs* are those expenses that can be directly related to a specific job, because they would not have occurred had the job not been done.

Fixed costs are identified and totaled at the end of each year and are allocated to jobs by the percentage of total sales volume the job occupies.

Job-related costs are allocated to the job on which they occur, by the use of three collection forms: the *daily labor record, daily expense record,* and the *daily material-use record.* The totals of these daily records are then logged in a journal of job expenses, to which the fixed costs are added at the end of the job.

The profit percentage added to costs in cost-plus pricing varies because of the size and scope of the job, the difficulty of the job, the job location, and guarantees and warranties specified. The ultimate goal is to produce the amount of net profit from a combination of differently priced jobs to enable the business to realize a proper return on equity invested in the business.

The *foreman's time and wages study* allows management to study the hours worked and hours paid to foremen, the total cost of their time, the use of their hours, and the revenue produced by each foreman, and by the foremen as a group. This form also enables the management of a business to compare the hours and cost of its supervisors to those of its laboring force.

The *laborer to foreman ratio* is an important calculation of the relative number of laborers supervised by each foreman throughout the year, on average. This ratio serves as a year-to-year gauge of the total labor efficiency of a business.

SUMMARY QUESTIONS

1. Why is it necessary, in a landscape nursery operation, to analyze labor thoroughly each year?
2. What type of jobs are normally done by a firm that uses a retail price method of pricing labor? Cost-plus method?
3. What is the major difference between the retail price method and the cost-plus method?
4. From which business record could you obtain the total hours of labor purchased by a business during a year?

5. Where would the *payroll taxes and insurance,* which directly relate to labor be found?

6. Which business form contains the total hours charged to customers in a retail pricing situation and the categories in which these hours were charged?

7. What is *overhead labor?*

8. What three calculations must be made in order to forecast the total labor cost, for the coming year?

9. When forecasting labor prices for the coming year, what factors must be considered to arrive at the targeted net gain on labor?

10. Why are machine charges subtracted from the total charges on the labor and machine work table to arrive at the net labor charges?

11. What is the difference between a fixed cost in a cost-plus pricing situation and a job-related cost?

12. Name the four reasons for variation of the profit percentage added on to costs for a cost-plus bid preparation.

13. Why do two foremen, who are receiving the same hourly pay and who are paid for the same total number of hours, cost a business a totally different amount?

14. Tom's Landcaping bought a total of 41,560 hours of labor during the year and sold a total of 19,840 hours to their customers. Calculate a labor efficiency percentage for Tom's Landscaping for the year.

15. Bill's Landscaping bought a total of 12,457 hours of supervisors' time during the year and an additional 19,674 hours of labor for their remaining work force. Calculate the laborer to foreman ratio for Bill's Landscaping for the year.

CHAPTER 13

Labor Analysis/Problem Study

Because of the complexity of the labor analysis system for those firms that use the retail price method of pricing labor and because of special applications the system has for problem solving, this chapter is devoted to the study of a special example of the proper use of labor analysis.

The examples used in the previous chapter were of landscape nurseries whose only enterprise was landscaping. Many landscape businesses are concerned with additional responsibilities, however, such as garden store operations and nursery growing fields. A properly executed labor analysis can deal effectively with these extra labor uses. It can also be an important tool in turning a business around, profitwise, and heading it in the right direction. The special problems in this chapter have been designed to demonstrate the value of labor analysis in solving specific business problems.

XYZ Nursery–General Information

XYZ Nursery, a fictitious firm, has a wide range of interests. This nursery operates a garden store, a landscaping business, and a nursery stock-growing operation, primarily for retail sales. XYZ Nursery is a single proprietorship, and the owner serves as general manager of all three phases of the business. Three assistant managers, one for each part of the operation, and a bookkeeper/receptionist assist with management.

As the business grew, it became apparent that little was known about the profitability of each segment of the business. All parts of the business were mixed together, so costs could not be attributed to any one segment accurately. Hourly rates were charged to customers for labor and competition somewhat limited the amount of those rates, but there was very little indication of whether profits occurred from labor, materials, or a proportionate amount from each.

As the garden store and the nursery stock production divisions grew, each consumed more labor. Consequently, the business was spending more for labor than it was receiving from labor charges, and the gap between the two was widening. The owner knew that it was logical to expect this because some of the labor he purchased was used in the production and sale of materials, but he also knew that control was lacking, and the production of profits was more speculative than he would like.

It was decided to separate the three distinct parts of the business into separate income and expense categories in order to determine the profitability of each segment and to aid in the analysis of labor and material sales. Whereas, in the past, only one profit and loss statement had been prepared at the end of each year, now there would be four such statements, one for each of the divisions and one for the entire business, which would be the sum of each of the others. A concentrated labor analysis would be conducted at the end of each business year, resulting in a definition of profits from labor sales, as well as materials sales. The labor analysis would also be used to aid in setting labor prices on a retail basis for each coming year. Studies would be implemented to determine the relative costs and values of supervisors' time, and that of the remaining laboring force.

The first task was to define each division of the total business, so determinations could be made regarding the division of sales, cost of goods, and expenses. The following definitions were made:

1. *Landscaping division.* This division is concerned with all sales that are service or installation oriented. All materials installed by the nursery are sold by this division. All new landscaping installations, lawn installations, sprinkler systems, landscape construction, and all lawn and garden maintenance services fall under this division.
2. *Garden store.* All retail sales from the firm's store, whether cash-and-carry or delivered, are sold through this division. Materials sold in the store and planted by personnel from the landscape division become sales for the landscape division. In return, materials sold by the store for delivery are distributed by personnel of the landscape division, but the sales belong to the garden store.
3. *Production and procurement division.* This division will be responsible for the production of nursery stock for both retail and wholesale purposes. It will also make all other purchases of plant materials to be sold by other divisions and handle all costs of shipping and stocking these materials. It will sell these materials, through a transfer procedure within the bookkeeping system, to each division as they sell materials to clients. Wholesale sales, though few, are made by the nursery and are recorded in the sales of this division.

Because the retail pricing of labor had been done by guesswork in the past and inadequate records had been kept to perform an immediate analysis of labor, a schedule of implementation had to be arranged to enable an accurate analysis to be made as quickly as possible. Following is the schedule decided upon, in chronological order, from the first day of the business year:

1. The new bookkeeping system was set up, and all sales, cost of goods, and expenses would be recorded by divisions throughout the year.
2. Job sheets were printed and were used on all jobs during the year. (See Table 12–20)
3. Time-use records were devised, and employees were instructed to fill them out daily. (See Table 12–1.) A special time-use record was devised for use by the landscape designer.
4. Records were started for each piece of equipment used by the nursery. The job sheet form was used to record all repairs and maintenance for the year.
5. The owner-manager kept informal time-use records to find out which divisions occupied his time, and to what degree. The same procedure was followed by the bookkeeper/receptionist.
6. Each pay period, which was two weeks in duration, the totals from the time-use records were recorded on a graph, so they might be visually compared in subsequent years with corresponding data.
7. Totals of hours charged were recorded as the jobs were billed, so these totals would be readily available at the end of the year.
8. At the end of the year all data was collected, so the labor analysis could be performed.
9. The labor analysis was completed, and a forecast for the coming year was made, along with the retail pricing of labor.

Profit and Loss Statements

The profit and loss statement is divided into three divisions by two means. Sales are recorded as they occur to each division by the use of different sales invoices. Expenses are allocated to various divisions by a check-coding system. Each division is given a code number, and as an expense is paid, the check is coded with the number of each division and the percentage of the expense that has been allocated to that division. Each expense is allocated by either percentage of usage, if that can be determined, or by percentage of total sales that are made by that division. For example, if an employee works specifically in the garden store, each paycheck issued to him will be coded with only the code number of the garden store, so all of his labor expense will be included in the profit and loss statement for the garden store division, in addition to the profit and loss statement for the entire business. An expense like *legal and accounting*, which is difficult to ascribe to a particular division, is allocated by the percentage of total sales. In this case, 63% of the prior year's sales for the entire business were landscape sales (an amount totalled from the previous year's sales tickets). Therefore, 63% of the total legal and accounting expense was allocated to the landscape division during the year. Each check made out for legal or accounting services was designated with the code number for the landscape division and 63% was written beside that code number. Similarly, the code numbers of each of the other divisions and their respective percentages of total sales were recorded on the check. Thus, the total 100% was recorded among the three divisions and on the profit and loss statement for the total business. For other expenses, division of the costs by percentage of sales is not equitable because nearly all of the expense is incurred by one division. For example, gas and oil and depreciation are two expenses that were estimated to be used in the amount of 80% by the landscape division, with the remaining 20% delegated to the production and procurement division. The garden store division, which owns no equipment and uses no gas or oil, will not be charged with any of these expenses. By the same token, the garden store division does the most advertising, so 70% of the total advertising is charged to that division, with the remaining 30% divided into 20% for the landscape division and 10% for the production and procurement division. These allocations are also made via the check-coding method.

The cost of goods sold are allocated to the garden store division and the landscape division by transfers, which are recorded as *cost-of-goods sold* in the division making the retail sale and as a *transfer sale* on the profit and loss statement for the production and procurement division. Since these transfer sales increase the cost of goods sold and the sales by the same amount on the profit and loss statement, they cancel each other out, leaving the true sales and the true cost of goods sold to affect the net profit. This enables each division of the business to have its own sales and its own cost of goods, in addition to its own expenses, so a net profit from each division can be determined.

Sample profit and loss statements are found in Tables 13–1, 13–2, and 13–3 for each division of the business, as they developed into a year-ending status. The corresponding profit and loss statement for the entire business is shown in Table 13–4.

Remember that the total sales and the total cost of goods sold on the profit and loss statement for the entire business are both inflated by the amount of the transfers of materials to divisions, but the net profit is accurate, because they cancel each other out. Those figures would not appear on an audited profit and loss statement for the entire business. Remember also that the transfer sales on the profit and loss statement

Table 13-1. Profit and Loss Statement—Landscape Division

XYZ NURSERY
PROFIT AND LOSS STATEMENT—LANDSCAPE DIVISION
Dec. 31, 1976

Sales

Plant materials	$ 84,083	
Hardgoods	81,030	
Labor	162,167	
Total sales		327,280

Cost of goods sold

Cost of goods—plants	$ 46,245	
Cost of goods—hardgoods	52,670	
Total cost of goods sold		$ 98,915
Gross profit		$228,365

Expenses

Wages	$159,109	
FICA and unemployment taxes	12,729	
Workman's compensation	4,773	
Retirement funds	1,591	
Other insurance	2,646	(63%)
Utilities	1,530	(63%)
Telephone	1,055	(63%)
Advertising	648	(20%)
Repairs and maintenance	6,678	(90%)
Gasoline and oil	5,698	(80%)
Postage	829	(63%)
Legal and accounting	1,386	(63%)
Office supplies	765	(63%)
Taxes	1,399	(63%)
Interest	781	(63%)
Depreciation	7,536	(80%)
Total expenses		$209,153
Net profit		$ 19,212

for the production and procurement division are not really sales at all, but are a means of transferring costs to divisions for establishment of profits for each division.

The percentages used to allocate expenses among divisions should be reviewed yearly and changed if necessary.

TABLE 13-2. Profit and Loss Statement—Garden Store Division

XYZ NURSERY
PROFIT AND LOSS STATEMENT—GARDEN STORE
Dec. 31, 1976

Sales

Plant materials	$68,206	
Hardgoods	71,730	
Total sales		$139,936

Cost of goods sold

Cost of goods—plants	$37,513	
Cost of goods—hardgoods	46,625	
Total cost of goods sold		$ 84,138
Gross profit		$55,798

Expenses

Wages	$32,050		
FICA and unemployment	2,564		
Workman's compensation	962		
Retirement funds	321		
Other insurance	1,134	(27%)	
Utilities	656	(27%)	
Telephone	452	(27%)	
Advertising	2,268	(70%)	
Postage	355	(27%)	
Legal and accounting	594	(27%)	
Office supplies	328	(27%)	
Taxes	599	(27%)	
Interest	335	(27%)	
Total expenses			$42,618
Net profit			$13,180

Allocation of Salaries

In order for the XYZ Nursery to perform a labor analysis, it was necessary for the salaries of management, sales, and clerical personnel to be allocated to divisions at the beginning of the year. These wages were then expensed to the different divisions during the year by the check-coding system. Since the assistant managers were occupied 100% of the time within their own divisions, their salaries needed no allocation. The

TABLE 13-3. Profit and Loss Statement—Production and Procurement Division

XYZ NURSERY
PROFIT AND LOSS STATEMENT—PRODUCTION AND PROCUREMENT
Dec. 31, 1976

Sales

Plant materials	$15,911	
Hardgoods	29,640	
Actual sales	45,551	
Plant transfers—landscape	46,245	
Plant transfers—garden store	37,513	
Total sales		$129,309

Cost of goods sold

Cost of goods sold—plants*	$10,342*	
Cost of goods sold—hardgoods	$17,784	
Total cost of goods sold		$ 28,126
Gross profit		$101,183

Expenses

Wages	$32,841	
FICA and unemployment compensation	2,627	
Workman's compensation	985	
Retirement funds	328	
Seeds and plants purchased*	35,207	(100%)
Freight	3,056	(100%)
Other insurance	420	(10%)
Utilities	243	(10%)
Telephone	168	(10%)
Advertising	324	(10%)
Repairs and maintenance	742	(10%)
Gas and oil	1,425	(20%)
Postage	132	(10%)
Legal and accounting	220	(10%)
Office supplies	121	(10%)
Taxes	222	(10%)
Interest	124	(10%)
Depreciation	1,884	(20%)
Total expenses		$ 81,609
Net profit		$ 20,114

*Since XYZ Nursery grows most of its own plant materials, the actual cost of the goods reflects only those plants purchased for resale. *Seeds and plants purchased* reflects those plants purchased for field replenishment.

TABLE 13-4. Profit and Loss Statement—XYZ Nursery

XYZ NURSERY
PROFIT AND LOSS STATEMENT
Dec. 31, 1976

Sales

Plant materials	$168,200	
Hardgoods	182,400	
Labor	162,167	
Actual sales	$512,767	
Plant transfers—landscape	46,245	
Plant transfers—garden store	37,513	
Total sales		$596,525

Cost of goods sold

Cost of goods sold—plants	$ 94,100	
Cost of goods sold—hardgoods	117,079	
Total cost of goods sold		$211,179
Gross profit		$385,346

Expenses

Wages	$224,000	
FICA and unemployment compensation	17,920	
Workman's compensation	6,720	
Retirement funds	2,240	
Seeds and plants purchased	35,207	
Freight	3,056	
Other insurance	4,200	
Utilities	2,429	
Telephone	1,675	
Advertising	3,240	
Repairs and maintenance	7,420	
Gas and oil	7,123	
Postage	1,316	
Legal and accounting	2,200	
Office supplies	1,214	
Taxes	2,220	
Interest	1,240	
Depreciation	9,420	
Total expenses		$332,840
Net profit		$ 52,506

owner-manager and bookkeeper/receptionist salaries were allocated to divisions as follows:

1. Owner-manager—$24,000 salary. One-half ($12,000) allocated to production-procurement, one-fourth ($6,000) to landscape, and one-fourth ($6,000) to garden store.
2. Bookkeeper/receptionist—$15,000 salary. One-half ($7,500) to landscape, three-tenths ($4,500) to garden store, and two-tenths ($3,500) to production-procurement division.

It should be noted here that ordinarily, in a single proprietorship, the owner's salary would not be listed as part of the wages on the profit and loss statements, but would show up as an increase in profits instead. For our purposes in this chapter, it is less confusing to show them as part of the total wages.

During the year prior to the first labor analysis for XYZ Nursery, the labor prices and categories used were as follows:

Labor	$8.00/hr.
Supervision	9.00/hr.
Push mowing	8.50/hr.
Rider mowing	9.00/hr.
Tractor	13.00/hr.
Pruning	9.00/hr.
Spraying	10.00/hr.
Powerrake	10.00/hr.
Rototiller	10.00/hr.
Loader tractor	14.00/hr.

As the year went by, information was collected on the timecards, time-use records, job sheets, and the divisional bookkeeping system, in preparation for the year-ending labor analysis.

The Labor Analysis for XYZ Nursery–Retail Price Method

The labor analysis for XYZ Nursery was done following the steps set forth in Chapter 12, and the labor and machine work table, as shown in Table 13–5 was made out for the year.

1. The total hours of labor purchased is calculated as being 27,233, which is entered in the totals column.
2. The total hours charged in each category is totaled from the job sheets, and each is entered in the proper category.
3. The time-use records are totaled.

TABLE 13-5. XYZ Nursery—Labor and Machine Work Table

1	2	3	4	5	6	7	8
Labor Category	Total Hours	Retail Rate	Total Charge	Machine Charge	Net Labor Charge	Labor Cost @ $5.75/hr.	Gross Gain or Loss on Labor
Labor	11,134	$8.00	$89,072	$ 0	$89,072	$64,020	$25,052
Supervision	4,579	9.00	41,211	0	41,211	26,329	14,882
Push mow	1,092	8.50	9,282	1,911	7,371	6,279	1,092
Rider mow	207	9.00	1,863	1,035	828	1,190	−362
Tractor	1,086	13.00	14,118	4,724	9,394	6,244	3,150
Pruning	303	9.00	2,727	0	2,727	1,742	985
Spraying	134	10.00	1,340	335	1,005	770	235
Powerrake	96	10.00	960	240	720	552	168
Rototiller	88	10.00	880	220	660	506	154
Loader	51	14.00	714	255	459	293	166
Lost time	5,652	0	0	0	0	32,499	−32,499
Equipment repair	519	0	0	0	0	2,984	−2,984
Building Maintenance	2,292	0	0	0	0	13,179	−13,179
						$156,587*	
Totals	27,233		$162,167	$8,720	$153,447	(156,588)†	−$3,140

Total hours sold:	18,770	Minus other expenses:	$15,336
Overhead labor:	$21,614	Net loss on labor:	($18,476)

*Total sum of categories @ $5.75/hr.
†Difference between two figures caused by rounding-off hourly cost to nearest whole cent.

a. Totals from the time-use records are synchronized with the totals from the job sheets. The following calculations are used:

$$\frac{\text{Total hr. chged. (job sheets)}}{\text{Total hr. chged. (time-use)}} \quad \frac{18,770}{20,183} = 93\%$$

Equip. repair hr. (time-use) $558 \times 93\% = 519$ hr.

Building maintenance hr. (time-use) $2,465 \times 93\% = 2,292$ hr.

b. The second synchronization of hourly totals, between the synchronized totals of the job sheets and time-use records and the total hours on the timecards, is made by subtracting the times listed in each of the labor sold and labor use categories, except lost time, from the total hours bought, as shown on the timecards. Total lost time, 5,652, is the result, instead of the 5,161 hours shown as total lost time by the time-use records. All of the hourly totals for categories of labor bought and sold are entered on the labor and machine work table.

4. The retail labor prices, shown earlier, are entered for each labor category on the labor and machine work table and multiplied by the number of hours in the category. This results in the total charges, which are then entered in column 4. The total charges are $162,167, which corresponds to total labor charges on the profit and loss statement for the landscape division. Note that these two totals do not always match: the completion of jobs with a set price distorts the hourly charges.

5. Machine charges are calculated and entered into column 5. These figures result from records kept during the year on job sheet forms and from depreciation schedules kept by the firm. The calculation for tractors is shown as follows:

Depreciation	$1,285
Gasoline	1,629
Oil and lube	600
Repairs and maintenance	1,210
Total cost	$4,724

6. Machine charges are subtracted from total charges, and the resulting net labor charge is entered in column 6.

7. Net labor cost is calculated.

   a. Wages for the landscape division ($159,109) are found on the profit and loss statement for the landscape division. Direct payroll taxes, insurance, and retirement funds of 12% are added to the wages to arrive at a gross labor cost of $178,202.

   b. Overhead labor is calculated.

      (1) The salaries of those identified in the sale or administration of materials sales are identified.

         A. Owner-manager—$6,000 landscape salary.

         B. Bookkeeper/receptionist—$7,500 landscape salary.

         C. Assistant manager–landscape division—$17,552, entire salary to landscape division.

         D. Landscape designer—$9,000 salary. Since 80% of his time (from his special time-use records) was spent doing landscape designs, 80% of $9,000 is $7,200, which is his landscape salary as it applies to overhead labor, for the sale of labor and materials.

      (2) The total salaries of the above ($38,252) must then be multiplied by the percentage of total sales that are materials sales, so that figure can be removed from the gross labor cost as overhead labor. The following calculations are made:

$$\frac{\text{Total labor sales } \$162,167}{\text{Total landscape sales } \$327,280} = 49.55\% \text{ Labor sales}$$

$$100\% - 49.55\% = 50.45\% \text{ Materials sales}$$

The 12% payroll taxes and insurance are added to the total of $38,252, for a gross of $42,842. This figure is then multiplied by 50.45% to result in $21,614, which is the overhead labor as it applies to materials sales.

c. The overhead labor of $21,614 is then subtracted from the gross labor cost of $178,202, resulting in $156,588, which is the net labor cost. This total is entered as the total, in parenthesis, of column 7 on the labor and machine work table.

d. The net labor cost is then divided by 27,233 hours to yield an hourly cost of $5.75 per hour purchased ($5.7499357).

e. The hourly cost of $5.75 per hour is multiplied by each of the hourly totals of both the labor sold and labor used categories, and those totals are entered in column 7. Because of a fractional remainder when the cost is divided by the hours, the totals of column 7 actually amount to $156,587.

8. The labor cost is subtracted from any net labor charges made for each labor category, and the difference is posted in column 8 as a gross gain or loss on labor.

9. All columns are totaled on the labor and machine work table, indicating a gross loss on labor of $3,140.

10. Other expenses are calculated. The profit and loss statement for the landscape division of XYZ Nursery shows total expenses of $209,153. From this total, the wages are subtracted, plus any expenses that relate directly to either labor or materials sales. These direct expenses, we find, are the FICA and unemployment taxes, workman's compensation insurance, and retirement funds, which total $19,093, plus $159,109 for wages. Subtracting these from the $209,153, we find the total overhead expenses to be $30,951. Labor's share of this amount is found by multiplying the $30,951 by 49.55% (percentage of labor sales), which results in a total of $15,336, the overhead expense as it applies to labor sales only.

11. The $15,336 is then added to the gross loss on labor of $3,140, resulting in a net loss on labor of $18,476.

The labor and machine work table is now complete, as shown in Table 13–5.

Evaluation of Previous Year

XYZ Nursery management can now more readily evaluate their labor pricing for the previous year. They sold a total of $162,167 in labor and paid $159,109, knowing, as they did, that some of that labor was used to sell and administrate the sale of materials. However, upon completion of the labor and machine work table, they find that they actually lost

$18,476 on labor sales. Since the only individual labor sold category showing a loss was the rider mower, they could assume that the overall pricing was too low or that the amount of lost time, building maintenance, and equipment repair was too high. Calculation of the *labor efficiency percentage* shows that 69% (18,770 hrs./27,233 hrs.) of the total hours of labor purchased by the landscape division that year were sold to customers. Since XYZ Nursery has not done a labor analysis in the past, there are no labor efficiency percentages from the past to compare with this year. However, management doubts that their efficiency was abnormally low during the past year. Therefore, they assume that the pricing must have been low.

Although it was apparent that adjustments would be necessary in order to realize the proper profits during the coming year, other labor facts needed to be investigated before decisions could be made by the XYZ management.

The total wages, including $24,000 for the manager's salary, were $224,000 for the year. From the timecards, the total hours of labor purchased for the entire nursery was found to be 46,879 hours, 27,233 of which were used within the landscape division. Adding the 12% payroll taxes and insurance cost to the wages, the total cost of labor for the entire nursery becomes $250,880, which, when divided by 46,879 hours, yields an average cost per hour of $5.35 ($5.3516499). Since the average cost of landscape labor purchased was earlier found to be $5.75/hour, it follows that each of the other divisions must have an average cost per hour less than $5.35 to bring the average down. This presents some questions for management to ponder. Why is there so much difference in the average hourly cost of each division? Is the average cost per hour in the landscape division too high to be made profitable? Why is the average so high in the landscape division? The answers to these questions can be found from the information gathered for the labor analysis and by evaluating more background information.

More Background–XYZ Nursery

The owner of XYZ Nursery has always firmly believed that good landscape work is accomplished by having good supervision over crews at all times. A strong effort has been made over the years to hire, train, and retain good landscape foremen: an effort that has required higher than normal salaries and such fringe benefits as paid vacation, paid holidays, paid sick leave, and a good retirement program. The management knows that these benefits are expensive, but since vacations come during slow periods and holidays are not working days anyway, they are not aware of just how much these benefits do cost. It was necessary, then, to complete the foreman's time and wages study to better analyze the relative costs of foremen versus laboring force.

Foreman's Time and Wages Study. Six landscape foremen were employed by XYZ Nursery during the year. Four of the six were eligible for the company paid retirement program, all were eligible for paid sick leave (which was mandatory) and paid holidays, and all received paid vacations, differing in length.

The time-use records, timecards, and the information on the labor and machine work table allow a good analysis of the foremen's time and cost versus their production. Table 13–6 is the foreman's time and wages study for XYZ Nursery for the year being analyzed.

For simplicity, the foremen of XYZ Nursery are designated by the numbers 1 through 6 on the foreman's time and wages study. The upper section of this study shows the hours worked by each foreman, the hours paid but not worked, and the total wages, payroll taxes, insurance, and retirement funds, for a total cost to the nursery of the individuals. Notice that Foreman 1, who is paid at a rate of $7.00/hour, costs the nursery $9.11/hour for every hour he actually works. This is because he does not work every hour for which he is paid, and the payroll taxes, insurance, retirement funds, and the amount of overtime worked all increase the amount of cost, which must be spread over the hours. Since the overhead expenses are not accounted for on this table, it is obvious that this foreman works at a loss for the nursery in each labor category.

Foremen 4, 5, and 6 are all paid at an hourly rate of $4.50/hour, but because of differing mixes of hours worked and differing amounts of sick pay, vacation, retirement contributions, and so forth, their actual cost to the nursery varies from $5.31/hour to $5.70/hour.

By adding the columns on this table, we find that the foremen for XYZ Nursery accounted for 12,847 hours of the total 27,233 hours of labor purchased by the landscape division. The total amount paid, including the retirement contributions, was $84,512, for an average cost of $6.59/ hour for the six foremen.

In the third section of the foreman's time and wages study, the times charged in each category were estimated, because management was interested in the total effect and not in the accuracy of each figure. The total net charges made for foremen's time were estimated to total $69,089, leaving a net loss on their time of $15,423.

In addition to the facts already mentioned, many other things can be learned about the landscape division labor of XYZ Nursery from the foreman's time and wages study.

TABLE 13-6. Foreman's Time and Wages Study

	1	2	3	4	5	6
Regular hours worked	1,901	1,935½	1,917¼	1,867	1,869¼	1,941
Overtime	181¼	130½	136¼	153¾	65½	52
Total hours worked	2,082¼	2,066	2,053½	2,020¾	1,934¾	1,993
Holiday, vacation sick leave	132	140	148¾	92	104	80
Total hrs. paid	2,214¼	2,206	2,202¼	2,112¾	2,038¾	2,073
Payrate	$7.00	$6.50	$6.00	$4.50	$4.50	$4.50
Total wages	$16,134	$14,763	$13,622	$9,854	$9,322	$9,446
Payroll tax and insurance	$ 1,936	$ 1,772	$ 1,635	$ 1,182	$ 1,119	$ 1,134
Retirement	$ 896	$ 681	$ 624	$ 492	$ 0	$ 0
Total cost	$18,966	$17,216	$15,781	$11,528	$10,441	$10,580
Average cost/hr. worked	$9.11/hr.	$8.33/hr.	$7.68/hr.	$5.70/hr.	$5.40/hr.	$5.31/hr.
Total hours charged	1,025½	1,183	1,319¼	1,442½	1,465	1,502
Building and grounds maintenance	517	313	374	278	176	212
Equipment repair	40	87½	73	26	52	19
Lost time	631¾	622½	436	366¼	345¾	340
Tractor time charged @ $13	$ 650	$2,600	$3,900	$4,550	$1,300	$1,118
Supervision @ $9	8,100	7,200	8,100	6,300	6,300	5,211
Pruning @ $9	270	585	1,008	360	360	144
Labor @ $8	364	944	58	2,820	5,000	6,568
Total revenue from charges	$9,384	$11,329	$13,066	$14,030	$12,960	$13,041
Minus machine charge	−217	−870	−1,305	−1,522	−433	−374
Net gain or (loss)	($9,799)	($6,757)	($4,020)	$980	$2,086	$2,087

Total hours paid—all foremen:	12,847 hours	Total net charge—all foremen:	$69,089
Total cost—all foremen:	$84,512	Total net (loss)—all foremen:	($15,423)

Of the total cost of labor ($178,202) for the landscape division, including payroll taxes, direct insurance, and retirement, $84,512 is attributed to the foremen and $42,842 is the total overhead labor as it applies to both materials and labor sales. This leaves a total of $50,848 as the cost for the laborer's hours. Subtracting the foremen's hours (12,847) from the total hours of the landscape division (27,233), we find a remainder of

14,386 hours. However, this total includes the landscape designer's time, and 80% of it was taken off as overhead labor because it was used for drafting landscape plans. The landscape designer worked a total of 2,010 hours during the year, so 80% of that total is 1,608 hours. This is subtracted from the 14,386 hours, leaving a total of 12,778 hours of laborer's time. Dividing the $50,848 cost of laborers by 12,778 hours, we find that the average cost of laborers was $3.97/hour.

Since XYZ Nursery offers a starting pay of $3.00/hour, it is apparent that many laborers have been given raises to the point that their wages now approach those of the lower paid foremen. Of course, the $3.97/hour average includes payroll taxes, insurance, and retirement, so if we reverse the procedure and remove these extra costs, the average becomes $3.54/hour ($3.97 ÷ 1.12).

The management of XYZ Nursery was able to learn several facts about labor from the completion of the labor and machine work table and the foreman's time and wages study.

1. Landscape division wages of $159,109 and labor sales of $162,167 accounted for a net loss of $18,476 on labor sales alone.
2. Six foremen accounted for nearly half of the total labor cost of the landscape division ($84,512 of the total $178,202). These same foremen accounted for 12,847 of the total 27,233 hours of the landscape division, for an average cost per hour of $6.59 per hour paid and $6.96/hour actually worked.
3. The remaining labor force for the landscape division cost an average of $3.97/hour, with average wages for that group of $3.54/hour.
4. The total cost of the six foremen exceeded the revenue generated by the sale of their time by $15,423.
5. The laborer-to-foreman ratio for the year was just under 1.00 (12,778 laborer hours to 12,847 foremen hours).
6. The labor efficiency ratio was found to be 69% (the percentage of hours purchased by the landscape division which were sold to customers).

Planning the Coming Year

Armed with the information just discussed and other information that is common knowledge to those involved in the management of XYZ Nursery, the following decisions were made in planning the upcoming year.

1. Retail labor rates must be raised, especially in some of the machine rate categories, where the average cost per hour of $5.75 for all land-

scape division labor purchased exceeded the difference between the hourly charge and the hourly machine charge.

2. An attempt must be made to utilize more lower cost labor along with the foremen presently employed, in order to substantially increase the laborer-to-foreman ratio. This would have the effect of lowering the average cost per hour for all labor purchased.

3. An attempt must be made to increase the labor efficiency ratio. It is not known whether this is possible, since this is the first year such a ratio has been calculated. Everything possible will be done to reduce the amounts of time purchased for the labor categories not sold: lost time, building and grounds maintenance, and equipment repair.

There are two choices of action to increase the laborer-to-foreman ratio. The first choice involves eliminating one or two of the foremen's positions, so the ratio can be improved without increasing the number of hours purchased or increasing the number of hours sold. The second choice involves a considerable increase in labor sales, so all foremen can be retained and the laborer-to-foreman ratio can still be increased. The second choice is much more desirable than the first, since it does not put anyone out of a job, while affording a chance at higher profits from increased sales volume. It then becomes a problem of deciding which option will work.

The assistant manager of the landscape division had done all of the sales work to this point and could handle no more. Yet, if another full-time salesman were to be hired, the additional cost would mean that sales would at least have to be doubled. Management doubted that this would be possible because of the market limitations and competition. They did not doubt, however, that sales could be increased substantially. As indicated earlier, their competition, while strong, was not dominant, and more potential sales were available. Collectively, they decided that it might be possible to increase sales by as much as 40% with a strong sales push, using the right personnel.

One of the six foremen had demonstrated the necessary traits and abilities for sales work. His time could be divided between sales and supervision to allow the necessary sales increase without hiring another full-time salesman. But how would they handle an increased sales volume, particularly in labor sales, without increasing their supervisory force?

As mentioned earlier, XYZ Nursery has a strong group of supervisors. The firm has paid good wages and benefits for years in order to keep the best possible foremen. Three of the six foremen are believed to possess the ability to supervise more than one crew at a time. Additionally, some of the laborers, whose payrates are responsible for substantially increasing the laborer's total cost, are deemed to have enough experience to guide a crew in a foreman's absence with very little direction. These employees can serve as crew leaders for those foremen who will supervise more than one crew at a time. The two diagrams in Figure 13–1 show the present situation and the future situation for personnel supervision.

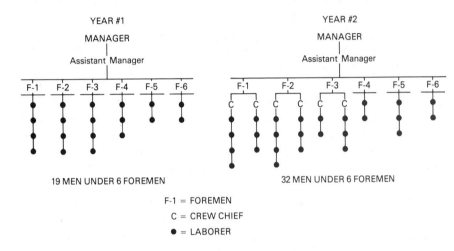

Figure 13-1. XYZ nursery—chain of command.

In these schematics, the numbers represent each of the firm's six foremen. Foreman 4 is the one deemed to have sales abilities. The dotted marks represent laborers, while the letters (C) represent those laborers who are to become crew leaders. By having three foremen supervise two crews most of the time, the business has a capability of nine crews, instead of six, as in the past. If this is accomplished, the laborer-to-foreman ratio will be increased substantially, and the additional labor sales the firm hopes to generate can be accommodated. Of course, these diagrams show the peak-season conditions only, since during the off-seasons there may be few laborers present.

Labor rates had to be set very carefully for the coming year in order to make labor sales profitable, while remaining competitive. The managers know that last year's labor rates were slightly lower than those of their biggest competitors and that rising costs will force their competitors to raise their rates for the coming year also. They also know that it would be foolish to continue selling labor at a loss, since material's profit margins cannot provide a good enough profit for a satisfactory return on the owner's equity investment.

Prior to setting the labor rates for the coming year, the costs for that year had to be anticipated. Cost-of-living raises were given to each of the foremen and each returning laborer in the amount of 5%. It was decided that the starting wages for laborers would remain at \$3.00/hour, because they felt that to reduce the starting wages would result in an inability to hire enough help, while increasing them would compound the problems unnecessarily.

Although they hoped to increase sales volume by 40%, it was felt that a more conservative estimated increase would be prudent for pricing purposes, so a 20% increase was anticipated.

A new, *projected* labor and machine work table was then prepared, and the projected increases in hours were entered for each category. The labor categories not sold were also increased in the same proportion, since the 69% labor efficiency percentage of last year must be assumed average until proven otherwise.

The following procedure was used to estimate labor cost increases for the coming year.

1. Determination of changes in labor cost as a result of pay raises and increased personnel.
   a. Pay increases of 5% given six foremen.

   $$.05 \times \$73,141 \text{ (wages only)} = \$3,657 \text{ increase}$$

   b. Pay increases of 5% given six laborers. These laborers totaled 8,100 hours the previous year, at \$4.10/hour avg.

   $$\$4.10 \times 8,100 \times .05 = \$1,661 \text{ increase}$$

   c. Increase of 20% in labor hours.

   $$27,233 \text{ hr.} \times .20 = 5,447 \text{ hours increase}$$

   $$5,447 \text{ hr.} \times \$3.00 \text{ (starting pay)} = \$16,341 \text{ increase}$$

   d. Pay increase of 5% for landscape designer.

   $$\$9,000 \times .05 = \$450 \text{ increase}$$

   e. Pay increases are totaled and added to last year's wages. Then the payroll taxes, insurance, and retirement costs are added on.

Last year's wages	\$159,109
Foremen's increases	3,657
Laborer's increases	1,661
Increased hours cost	16,341
Landscape designer raise	450

Total projected wages	$181,218
Plus 12% payroll taxes	21,746
Projected gross cost	$202,964

2. Changes in overhead labor are calculated. Since the only projected change in overhead salaries is the landscape designer's increase, that change needs to be reflected. The additional sales time of the foreman who will assume sales duties also must be added to last year's overhead labor. Management decides to anticipate that he will spend 30% of his time making sales and 70% supervising.

Foreman 4, last year's salary	$ 9,854
Plus: 5% increase	493
Total projected wages	$10,347

$10,347 \times .30 = \$3,104$
$\$3,104 \times .5045$ (anticipated materials %) = $1,566

Therefore, $1,566 is the contribution to overhead labor applying to materials sales.

Landscape designer—last year's salary	$9,000
Plus: 5% increase	450
Total projected wages	$9,450

Since 80% of the landscape designer's salary applies to the sale of materials and labor, 50.45% of which is anticipated to be materials, the following calculation results in the increased contribution to overhead labor.

$$\$450 \times .80 \times .5045 = \$182$$

Foreman 4 overhead labor	$1,566
Landscape designer increased overhead labor	182
	$1,748

$\$1,748 \times 1.12 = \$1,958$ overhead labor (including payroll taxes, insurance, and retirement)

Last year's overhead labor	$21,614
Plus: new contributions	1,958
Projected overhead labor	$23,572

Now, since the total gross labor cost has been anticipated for the coming year, the overhead labor has been adjusted, and the hours of labor usage for each category has been estimated, the average cost of labor per hour can be calculated, and the various amounts of labor cost filled in column 7, for labor cost.

Total projected gross labor cost	$202,836
Minus: projected overhead	23,572
Projected net labor cost	$179,264

$179,264 \div 32,679$ (projected hours purchased) $= $5.49/\text{hour}$ cost
(5.4856023)

Forecasting Profits

The next step in forecasting and pricing for the coming year is the determination of the desirable net gain on labor for the coming year for XYZ Nursery, along with the updating of the other expenses anticipated for the coming year.

Other expenses are expected to increase for two reasons during the coming year. First, the additional sales are bound to influence the amounts of all expenses, although many of these expenses are fairly stable, and they do not fluctuate in relation to the sales. Secondly, costs fluctuate with the economy, so this fluctuation must be anticipated. XYZ management decides that they will anticipate a total increase of 20% in the overhead expenses for the coming year, so that portion which applies to labor is expected to be $18,403.

The determination of the desirable net gain on labor begins with an assessment of the total equity invested in the business by the owner. From the balance sheet for XYZ Nursery, prepared on the last day of the previous year, the owner's equity is found to be $500,000. The owner desires an 18% return on his equity, meaning that $90,000 in profit would have to be realized by the entire business during the coming year in order to reach that goal. The landscape division, which accounted for 64% of the total sales made by the business during the past year, would have to account for $57,600 of that amount. Since labor accounted for 49.55% of the landscape sales, it follows that 49.55% of the expected profits, or $28,541, would have to be generated by labor sales. But to go from a net loss on labor of $18,476 in one year to a net gain of $28,541 the next year would be highly improbable. Thus, management decides that they should shoot for a much more realistic goal and hope to improve the situation each year.

The more realistic goal agreed upon is a net gain on labor of $10,000. Prices are then set for the various categories of labor, which would allow the $10,000 net gain to be realized, if the sales increase of 20% is realized and if all projections for costs during the coming year are accurate. The machine charges are set first, since they were established to be in need of the most adjustment. Labor is the last category to be adjusted because it is the largest category, and the one most subject to being affected by competition. After the new rates are set, which will allow a net gain of $10,142 if all projections are accurate, the projected labor and machine work table, as shown in Table 13–7 is completed.

TABLE 13-7. XYZ Nursery Projected Labor and Machine Work Table

Labor Category	Total Hours	Retail Rate	Total Charge	Machine Charge	Net Labor Charge	Labor Cost @ $5.49/hr.	Gross Gain for Loss on Labor
Labor	13,361	$ 9.00	$120,249	$ 0	$120,249	$ 73,352	$ 46,897
Supervision	5,495	10.00	54,950	0	54,950	30,168	24,782
Push mow	1,310	9.00	11,790	2,358	9,432	7,192	2,240
Rider mow	248	12.00	2,976	1,240	1,736	1,362	374
Tractor	1,303	15.00	19,545	5,864	13,681	7,153	6,528
Pruning	364	10.00	3,640	0	3,640	1,998	1,642
Spraying	161	12.00	1,932	402	1,530	884	646
Powerrake	115	12.00	1,380	287	1,093	631	462
Rototiller	106	12.00	1,272	291	981	582	399
Loader	61	16.00	976	315	661	335	326
Lost time	6,782	0	0	0	0	37,233	−37,233
Equipment repair	623	0	0	0	0	3,420	− 3,420
Building maintenance	2,750	0	0	0	0	15,098	−15,098
						$179,408*	
Totals	32,679		$218,710	$10,757	$207,953	($179,264)†	$28,545

Total hours charged:	22,524	Minus other expenses:	−18,403
Overhead labor:	$23,572	Net gain on labor:	$10,142

*Sum total of categories @ $5.49/hr.
†Difference between two figures caused by rounding-off hourly cost to the nearest whole cent.

Monitoring

All of the labor forecasting and pricing have now been completed for XYZ Nursery for the coming year. Now the guidelines are followed as closely as possible during the year. The results are monitored during the year by monthly profit and loss statements, totals taken from time-use records, and totals of hours sold as they are removed from the job sheets. A graph is kept of the totals from the time-use records of each pay period, along with the totals of the same records for corresponding periods of the previous year. The graph indicates some interesting happenings. The hours of labor purchased and labor sold are indeed going up dramatically during the year, particularly during the peak periods of the seasons. The hours of lost time, building and grounds maintenance, and equipment repair, although they are also increasing, do not increase proportionately. Management is heartened by this fact, an indication of increased efficiency.

They are surprised to find that most of the increased labor sold is taking place in three categories, but after further consideration, the reasons become obvious. The additional sales work being done has resulted in additional sales that would affect the sale of labor, supervision, and tractor work. Sales of pruning, mowing, and other categories are made mostly from call-in orders.

Second Year Analysis

At year's-end, another labor analysis was made, resulting in another labor and machine work table, as shown in Table 13–8.

TABLE 13-8. XYZ Nursery Projected Labor and Machine Work Table

Labor Category	Total Hours	Retail Rate	Total Charge	Machine Charge	Net Labor Charge	Labor Cost @ $5.36/hr.	Gross Gain or Loss on Labor
Labor	16,535	$ 9.00	$148,815	$ 0	$148,815	$88,628	$60,187
Supervision	5,975	10.00	59,750	0	59,750	32,026	27,724
Push mow	1,081	9.00	9,729	1,946	7,783	5,794	1,989
Rider mow	173	12.00	2,076	865	1,211	927	284
Tractor	1,275	15.00	19,125	5,733	13,392	6,834	6,558
Pruning	356	10.00	3,560	0	3,560	1,908	1,652
Spraying	156	12.00	1,872	390	1,482	836	646
Powerrake	98	12.00	1,176	245	931	525	406
Rototiller	139	12.00	1,668	382	1,286	745	541
Loader	55	16.00	880	283	597	295	302
Lost time	6,638	0	0	0		35,579	−35,579
Equipment repair	597	0	0	0	0	3,200	− 3,200
Building maintenance	2,597	0	0	0	0	13,920	−13,920
						$191,217*	
Totals	35,675		$248,651	$9,844	$238,807	($191,384)†	$47,590

Total hours sold:	25,843	Minus other expenses:	−19,631
Overhead labor:	$24,430	Net gain on labor:	$27,959

*Sum totals of categories @ $5.36/hr.
†Difference between two figures caused by rounding-off hourly cost to nearest whole cent.

Tremendous changes had occurred during the year. The total hours purchased by the landscape division had increased by 31% over the previous year to a total of 35,675 hours, exceeding the practical goal of 20%, but short of the ultimate goal of 40%. Lost time had increased by only 17%, largely because most of the extra labor was purchased seasonally and laid off during the off-season. Equipment repair hours increased by 15%, and building and grounds maintenance hours increased by 13%, both indications that the increased labor sales do not necessarily increase expenses proportionately.

The most dramatic increases in labor sales were 48.5% in the labor category and 30% in the supervisor's category, where crew leaders were able to charge their time as foremen would. Push mowing and rider mowing both showed slight decreases. The push mowing decrease might have been due to weather-related factors, but it was presumed that the decrease in rider mower time was due to the $3.00/hour increase in hourly charges. Still, it was better to sell less time, at a profit. All other categories showed a gain, although most of them were slight.

The most significant figure on the labor and machine work table was the net gain on labor, which was an incredible $27,959. The extra 11% increase over the 20% increase anticipated in hours purchased (2,996) hours) were all of the lowest priced labor, and some 3,319 more hours were sold than projected. The labor efficiency ratio increased from 69% to 72.4%. The average cost per hour of landscape labor decreased from $5.75/hour to $5.36/hour ($5.3646531), again because most of the increase in hours purchased was lower priced labor.

The total charges made for labor and machines increased by $86,484 from one year to the next, but only $27,372 of that amount was due to increased hourly rates. The remaining $59,112 increase was due to the additional hours sold, an indication of the competitiveness of XYZ Nursery.

Another highly satisfying result of the adjustments made by XYZ Nursery is that none of their employees were lost or took a reduction in salary. In fact, several cost-of-living raises were given, and additional responsibilities given employees increased their capabilities.

It would be wise to remember several factors at this time. XYZ Nursery is a totally fictitious firm, and all figures used in the examples were made up by the author to show specific results. In order for the improvements to have occurred as demonstrated, the nursery had to have the necessary personnel to effect such changes, enough potential for the additional sales to be made, and the weather had to be cooperative. However, such changes, some less dramatic, can be continuously effected by careful record keeping and a sound labor analysis at the end of each year, followed by an equally sound job of forecasting costs, conditions, and prices for the coming year. Each year, there is less risk in forecasting, because there is more sound information from past records on which to base such forecasts.

SUMMARY

With a good, sound labor analysis system, many labor-related management problems can be solved.

XYZ Nursery, a fictitious firm, was devised with several specific problems, including a retail pricing schedule in which the prices were too low, a top-heavy pay range, which included a too low laborer-to-foreman ratio and too many laborers with pay rates approaching those of the foremen. The firm's accounting system gave no indication of the profit-producing capabilities of each of its three divisions, and there was an uncertainty about the efficiency of the business.

The three segments of the business were defined: garden store, landscape, and production and procurement. Each of these divisions was set up with its own profit and loss statement, which was a portion of the profit and loss statement for the entire business. A divisional bookkeeping system was devised in order to judge the contributions of each division of the business to its total profit or loss.

Job sheets, time-use records, and timecards are all instituted to record the necessary information for a year-ending labor analysis.

Upon completion of the labor and machine work table at year's end, XYZ Nursery found that, although they had sold $162,167 in labor, and wages for the landscape division were $159,109, the division actually lost $18,476 on labor for the year, after all adjustments to labor cost had been made.

The completion of the foremen's time and wages study revealed several other facts about labor. The foremen accounted for nearly half of the total labor cost and nearly half of the total labor hours purchased. The laborer-to-foreman ratio was found to be just under 1.00. The foremen cost the business an average of $6.59/hour, while the remaining labor force averaged $3.97/hour.

Management decided that the laborer-to-foreman ratio had to be improved during the coming year and the average cost per hour for labor had to be decreased. If, at the same time, the retail prices for labor were increased, this would produce a double effect on increasing the labor profits.

The decision was made to attempt to increase sales of labor by 20% during the coming year. One of the foremen who possessed the necessary traits to make sales would spend 30% of his time making sales. In order to do more volume with less supervision, three of the foremen were asked to supervise more than one crew at busy times. Crew leaders to serve under these foremen were selected from the most experienced laborers.

Prices were increased in all categories, with the highest increases in the machine categories. A goal was set for a net gain on labor of $10,000 for the year, although the ultimate goal for a proper return on invested equity would have been $28,541. It was felt unrealistic to aim for that much change in one year's time. A projected labor and machine work table was made out, with prices which would allow a $10,142 net gain on labor, if a 20% increase in labor sales was realized.

Startling results occurred during the year. The increase in labor sales actually increased by 31%, and since the increased labor purchased was of the lowest priced variety and those laborers were laid-off during the off-season, the net gain on labor climbed to $27,959. Total labor revenue increased by $86,484, of which only $27,372 was due to price increases, while $59,112 was due to increased hours sold. The labor efficiency percentage climbed from 69% to 72.4%, again because the additional labor was largely seasonal in nature.

All of the accomplishments of the year were made without any employees losing their jobs, suffering a loss of pay, or losing responsibility. In fact, they received cost-of-living increases and gained a higher level of responsibility during the process.

SUMMARY QUESTIONS

1. What advantages does a divisional bookkeeping system offer a multifaceted business?

2. What are transfer sales, and how do they affect net profit or loss?

3. How does the laborer-to-foreman ratio affect the average cost per hour of labor?

4. How does the labor efficiency percentage affect labor profits?

5. What effect does multiple-crew supervision have on the average cost per hour of labor?

6. Why, in the special example in this chapter, did the lost time, building and grounds maintenance, and equipment repair times not increase in proportion to the labor categories for time sold?

7. Why did some of the labor categories sold increase more than others?

CHAPTER 14

Pricing Materials

Most hardgoods come to the retailer with a suggested retail price either written on the package or included in the catalog description of the product. If no such price is given, the retailer uses a markup to calculate the retail selling price. The *markup* is a percentage, developed over the years primarily by manufacturers, which allows enough margin between the wholesale cost of a product and the revenue received by sales of that product to account for all associated business costs and still allow a profit to remain. Markups on most hardgoods vary from 20% to 50%, based on the retail price. While some of the higher priced items, such as lawnmowers and garden tractors, have the lowest percentage markups, most of the hardgood products sold by landscape nurseries average about 40% markup on the retail price.

Manufacturers have done much research over the years to determine their suggested markups. It is in the best interests of these manufacturers to guide their retail sales outlets to sell their products profitably, but competitively. The more successful the retail outlets are, the more of the product the manufacturer will be able to produce and sell at wholesale to the retailer. Markups are based on average business costs; but they will not work for every business. The large discount chains, for example, by selling large volumes of goods, have been able to reduce the cost associated with each sale. As a result, they are able to make a satisfactory profit by using a lower markup.

It is important to realize that the markups are usually based on the retail selling price, rather than the wholesale cost. If an item costs the retailer $1.00, and he sells it for $2.00, he realizes a 50% markup based on the product's retail price. The same markup, based on the wholesale cost, would be 100%.

Calculation of Markups

To calculate markups based on the retail price when only the wholesale cost and the percentage of markup is available, the following formula is used:

Wholesale cost ÷ (100%−markup %) = Retail price

For example, if the wholesale cost of a hardgood is $13.50 and the markup is 40% of retail, the calculation looks like this:

$13.50 (wholesale cost) ÷ .6 (or 100 − .40) = $22.50 (retail price)

The calculation can be easily checked by applying the markup percentage to the retail price to find the margin, then subtracting the margin from the retail price, which will leave the wholesale cost as a remainder.

$22.50 × 40% = $9.00 (margin between retail price and wholesale cost)

$22.50 − $9.00 = $13.50 (wholesale cost)

Markups have not been so clearly identified for plant materials. The wholesale nurseryowners who produce the plants generally do not suggest a retail price for their plants, nor do they suggest a markup. There are good reasons for this, which can best be detailed by a closer study of the criteria for pricing materials.

Costs of Materials Sales

The wholesale price paid for a product to be resold is by no means the entire cost of that product to the retailer. Many other business operational costs are encountered before that product reaches the consumer. These costs vary from product to product; hence the difference in suggested markups. The variation from hardgood products to plant materials is great, as is the variation between plant materials.

Some of the costs encountered are shared by any product to be sold, be it hardgood or plant material. Some of these costs are listed as follows:

- Freight costs from producer to retailer
- Unloading and stocking costs; potting costs for bare-root plants
- Labeling, pricing, and inventorying costs
- Cost of storage facilities
- Cost of land space occupied by storage, shelf space, etc.
- Care of product until it is sold
- Overhead expenses, as they apply to materials sales
- Sales expenses

- Cost of guarantees and shrinkage
- Interest on money invested while the product is owned by the business

Freight costs are encountered in the transfer of any product from the manufacturer, or jobber, to the retailer. Sometimes this freight is paid by the wholesaler, but if it is, that payment must be reflected in the price paid for the product. The payment of freight by the wholesaler might also be reflected in a lower suggested markup for the product, since it reduces the retailer's costs. Freight costs are normally based on the weight of the product.

Although costs are encountered in the unloading and placing in storage of any product, these costs are widely variable. Plants and fertilizers are much more difficult to unload than cases of hardgoods, for example. Perhaps the most variable cost in this area is the placement of the goods in storage. While most hardgoods can simply be placed and forgotten, plant materials may have to be healed-in, or potted, and watered. Sometimes it may be necessary to prune branches damaged in transit or reburlap plants with rot-proof burlap. All of these costs must be calculated using total labor costs, as determined by a recent labor analysis, instead of raw wages.

The retailer receives many hardgoods with retail prices and necessary consumer information marked on the bag. Plants and other hardgoods, however, might have to be labeled with information and prices at some time before they are sold. Usually, an inventory system is maintained for all materials, so time is required to enter newly received materials in such inventories. Again, true labor costs, not wages, should be used to record these costs.

The cost of storage facilities for materials, such as retail stores, warehouses, polyhouses, cold storage facilities, lathhouses, or greenhouses, must be considered a sales cost of the materials because there is no other reason for such structures to exist. Depreciation, repair and maintenance costs, and interest on the investment in these structures must be considered. Taxes and insurance are most likely to be included later in overhead expenses.

Land has a value to the business for other production or as a rental property. This value must be considered as a cost for selling products. The land space occupied by storage and sales areas must be computed, if the land is owned by the business. If the land is rented, the rental amount is the expense.

All of the care given materials from the time of their arrival at a business until they are sold must be considered as a sales cost. Most hardgoods require very little care from the time they are placed in storage. Still, it might be necessary to move some materials from one

Figure 14-1. Hoeing in weed control chemicals in a young planting of nursery stock. Just one of the many costs of growing nursery crops.

location to another, dust off fertilizer bags, or provide some other care during the storage period. On the other hand, plants require very frequent care. Watering during the spring, summer, and fall, protective covering during the winter, and replacement of rotten burlap are just some of the tasks involved in regular care of plant materials.

Overhead expenses are all of the expenses that cannot be practically tied to individual materials, such as advertising, accounting, utilities, postage, and so forth. These expenses must be allocated to either materials or labor sales in an equitable fashion, since they do not apply directly to either.

The cost of selling materials must be considered. Primarily this is a labor expense for sales and administration, since other related costs, such as advertising, are more easily included in the overhead expenses.

Guarantees are offered on most products sold today, including plants. The cost of a guarantee on a hardgood is often absorbed by the manufacturer, although that cost is transferred in the wholesale cost and may be reflected in the suggested markup. The cost of plant guarantees is more variable than the cost of hardgoods guarantees because the weather and customer's care for the plants are highly variable.

Loss of inventory is a reality most businessmen fight with a vengeance, but it persists nevertheless and must be dealt with. Theft by shoplifters and employees, deterioration of packages through aging, and, in the case of plant materials, death, are some of the reasons an inventory of goods shrinks while in storage.

Finally, the business has money invested in its inventory of hardgoods and plant materials until the time these materials are sold and collection is made. Interest must be charged against this investment. If the money is borrowed, the interest rate being paid is the rate used to charge against the materials, and if the money is not borrowed, current interest rates being charged by banks should be used.

When a business prices its goods for sale by using a markup percentage or amount specified by the manufacturer, it is assuming that all of the costs just discussed have been considered and that the average costs plus a profit percentage can be covered by that margin. Perhaps it is not wise to make such an assumption. All businesses are very different, and each encounters different costs. At the very least, each business should monitor its own costs, so the suitability of prescribed markups will be known. Better still, each business should keep its own cost accounting records and identify the most suitable markups for its own products. It might not work to charge higher than specified prices on a bag of fertilizer, which is labeled at the factory, but other prices might be increased, if needed. More importantly, a highly efficient business might be able to take advantage of that efficiency by reducing the markup to gain a competitive advantage.

Collecting and Assembling Costs

Compiling cost records, which allows a firm to price its own goods properly, is largely a matter of recording essential data and then processing it in the correct order. The order is important because some of the costs are taken as a percentage of the sum of the other costs at that time. If not all of those costs have been previously accounted for, these percentages will produce amounts lower than the actual cost. Examples of such percentages are in replacement and shrinkage costs and interest on the money invested in goods. The cost list on page 326 shows the order in which the costs need to be compiled.

By compiling all of these costs for goods in the proper order, then adjusting them so they are proportionate to the dollar values of the wholesale prices, these costs can be added to a profit amount to set retail prices. In doing these calculations, the business will have set a markup of its own, which suits its own profit requirements. The costs can all be assembled for a group (for example, plants) and a markup created for that general group, or markups can be created for the individual units (the individual plants) within the group. Both methods will be demonstrated in this chapter. Plants will be used for the pricing examples because their costs are generally more difficult to assess accurately, but the same methods will work for hardgoods.

Two types of plant materials are sold by nurseries: those which are purchased at wholesale from other nurseries and those which the nursery produces. While many nurseries buy all of their plants from others, some grow at least part of their own stock. Some of the reasons for growing their own include: a belief that higher quality is achieved by growing some varieties, problems encountered with getting delivery promptly, inability to get the varieties needed, or plants arriving in poor condition. A decision by a retailer to grow at least some of his stock must always be based, in part, on a cost comparison. Generally, the wholesaler should be able to produce plants for less cost than the retailer can on a part-time basis. The best way to make a decision about growing plants is for the retailer to calculate costs both ways, then compare.

Pricing Plants For a Standard Plant Markup

Pricing plants by a standard markup offers the same advantages as the retail price method of pricing labor. The markup may be calculated during the off-season, based on the prior year's experience and on any necessary current price adjustments. Then as new plants arrive, the markup is simply applied to the wholesale price, and the retail price is established. Pricing plants individually, as they arrive, could be compared to the cost-plus method of pricing labor, which is more time consuming, but also might be more accurate.

Pricing for a standard markup involves the collection of expense data throughout the year, as it applies to the cost of plant materials, then breaking down these costs into individual applications. With each load of plants delivered, the information necessary for accumulating costs is assembled. Freight costs are entered into a log to be totaled at the end of the year. Unloading, stocking labeling, pricing, inventorying, and potting times are recorded. After several loads have been timed, it might be possible to select an average time to be used thereafter, and the only subsequent timings required would serve as efficiency checks. Times are kept during the growing season to determine the amount of time required to water and otherwise care for the plants. Inventory records are kept during the year, so the guarantee and shrinkage losses can be determined.

At the end of that first year, all of the costs and times are totaled by category. Freight, for example, will be a total dollar volume, while the times required for unloading, stocking, labeling, pricing, inventorying, and potting will be recorded in hours. The costs of potting soil, pots, burlap, and price labels, along with any other materials used, must be collected also. Inventory figures for shrinkage and guarantee will show up as discrepancies in the balance of the inventory when a physical count of plants is made. Replacement plants that fulfill the obligations of a guarantee should be tabulated so these losses can be distinguished from shrinkage. Records are also kept regarding sales time, but if a labor analysis is currently being done, such records will be available already. All other information necessary will be available at year's end from the firm's profit and loss statement.

Sample Calculations

At the end of the year, when all information has been accumulated and the final profit and loss statement has been prepared (or when such figures can be reasonably anticipated), the costs are compiled. As mentioned previously, it is important that costs be compiled in the order listed on page 326. To facilitate a demonstration of such a compilation of costs, we will use the fictitious company, Green Tree Nursery.

1. The wholesale price of plants ordered for the coming year is obtained from the catalogs of wholesalers from whom the business buys. The freight charges for the delivery of these plants is anticipated, based on the charges made for last year's deliveries, the comparative number of plants ordered during the two years, and the comparative freight rates being charged during the two years. Green Tree Nursery, let us assume, orders the same number of plants for the coming year that were purchased during the last year, at approximately the same mix of size and variety. Freight prices are anticipated to increase by 10%, based on information given Green Tree Nursery by the freight companies. As shown in Table 14–1, records kept during the past year by Green Tree Nursery indicate the plant mix that was purchased and the total wholesale and freight costs.

TABLE 14-1.

Quantity	Plant Type	Average Weight	Total Weight	Total Plant Cost*	Total Freight†
800	Large shade trees	200 lb.	160,000 lb.	$20,000	$2,400
1,200	Small shade trees	100 lb.	120,000 lb.	14,400	1,800
1,000	Ornamental trees	75 lb.	75,000 lb.	8,000	1,125
3,500	Evergreen and broadleaf	50 lb.	175,000 lb.	24,500	2,625
1,500	Shrubs	—	—	1,450	112
8,000	Total plants		530,000 lb.	$68,350	$8,062

*These prices and weights are already adjusted for the coming year. The projected 10% freight increase and current catalog prices for plants have been included.

†Weight was not a factor in these freight charges for bare-root plants.

2. Total unloading and stocking time was found to be 387 hours. The current year's labor analysis projects an actual cost per hour of $5.00 for labor, so the total cost for unloading and stocking the plants during the coming year is expected to be $5.00 × 387 hours = $1,935. Potting costs are expected to total $1,500, again based on updated prices from last year's costs for materials and labor, so the total for this cost category is $1,500 plus $1,935, or $3,435.

3. A total of 160 man-hours were used during the past year to price, label, and inventory the plants purchased. By multiplying that figure by the $5.00 per hour average cost of labor, it is found that $800 will be the expected labor cost in this category. Additionally, the labels will cost $.01 each; labels for 8,000 plants will total $80. The total cost expected during the year for pricing, labeling, and inventorying plants purchased will be $880.

4. The cost of storage facilities is calculated next. The only storage structure owned by Green Tree Nursery is a lath shade. The total cost to build this structure was $2,000, and it is expected to last for 10 years and have no salvage value at the end of that time. Records were kept of repairs and maintenance during the past year which indicate that about $300 will be spent on maintenance during the coming year. Current interest rates are 9%. The following calculation is made of the cost of the storage facilitiy.

Depreciation ($2,000 ÷ 10 years)	$200/year
Maintenance	300/year
Interest (9% of $2,000)	180/year
Total cost of lath shade	$680/year

Had the Green Tree Nursery owned cold storage or other plant storage structures, their cost would have been calculated in similar fashion.

5. Plant storage areas at Green Tree Nursery occupy about one-fourth of an acre of ground. Some 2,000 plants are stored here at one time. The lath shade area covers part of this land. The total current value of this land is $2,500, and it is estimated to have a rental value of some $225 per year, which is 9% of its total value. The $225 then serves as the land cost, as it applies to the sale of plant materials.

6. Records kept during the past year indicate that a total of 420 hours were required to water, weed, spray, and otherwise care for plants in storage awaiting sale. Applying the $5.00/hour anticipated labor cost, the total cost for this care is found to be $2,100. Chemicals used to spray the plants and treat the ground under the plants to prevent weed growth are anticipated to be $60. The water used to water plants in storage at Green Tree Nursery is supplied by a well, which originally cost $1,000 and is expected to have a 10-year life. The pump in the well costs $300 and is also expected to last 10 years. Current replacement cost of all pipes, hose, and sprinklers used is estimated to be $1,500, and again these are expected to have a 10-

year life. Yearly maintenance, calculated from records kept, is anticipated to be $140 during the coming year. The cost of the water can then be calculated as follows:

Well ($1,000 ÷ 10 years)	$100/year
Pump ($300 ÷ 10 years)	30/year
Pipe, hose, etc. ($1500 ÷ 10)	150/year
Repairs, maintenance	140/year
Yearly cost of water	$420/year

The anticipated cost of caring for plants in storage for the coming year is $2,100 (labor) plus $420 (water) plus $60 (chemicals), for a total of $2,580.

7. To determine the anticipated overhead expenses, the profit and loss statement for the end of the previous year must be consulted. If the plant pricing must be complete before the last profit and loss statement is issued for the year, it might be necessary to anticipate the expenses of the last month. The calculation of these overhead expenses as they apply to plant sales involves answering three questions:

a. Which expenses are *overhead expenses?*

b. What is the total of these overhead expenses?

c. What percentage of the total sales are plant sales?

The answer to the first question lies in the profit and loss statement listing of expenses. Remember that overhead expenses are those expenses that cannot be directly attributed to either materials or labor sales. Looking at the sample profit and loss statement shown in Table 14–2, each expense can be analyzed to see if it belongs in the overhead expense category.

Wages, as they apply to plant sales, are already being considered regularly in the calculation of other expenses, so they are not part of the overhead expenses. Payroll taxes have been considered along with the wages, since the cost figures used came from the labor analysis.

Seeds and plants purchased is not part of the overhead expenses because this expense, being the invoice price of all plant material purchased, has already been considered.

Gas and oil, telephone, utilities, postage, office supplies, taxes, legal and accounting, and advertising are all expenses that would be part of the overhead expenses, since none of them have been applied as a direct cost of the plants and are not a direct cost of labor either.

Machine hire is an expense that is directly related to labor, and the portions of repairs and maintenance which apply to plant sales have already been included in such things as repairs and maintenance of watering equipment, pumps, and storage facilities. Interest, as it applies to plant sales, will be considered separately later.

The addition of all of these expenses considered to be overhead

TABLE 14-2. Profit and Loss Statement

GREEN TREE NURSERY
PROFIT AND LOSS STATEMENT
(Date)

Sales		
Hardgoods	$100,670	
Labor	82,162	
Plant materials	134,968	
Total sales		$317,800
Cost of goods sold		
Cost of goods sold—hardgoods		78,435
Gross profit		$239,365
Expenses		
Wages	$102,600	
Payroll taxes	9,234	
Seeds and plants purchased	57,605	
Gas and oil	6,200	
Telephone	3,880	
Utilities	2,400	
Postage	1,200	
Office supplies	970	
Machine hire	6,230	
Interest	4,600	
Taxes	1,100	
Repairs and maintenance	3,100	
Legal and accounting	2,200	
Advertising	6,100	
Total expenses		$207,419
Net profit		$ 31,946

reveals a total of $24,050. To allocate the portion of that total to plant sales, the percentage of total sales that are plant sales, is calculated. From the profit and loss statement, we find that of the total sales for the year for Green Tree Nursery of $317,800, $134,968 was plant sales. By dividing the total sales into the plant sales, the sales percentage is found to be 42.5%. The total overhead expenses of $24,050 are then multiplied by .425, resulting in $10,221, which is the overhead expenses as they relate to plant sales alone.

8. Sales and administrative labor can be calculated quite easily if a labor analysis has been done for the year. The overhead labor calculated as part of that labor analysis in a retail pricing scheme is the sales and

administrative labor for the sale of all labor and materials. The only requirement is to apply the plant sales percentage of 42.5% to the total overhead labor, resulting in the sales expenses for plant sales.

Assuming that Green Tree Nursery had done such a labor analysis and that the total overhead labor was calculated to be $50,811, the plant sales expenses would be $21,594 ($50,811 × .425).

9. Before the cost of guarantees and shrinkage can be calculated, the plant costs determined to this point must be totaled. From sales tickets, Green Tree Nursery can find that a total of 320 plants were replaced during the past year out of 8,000 plants sold. Dividing the 320 by 8,000 reveals a replacement percentage of 4%. Remaining unaccounted for on inventory cards are some 160 plants, which represent the plants that disappeared from the inventory by "shrinkage," during the year. The percentage for shrinkage can then be calculated as 2%.

Those plants lost as replacements or through theft, death, or other circumstances cost the business the same as all other plants which are eventually sold. Thus, the total costs accumulated thus far must be added together before these percentages can be applied, resulting in dollar figures for replacement and shrinkage. All of these costs are added together as follows:

Wholesale cost of plants	$68,350
Freight	8,062
Unloading, stocking, potting	3,435
Pricing, labeling, and inventory	880
Storage facilities	680
Cost of land	225
Cost of care during storage	2,580
Overhead expenses	10,221
Sales expenses (labor)	21,594
Total plant cost to this point	$116,027

Now, the replacement cost can be figured by multiplying the 4% replacement percentage by the $116,027, yielding a total of $4,641. Similarly, the cost of shrinkage is found to be $2,320. Had the percentages been multiplied by the wholesale price of the plants alone, the replacement cost would have been thought to be only $2,734 and the shrinkage cost only $1,367.

10. Interest is the last cost to be calculated. Current rates are determined to be 9%. The interest rate cannot be applied to the entire amount just totaled because not all of the plants were owned the entire length of time and not all expenses were encountered at the beginning of the year. There must be some means of determining the length of time that interest should be charged. The best means available is the *rate of turnover* calculation. This calculation reveals the average number of times during a year that the average plant inventory is sold, or turned over.

Earlier, we assumed that the plant storage areas at Green Tree Nursery held 2,000 plants at one time. This number is usually determined by physical count of the plants in an average population, in the storage areas. We also assumed that the business sold a total of 8,000 plants during the entire year. The rate of turnover is calculated by dividing the average population into the total number sold, (8,000 ÷ 2,000 = 4). Since the rate of turnover in this case is four, the interest can be figured on the entire amount for one-fourth of the year, or one-fourth of the total cost for the entire year.

The cost of replacements ($4,641) and shrinkage ($2,320) is added to the other costs ($116,027) for a total of $122,988. Interest on $122,988 at 9% is $11,068 for one year. One-fourth of $11,068 is $2,767, which is the interest to be charged against plant ownership and associated expenses for the year. The total cost of plants purchased to be resold during the year then is $122,988 plus $2,767, or $125,755.

The process of determining the cost of plants is now complete. The next procedure in the determination of appropriate markups is to decide how much profit is necessary from the sale of plants.

Determining Necessary Profit and Setting Markups

The determination of the necessary profits from plant sales begins with a review of the firm's year-ending balance sheet. The amount of profit required for a necessary return on equity (as discussed in Chapter 11) is determined by first finding the equity invested in the business, which is shown in the capital account of the balance sheet, then determining the desired percentage of return. Let us assume that Green Tree Nursery's balance sheet reveals an equity of $245,735 and that the profit goal of the business is a 15% return on that equity, or a total net profit during the coming year of $36,860. Unless there are circumstances that dictate that the profits should not be produced in the same proportion as sales, it could be assumed that, since the plant sales accounted for 42.5% of the total sales, and could be expected to account for a similar percentage during the coming year, those sales should also account for 42.5% of the net profits, which would be $15,665.

Having made the determination that $15,665 in profits should be generated during the coming year by plant sales, that amount can then be added to the total anticipated cost of plants ($125,755). This total ($141,420) must be generated in revenue by plant sales.

Since we now know that it will be necessary to generate $141,420 in revenue from plant materials that cost $68,350 at wholesale, it is now possible to calculate the average markup necessary to realize the $73,070 margin of difference between the two. Dividing the margin of difference by the total revenue desired provides the percentage to be used as a markup on retail.

$$\$73,070 \div \$141,420 = 52\% \text{ Markup on retail}$$

By applying the 52% markup to all new plants arriving during the year, Green Tree Nursery should be able to realize the profit goals set for plant sales, unless those sales drop off considerably from the previous year or expenses increase significantly. Groundcovers were not included in this study, because their cost is so much lower per plant and the numbers sold are normally much higher. To include them might distort the calculations. The same markup can be applied to groundcovers with success, however, unless it is known that they experience much higher replacement percentages or other significantly different cost factors. Potting cost should be added to the wholesale price of a plant before the markup is calculated, because the potting significantly changes the product offered.

Suppose that Green Tree Nursery receives, among other plants, a group of red oaks 1"–1½" caliper, a group of compact pfitzers 18"–24", and a group of forsythia 2'–3', in a load of plants. The oaks and compact pfitzers are balled and burlapped, while the forsythia are bare-root, but the nursery will pot them before they are offered for sale. Potting cost is known to be $1.00 each for plants of that size. The wholesale price paid for the plants are: $32.00 each for the red oaks, $7.00 each for the compact pfitzers, and $1.40 each for the forsythia. Markups are calculated as follows:

Red oak 1"–1½" cal. cost $32.00 ÷ .48 (or 100%−52%) = $66.67 retail

Compact pfitzer 18"–24" cost $7.00 ÷ .48 = $14.58 retail price

Forsythia 2'–3' cost $1.40 + $1.00 potting = $2.40 ÷ .48 = $5.00 retail

Of course, the retail prices established here might be adjusted somewhat for customer appeal. The red oak, for example, might sell for $66.95 or $66.50, and the forsythia might be priced at $4.95. Prices also might need to be adjusted slightly in order to appear more competitive when compared to other's prices. If plant pricing is done this carefully over a period of years, however, the competition is likely to be following, instead of leading.

Limitations of Standard Markups

Pricing for a standard markup does have its limitations. All costs are spread over the entire plant population sold, leaving no adjustment for individual costs for certain varieties, which might vary considerably. Replacements, for example, were 4% for the entire volume of plants sold by Green Tree Nursery, in the example used, so the costs of replacements were allocated to red oaks at a 4% cost figure. It might be, though, that in certain parts of the country, a nursery might experience 6% or 8% replacements on red oaks. It also costs no more to price, label, and inventory a group of red oaks that cost $32.00 than it does to price, label, and inventory a group of forsythia that cost $2.40, after potting costs have been included. Using the standard markup though, the red oaks are charged more than the forsythia for these tasks, because those costs are part of the 52% markup required to cover all costs, and when the wholesale cost is higher, all costs recovered by the markup will be proportionately higher. It can be argued that other costs balance out. For example, it might require considerably more sales expense to sell the red oak for $66.67 than to sell the forsythia for $5.00; even more than the percentage system allows. Still, in some cases, it is more desirable to price each plant individually by a cost-plus percentage system, much the same as the cost-plus system used in labor pricing (see Chapter 12).

Cost-Plus Percentage Plant Pricing

Cost-plus pricing of plants, much like cost-plus pricing of labor, might be most valuable to the landscape contractor who obtains most of his work by submitting bids. The jobs he does are likely to be larger and fewer, and are more likely to vary because of different specifications and locations. Bidding for these jobs might be highly competitive, and cost-plus pricing allows the contractor to be sure he is presenting the most competitive prices possible.

The same costs occur to a business selling plants by the cost-plus method, but they are considered on more of an individual basis. Costs that apply specifically to the job a contractor is working on are assimilated and added to the original wholesale price of the plant. Some of the costs do vary a bit. For example, it might not be necessary to tag and price a plant the way a retailer would for the public's information. It might be necessary to tag the plant with information for inspectors, however. Plants might be stored on the jobsite, eliminating any cost for permanent storage facilities at the contractor's home base. Instead, he might encounter special costs to protect and care for the plants at the jobsite. Replacements and shrinkage might be more variable from one jobsite to another.

Data Collection Forms

Three forms are useful in the collection and assimilation of costs in a cost-plus plant pricing scheme. The *Daily Materials Report* and the *Daily Expense Report*, shown in Tables 14–3 and 14–4 are used to capture all materials costs each day, as materials arrive at a jobsite, and all expenses as they are encountered. The *Materials Cost Assimilation Form*, shown in Table 14–5 is used to combine the wholesale cost of the materials purchased with all of the other costs associated with that material.

TABLE 14-3. Daily Materials Report

Job No. _____	DAILY MATERIALS REPORT						Date __/__/__	
P.O. No	Material	Size	Quantity	Unit Cost	Freight	Total Cost	Vendor
Total daily materials used							

TABLE 14-4. Daily Expense Report

Job No. _____	DAILY EXPENSE REPORT		Date __/__/__	
P.O. No.	Expense	Vendor	Amount of Invoice	Explanation
Total daily expenses				

TABLE 14-5. Materials Cost Assimilation Form

Material Name _____			
Job No. _____ MATERIALS COST ASSIMILATION FORM Date __/__/__			

Key	Cost Category	Quantity	Total
	Purchase price		
	Freight		
	Unloading, stocking, potting		
	Label, price, inventory		
	Storage		
	Land		
	Product care		
	Overhead expenses		
	Sales and administrative expenses		
	Guarantees and shrinkage		
	Interest		
	Miscellaneous		
	Total cost		
	Profit factor		
	Selling price		

On the daily materials report, each material received on a jobsite is recorded as it arrives, along with the size, quantity received, unit cost, or wholesale price, freight, and the name of the vendor. These are filled out each day, and later this is transferred to the materials cost assimilation form, along with the corresponding expense information from the daily expense reports, so the costs can be completely calculated.

The materials cost assimilation form contains a column on the left-hand side labeled *Key*. Any key that is used in the calculation of costs for the entire plant group as a whole, such as replacement or shrinkage percentages, pricing and labeling costs, or constant costs, like administrative labor and sales labor, can be entered in this column on each of these materials cost assimilation forms. This prevents recalculating these keys, or looking them up each time they are needed. Note that each form is used for one specific material.

The second column contains a listing of all of the various cost categories. The third column contains the quantity used of that particular material, which is multiplied by the key, if there is one, to result in the total of the cost in that category. If there is no key, the cost is simply totaled as a lump sum from the daily expense report forms, or is entered as a lump sum from estimated or known costs.

At the bottom of the materials cost assimilation form, spaces are provided for the total of all of the costs, the profit percentage, and the selling price. The profit amount is the amount actually realized. This same form is used in the preparation of a bid, at which time the profit factor desired is entered to arrive at a selling price on which to base the bid. The form used after completion of the job then indicates how successful the company was at anticipating costs and pricing the materials. Comparison of the materials cost assimilation forms prepared during the bidding process with those completed after the job is finished serves as the basis for future bids (see Chapter 15).

The materials cost assimilation form cannot be completed until the job is finished because various expenses encountered must be apportioned to materials, and that cannot be accomplished until all expenses are totaled. The assignment of various amounts of these expenses to materials is accomplished in similar fashion to the standard markup method earlier discussed. However, the cost-plus method does allow more freedom. Guarantee and shrinkage percentages can be applied for different materials, which reflect true experience percentages for a particular variety of plants, for example. Overhead expenses must be applied on some basis that reflects the total year's activity. A calculation of the percentage of the total working time a particular job occupies of the total working time of the business for the year, or a percentage of the total sales volume produced by a job, of the total sales volume expected during the year, can be used to apportion the overhead expenses to a particular job. In other words, if the volume of one job is $40,000, and the total sales volume of the business for the year is expected to be about $400,000, then 10% of the overhead expenses expected to be encountered during the year might be assigned to that job. Similar apportionments can be accomplished for such expenses as sales and administrative labor, unless such labor can be directly tied to the job. If an expense can be tied directly to a particular job, it is called *job-related cost*, while general expenses, not related specifically to one job, are called *fixed costs*.

Expense Apportionment

There are two ways to apportion expenses to materials, other than dividing the total number of materials into the cost and giving each material an equal share. Those expenses that relate to the size of materials might be apportioned according to their proportionate weight. The unloading and storing of plants might be directly related to their weight, for example. Therefore, the total weight of all plants can be calculated and then a key factor can be determined, which in this case would be a cost per pound. Consider a load list of plants that might be received on a job. The 575 plants on the load weigh a total of 50,000 lb., and individual weights are listed for each type of plant. Assume now that a total of 36 man-hours are spent in unloading and storing the plants, at $5.00/hour cost, for a total cost of $180. The $180 cost can be then by divided by the 50,000 lb. total weight, to determine a charge of $.0036/lb., which would then be entered in the materials cost assimilation forms for all plants as the *key* for that cost category. Then, each tree weighing 200 lb., or thereabouts, would be apportioned a total cost of $.72 (200 lb. × .0036) for unloading and storing costs, while a 50 lb. evergreen would only be charged $.18 (50 lb. × $.0036).

The second method of apportioning cost, other than equal distribution, is by adding the total wholesale value of plants purchased for each job and dividing that total into one dollar, resulting in a percentage factor. That percentage is then multiplied by the number of dollars paid for each plant at wholesale to arrive at the "key" number, which is placed on the materials cost assimilation form. If the total wholesale cost of the plants for a job is $4,000, the percentage number would be .00025 (or $1 ÷ $4,000). A red oak costing $32 would then be valued at .008 (or 32 × .00025), while a compact pfitzer costing $7 would be valued at .00175 (or 7 × .00025). If there are 30 red oaks of that size on that job and 80 compact pfitzers, then the red oaks would share a total of .24, or 24%, of the apportionment for an expense, while the compact pfitzer would share .14, or 14%, of that total expense (.008 × 30 = .24; and 80 × .000175 = .14). This method of apportionment might be used for such expenses as overhead, interest, care of products, and sales and administration, which are usually more related to the cost of a material than to its size. The expenses, such as freight, unloading and storing, storage facilities, and land space might be more related to the size of a plant, so the cost per pound factor might be used for these.

It is important to remember that, while the method chosen to apportion expenses to individual materials might change the costs of that particular material somewhat, it will not change the total cost. Total costs are total costs; it is just a matter of to which material those costs are assigned.

Allocation of Profit to Individual Materials

The amount of profit required from each materials group is also determined by the percentage factor based on the wholesale price. After the necessary profit has been determined for the entire job, by the same means as earlier discussed for the standard markup method of pricing materials, this percentage factor is multiplied by the entire profit requirement to determine the amount of dollars of margin required of that group of materials. That dollar amount is then added to the total cost of those materials to arrive at the selling price. Dividing the total selling price by the quantity of the material reveals the individual selling price for one unit of the material.

Pricing Home-Grown Plants

The pricing of plants grown in a firm's own nursery is much more involved than pricing those bought at wholesale from another nursery. The price paid for the plants, instead of just being an item on an invoice, becomes expenses incurred over a period of years while the plant has been growing. After the plant has been harvested, the expenses thereafter are much the same as for those purchased at wholesale, except that freight is usually not a factor. Often, the other expenses are reduced as well, since the plant might not be harvested far in advance of its sale and subsequent removal from the business's property.

The additional costs for plants grown by a nursery, which replace the purchase price, are listed as follows:

- Cost of liner originally planted out in nursery
- Cost of planting liner
- Costs of watering, pruning, spraying, cultivating, and otherwise caring for the plant until it can be harvested
- Harvesting cost
- Interest on the land investment
- Cost of wasted plants not harvested

The small plants first planted in a nursery, often called *liners*, are usually not a large part of the total price of the eventual plant that is sold. Still, that cost must be considered as part of the whole, and it becomes more significant if a large number of liners die. The amount paid for these liners also becomes more significant because the liner usually is owned by the nursery for several years before the plant is sold and harvested.

The cost of planting liners can be found by timing the hours required for such planting and multiplying that cost by the average cost per hour of labor as found by labor analysis. The cost can then be divided by the number of liners planted to arrive at the cost per plant. This assumes that it takes an equal amount of time to plant all types of liners. After timing one or two planting operations, an average planting time per plant can probably be deduced, so thereafter only the current labor cost must be applied, as long as the planting methods remain the same.

The cost of caring for plants until they are harvested can be a very involved procedure, if separate figures are kept for each variety. Most of the maintenance operations are fairly standard for all varieties. Variation does occur in the cost of pruning or spraying. Some plants require very little of either, while some require a great deal of each. The required spacing between plants will affect the per plant price of cultivation. Other costs, like staking, are encountered only for trees; shrubs do not require staking. Considering everything, it is probably in the best interests of those nurseries whose primary interests are not growing plants to keep records of all maintenance activities in the nursery and divide them by the average population of plants. The number of years a plant is grown needs to be considered also.

Harvesting costs include the tying up of the top of the plant, the digging, whether bare-root, balling and burlapping, or field-potting, loading and transporting, backfilling the hole, and materials used. Often, as in the case of the larger shade trees, this harvesting cost is a very significant part of the total cost of the plant.

Land is valuable, because if it is not being used for a nursery, there are other commercial benefits of owning it. The cost of owning the land must be spread over the plants grown on that land.

The most astute forecaster could not possibly know four or five years ahead of time how many trees of a particular variety will be required. At planting time, only an educated guess can be made about the numbers. Ultimately, either shortages of those varieties or excesses will result. The excess plants normally have to be removed, which involves a cost, as well as the cost of planting and maintaining those plants for years with no return. These costs must be spread over those plants which are harvested and sold.

Sometimes, a retail nursery, which grows a few plants for various reasons but is not primarily involved in growing, will keep only sketchy records of the costs for growing these plants, for comparison with wholesale prices. Wholesale prices, from other sources of the same material, are used in setting the retail prices for the plants, however, because the retailer feels that the prices set by that wholesale source are probably more reliable. The time spent in costing the growing operation is reduced to almost nothing when this method is used, but of course, the results are minimal also.

All of the examples used in this chapter, as in others in this text, are completely fictitious and are not intended to be considered average. The pricing processes, however, will work for any nursery, and each is likely to have a set of figures completely different from those discussed here.

It also should be remembered that, although the examples in this chapter were for pricing plants, the same methods will work for pricing other materials as well. Plants were used because they are more difficult to price.

SUMMARY

When a business uses a markup established by a manufacturer for a product, it is assuming that the manufacturer has allowed enough margin between the wholesale price and the retail price to allow for all expenses incurred, plus a profit percentage. Markups vary considerably, but, while most manufacturers of hardgoods supply them, plant wholesalers seldom do.

Most markups are based on the retail selling price, instead of the wholesale cost. The formula for the calculation of markups is as follows:

Wholesale cost ÷ (100% − markup %) = Retail price

There are 10 cost groups associated with any material purchased for resale in addition to the wholesale price paid; for example, freight costs from producer to retailer, unloading and storing costs, labeling, pricing, and inventorying costs.

It is important to calculate the costs in the order discussed earlier in the chapter; some costs must be based on the total amount of all of those which precede them.

There are two methods for pricing materials: the standard markup method and the cost-plus profit percentage method.

The *standard mark up method* of pricing materials involves totaling all expenses associated with a group of materials, along with the purchase price; then adding the necessary profit margin and subtracting the wholesale price of the materials from that total to find the margin necessary between the wholesale cost and the retail price. The margin is then divided by the total cost figure, resulting in a percentage of markup, which can be used to price all materials received within that material's group. The advantage of this pricing method is that markups can be determined at one time of the year, to be used in pricing during the remainder of the year.

In the *cost-plus profit percentage* method of pricing materials, the costs are assimilated as they occur, and plants are priced individually, instead of as a group. This method is used primarily by landscape contractors.

Three forms are used in the cost-plus method of pricing materials. The *daily materials report* is used to capture the materials used on a daily basis, along with the associated freight cost. The *daily expense report* captures all expenses as they occur on a job. These expenses and materials are transferred to a *materials cost assimilation form* at the end of a job, so all costs of the materials can be calculated. This form is used once by the contractor in the preparation of a bid, then it is used again at the end of the job to calculate the actual cost of the materials. The comparative results can then be used in the preparation of future bids.

Two types of costs are encountered in materials pricing. Job-related costs are those which specifically relate to one job. Fixed costs relate to the business in general. They must be apportioned to various materials either by percentage of their value as compared to the total value of similar materials purchased during the year, or by percentage of weight, as compared to the total weight of materials purchased during the year. The apportionment method chosen will have no effect on the total costs of materials, but only on the costs assessed to individual materials.

Home-grown plants encounter most of the same costs as those purchased at wholesale prices. Instead of paying wholesale prices, however, the nursery encounters another group of costs over the period of years the plant is being grown; for example, the harvesting cost, maintenance costs, and so forth.

SUMMARY QUESTIONS

1. What is the distinction between a *markup* and a *margin?*
2. Are markups normally based on the wholesale cost or retail price?
3. A material is purchased for $6.70. Calculate the retail price, using a 40% markup on the retail price.
4. Why are land and storage facilities considered costs of selling materials?
5. Why must materials costs be calculated in a specified order?
6. What are *overhead expenses?*
7. Why is it important for each firm to calculate its own materials costs, instead of automatically assuming manufacturer's markups to be correct?
8. What does pricing for a standard markup mean?
9. Why might the unloading and placing in storage of plants be best apportioned by comparative weights of plants?
10. Why must true labor costs from a labor analysis be used in pricing materials instead of wages?
11. What information is required from the firm's profit and loss statement for establishing a standard markup?
12. What is *shrinkage?*
13. What is the *rate of turnover?*
14. How does cost-plus pricing differ from the standard markup pricing?
15. Why can the materials cost assimilation form not be filled out until the job is completed?
16. How do job-related costs differ from fixed costs?

CHAPTER 15

Bidding and Estimating

When a customer walks into a retail store, the products offered for sale usually have prices written on them. Most consumers want to know how much something will cost before they buy it. Landscape nurseries must also price their products and services to their customers, but it is not easy to hang tags on everything they have for sale. There are really only three possible ways to present a price to a customer, although variations of each exist.

- The *time plus materials* method
- The *cost estimate*
- The *bid*

Time Plus Materials Method

The time plus materials method can be used by a business that prices its materials and labor by retail price or by cost-plus profit percentage methods. In the former case, the business has established set prices for all materials and hourly or daily retail rates for labor and machine work. To arrive at these set prices and rates the business has used either the labor analysis and materials pricing methods discussed earlier or some other means. The customer is simply told that accurate records will be maintained of all materials and labor used in the completion of a job and that he or she will be charged the normal retail rates for these products and services. The customer might be told the hourly rates for labor and machine work and the individual prices for materials, but no figure is given for the cost of the total job.

If a cost-plus method of pricing labor and materials is used, the customer is told that, again, adequate records of the time and materials consumed during the job will be kept and the associated costs will be captured. On completion of the job, a profit percentage will be added, and the total amount will be charged to the customer. Sometimes, the customer is told the amount of profit percentage to be added and nothing more. The customer has no real idea of the total cost of the job.

Regardless of the pricing method used by a business, the time plus materials basis is probably the safest way to present prices to a customer. It offers business the most protection against poorly made estimates. Since no estimation of total cost is made, the business can feel perfectly justified in charging whatever the records show as totals for labor and materials at the end of the job. Any difficulties encountered in the completion of the job will pose no problem as far as the pricing of the job. The time and materials used to handle these difficulties will automatically be recorded and subsequently charged. This constitutes the primary advantage of the time and materials method of pricing for customers.

The method does have drawbacks, however. Even though a customer has been told the individual prices for materials and hourly or daily prices for labor, he might have formed his own idea of the length of time required to complete the job. If a cost-plus method is used, the customer might question the costs at billing time. Customers often equate wages paid with total labor costs, for example. In other words, while a business that bases its customer charges on time and materials rates has every right to charge its normal retail rates for all time and materials used, misunderstandings can occur because of prejudgments made by the customer. Such misunderstandings can lead to poor customer references, which are detrimental to future business.

Cost Estimates

The cost estimate is an attempt to prepare the customer for the final bill without restricting the business to accepting all contingencies. The price may be quoted as a total or as a price range. Usually, if a price range is given, the lower price quoted is contingent on the smooth progress of the job. The higher price will allow for poor working conditions or any unforeseen problems that may be encountered.

The cost estimate involves combining all materials expected to be used on a job with all labor and machine work necessary to arrive at a total price to be charged to the customer. Sometimes, the business might add a percentage for unexpected problems before giving the price to the customer; hence the price range. In any case, the fact that it is just an estimate should be clearly stated. The customer will interpret any total price as a firm bid, unless the business makes it clear that variable factors can change that total price. Even then, the business should make every attempt to charge within the price range, if at all possible.

Bids

A bid is a firm price. When a business presents a bid for a job, it agrees to provide the materials and complete the work required for the price specified, regardless of conditions. Normally, if any work or materials are later added to the job, these will be provided at extra cost. But anything that falls under the original conditions of the agreement is part of the bid price, and the business is obliged to provide it.

Bids are usually associated with large contracts, for which plans and specifications are prepared. But many companies submit bids to customers as a matter of course. These firms feel that their customers are more comfortable with a bid, and there is less chance for misunderstanding. Such businesses also have a high degree of confidence in their ability to price work accurately, and they believe their customers will recognize and appreciate that confidence. This is not to say, of course, that businesses which do not price all of their work with bids are not confident of their work or deserving of their customer's confidence.

Estimating

The cost estimating procedure must be very precise because the development of either a profit or a loss is possible on every job. Although weather, organization, delivery of materials, performance of workers, and acceptance by the customer are all factors influencing the profitability of a job, the cost estimate is the *first* opportunity to make a job profitable. If a job is sold based on a poorly conceived estimation of costs, no amount of efficiency can restore the potential for profit.

Cost estimates require a rigid adherence to details, in a specified order. To neglect one detail on a cost estimate for a large landscaping job can cause the loss of all profit, or worse.

There are different types of cost estimations. The ones based on a firm's own plans and specifications are the most easily made, since the estimator is already familiar with the required procedures of the work. Estimations of cost, based on the plans and specifications of others, are more difficult and more risky. The estimator must first learn how the authors of such plans and specifications wish the work to be done and what results are expected. A third degree of difficulty is encountered when the estimator must take the separate plans and specifications of several others and calculate the work to satisfy all parties.

Reading Plans and Specifications

Looking at landscape plans can be exciting and enlightening, but to undertake a meticulous study of these plans might seem dull and uninteresting. Nevertheless, any set of plans upon which a bid or estimate will be based must be thoroughly scrutinized in a systematic fashion. Presumably the designer has already checked his plans for mistakes, but the only way the estimator will know if they are correct is to check them himself. This checking should be done in an organized manner, so nothing will be neglected. Following is a suggested list for checking plans.

1. Check the scale used in the drawings. Does the scale vary on different sheets? Do the spacings vary among plants of the same variety? Do the spacings between plants correspond with normally expected spacings for that variety? If it is possible, the estimator should visit the property and take sample measurements of the building, lot, sidewalks, or other physical features. These measurements can then be checked against the plan. Any discrepancies should be clarified at once with the designer, and any necessary revisions made.

2. Check the materials lists on the plans. Is it clear which materials are wanted by the designer? Do the botanical names correspond with the common names he has used? Do the numbers of materials listed correspond with the actual count of these materials on the plan? This is most important; especially since most specifications state that when a discrepancy exists between the numbers represented on the plans and those represented on plant lists, the actual count will rule. Are all materials represented on the plans also represented on materials lists? Check carefully to see if gravels, groundcovers, edgings, and so forth, which are drawn on the plans, are represented on materials lists. If they are not, the estimator must make sure they are included in his final list of materials to be priced. Also, the estimator must make sure that the edgings, etc., are designated in the same way throughout the plans and specifications. If the estimator notices inconsistencies, he must seek clarification from the designer.

3. If detailed drawings are included in the plans at a larger scale than the general plans, these should be scrutinized carefully. Are there details on these which are not included on the general plans? Do the detailed drawings provide enough information for the estimator to understand exactly how the work is to be completed? When the two scales are compared, do the measurements in the detail correspond with those on the general plan?

4. All written notes, instructions, and references on the plans should be carefully read and understood. These should later be compared with corresponding writings in the specifications to make sure there are no inconsistencies.

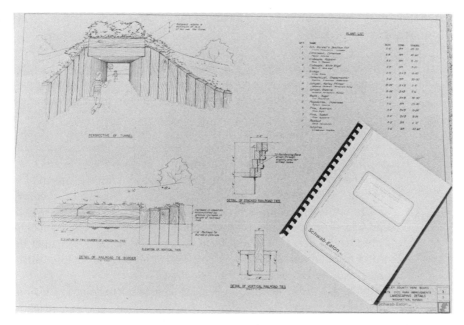

Figure 15-1. A set of landscape plans and the accompanying specifications.

5. The date on the plans should be checked to ensure that no further revisions have been made and the plans in possession are those to be used. The date of the most current revision is usually noted in either the specifications or the bidding instructions.

The order in which the plans are checked is of no importance. But if the estimator habitually follows the same order each time he makes an estimate, he will reduce the likelihood of anything being forgotten. The estimator should never hesitate to call the designer for clarification of any ambiguity in the plans. The designer is responsible for making his plans understandable. Once the estimator has presented his estimate or bid, however, it is assumed that the plans are understood completely. It is also understood that the estimator has verified the plans and specifications and is responsible for completing the work satisfactorily. By the time the estimator completes an estimate, he should be as familiar with the plans as is the designer.

Specifications can be even more difficult to read and understand than plans. They are written to protect the client and to assure quality levels, regardless of the source of materials or services. Unfortunately, the language in which they are written often simulates the legalese used by lawyers and is difficult for laymen to understand. Still, it behooves the estimator to thoroughly understand these specifications before pricing a job. Following is a list of considerations that should be given to the specifications accompanying landscape plans. Again, the order is not important, except that the same order should be used each time.

1. Check the date to be sure the specifications correspond to the plans being studied. As with plans, revisions are sometimes made in specifications, and the estimator is responsible for having the current information.

2. Bidding qualifications and instructions should be studied. Sometimes, an estimator might find something in these areas which would preclude any participation by his firm. For example, there may be some restrictions concerning the size of the business, the extent of its previous experience, bid bonds or performance bond requirements, and amount of insurance coverage. When this is the case, there is no need to study the specifications any further. This section will also state the bid date, time, and location, and the manner in which the bid is to be given. If no bid is required, the method for presenting prices will be discussed.

3. All materials lists should be checked against corresponding lists on the plans. A determination should be made as to which list rules—the plans or the specifications. Any discrepancies should be checked with the designer for verification.

4. Materials availability should be checked. The specifications will give sizes, conditions, quality standards, and quantities for all materials. The estimator should make sure his company can supply materials that will meet all of those standards. Sometimes, specified materials are unavailable. In such a case, the designer should be consulted to determine whether he will make a substitution or whether the bidders are to suggest substitutions. The specifications usually spell out the procedures to be followed when substitutes are necessary. It is not a bad idea to have the designer, or his representative, who will do the inspecting of materials on the job, look at sample materials before the bid is entered. The bid can then be presented with secure knowledge that materials will not be rejected later when the job is in progress.

5. The installation specifications should be scrutinized thoroughly. Variations in hole size, topsoil requirements, staking procedures, maintenance periods, and other factors have a vast influence on the labor requirements for a job. A business should never install a landscape contrary to the specifications, even though they might feel they are using superior methods, without the written permission of the designer. To do so will invite rejection of the job.

6. All conditions of any guarantees or warranties should be checked thoroughly. Are the plant guarantees unconditional? Does the company have to replace plants, for example, that were damaged by a hailstorm? Do the replacement plants also have to be guaranteed?

Will manufacturer's warranties cover the hardgoods being used or will the contractor be responsible for them? The maintenance specifications will affect the impact of guarantees and warranties, also. For example, if the contractor is responsible for the maintenance for only a 30-day period, but the guarantee period runs a full year, the number of plants that may require replacement will be in large part affected by the quality of some other person's maintenance practices. The estimator must try to determine the maintenance capabilities of those responsible during the remainder of the guarantee period.

7. As mentioned earlier, the maintenance section of the specifications requires close scrutiny. Exactly which maintenance operations will the contractor be responsible for? Sometimes, the contractor might be responsible for watering, fertilizing, and spraying grass, for example, while the owner is responsible for mowing and trimming. If the specifications are vague in this area, the designer should be contacted for clarification.

8. Terms for payment will be specified. This is an important consideration because it determines how long the company must have money invested in the job before it is paid. At this point, it is also wise to check on the credit record of the client. Many specifications state that the contractor will be paid 90% of the total contract upon completion of the job, with the remaining 10% withheld until the guarantee period has expired and conditions of the guarantee are satisfied. The withholding of that 10% for a year-long guarantee period amounts to a significant cost.

9. Specified wage requirements should be checked. If the job involves federal funding or control, for example, the contractor is told that he must pay specified wages for each type of labor utilized on the job, plus specified fringe benefits. These wages and benefits might exceed those normally paid by the contractor and will greatly affect the total cost of doing the work. Additionally, the paperwork on such jobs is considerable, so allowances must be made for more administrative work than normal. The possibility of union labor requirements is also a necessary consideration. Union involvement might increase the costs significantly and might even limit the workers who can work on the job.

10. Any and all other aspects of the contract, which are covered in both the plans and specifications, should be checked for synchronization.

Checking the plans and specifications in such detail might seem to require a great deal of time. Actually though, if such checks are made in a systematic fashion, following the same order each time, they can all be made very quickly. *The main thing, though, is not to overlook any of them.*

The Take-off

As soon as all plans and specifications are clearly understood, the estimator can then begin a listing of all materials and labor required to finish the job. This is called the *take-off*, and it is a necessary part of making any estimation, regardless of the source of these plans and specifications. Even a simple lawn estimate, done quickly on a homeowner's premises, requires such a listing of material and labor requirements.

The take-off can be done on a scrap of paper, if desired. It is probably better, however, to use some type of standard form or standard size paper, so an efficient filing system can be maintained. Copies of all estimates made should be filed so they can be quickly retrieved should questions arise. To make sure that file copies are made some firms find it convenient to use a standard form, with carbon copies. These forms can often be used as a simple contract form between the business and the client. One such sample take-off form is shown in Table 15–1.

When the estimator completes the take-off he must be very systematic to avoid overlooking anything, he should follow some predetermined order. One suggested order for take-off is listed as follows:

1. List all plant materials, along with the quantities and sizes.
2. List all gravels, barks, or other artificial groundcovers. Measure areas to be covered and calculate amounts needed. Calculate plastic required under these materials and list it.
3. Measure and list edging required.
4. Calculate and list all soil amendments required.
5. Calculate and list all staking or guying materials, along with tree wraps or other materials necessary to finish plantings.
6. List any other hardgoods required for the job, such as stepping stones, statuary, or boulders.
7. Calculate any landscape construction work to be completed as a unit.
   a. Itemize materials to be used and calculate quantities.
   b. Secure estimates of any necessary preliminary work to be subcontracted (e.g., excavation by a bulldozer).
   c. Estimate time requirements for completion of the construction work.
8. Calculate time required to stake out plantings, beds, and other landscaping features.
9. Calculate the length of time required for bed excavation and preparation.
10. Estimate planting time.
11. Estimate the time required to install gravel and edgings.
12. Estimate the time requirements for staking, guying, and wrapping trees.

TABLE 15-1. Estimation Take-Off Form for Those Using Retail Price Methods

Client _____ Address _____ Ph. _____

Type of work: (circle) lawn seeding   lawn sodding   sprigging   plugging

Landscape: planting   groundcovers   gravelbeds   edgings

Construction: fence   walls   deck   patio   walks   sprinkler system

Plant Materials

Name	Size	Quantity	Unit	Total	Name	Size	Quantity	Unit	Total

Total–plant materials _____

Hardgoods

Name	Size	Quantity	Unit	Total	Name	Size	Quantity	Unit	Total

Total—Hardgoods _____

Labor

Lawn: tractor __ hrs @ __ = __   Landscaping ____ manhrs @ __
labor __ hrs @ __ = __
machines _____   Construction ____ manhrs @ __

Total ____   Total labor _____

Total materials and labor _____

13. Estimate the time required for pruning, removing tags, making saucers, and other finishing operations.
14. Estimate grading, seeding, sodding, or other lawn establishment procedures.
15. Estimate cleanup time.
16. Estimate maintenance for any specified period.
    a. Materials required.
    b. Labor requirements
17. Price everything taken-off and total prices.
18. Add necessary sales taxes.

Again, it makes very little difference if this listed order is followed, but the same order should be followed each time an estimate is made.

Labor estimates may be made in many ways. Businesses that have many experiences at each type of operation might be able to forecast average times or average cost percentages related to materials prices. Many nurseries estimate the cost of planting plants by multiplying a percentage by the total cost of the plants. Others consider average times for plants of a certain size category. The latter method is probably more reliable, because, while two trees, each 2″ in caliper, will require similar planting time, their retail prices can be widely variable. Still other contractors might estimate the various labor requirements strictly by group time expectations. For example, it might be estimated that a crew of five, including the supervisor, can install 40 plants of mixed species and sizes in a day's time. Regardless of the method selected, estimators must be thoroughly familiar with their crews' capabilities. Each job requires different time considerations because of soil types, location, time of year, job difficulty, and other factors. Those who base estimates on averages, either of time or on percentages of materials costs, are doing so with the knowledge that all of the variables even out during a year's time. To my knowledge, there has never been a time-requirement chart for doing any type of landscaping work that was accurate under all circumstances.

Evaluation of Conditions

Some businesses incorporate an evaluation of conditions checklist in the estimation forms to make sure their estimators consider all aspects of completing the work. The topics covered in this evaluation section might include the following:

1. Surface rock
    _____ Thick, unbreakable layers

_____ Thin, breakable layers

_____ Small, flinty

_____ Deep, not a problem, except for largest holes

_____ No surface rock

2. Soil type

_____ Loam—easy digging

_____ Sand—extremely porous; might require more amendment

_____ Clay—not too tight

_____ Tight clay—compacted

3. Surface of ground

_____ Grass—tight sod

_____ Grass—poor quality; sod will not lift

_____ Bare soil

4. Accessibility

_____ Excellent—adjacent drive; no fences, walls, etc.

_____ Good—adjacent drive; fence around backyard

_____ Fair—front accessible; no adjacent drive; walls in back

_____ Poor—steep slope in front; walls and fence in back

5. Location

_____ Under 5 miles from shop

_____ 5 to 10 miles

_____ 10 to 25 miles

_____ Over 25 miles; calculate exact mileage

Different factors might be considered for different types of jobs. For example, an estimation of lawn seeding costs depends a great deal upon the terrain and surface soil conditions; the construction of a deck might be only mildly affected by these conditions, but greatly affected by the subsurface conditions and the accessability for the delivery of materials. Although a good estimator will always consider all of the conditions, it can be faster and easier, not to mention safer, to use a form to remind him.

Evaluating Estimates

One extremely important part of estimating work is the post-completion evaluation of estimates. If the estimator never compares the actual cost of a project with its estimated cost, he cannot possibly improve his accuracy. The *materials cost assimilation form,* used for cost-plus pricing of materials (see Chapter 14), can also be used in estimating jobs. The estimator uses the form to list all anticipated costs for each material, plus the desired profit percentage, to arrive at a total price to be charged for each material. After completion of the job, a materials cost assimilation form is filled out for each material used, with actual costs listed. These costs can then be compared with the estimated costs to improve future estimates. If the job is done on a retail price basis, the costs of the entire job can be calculated on the job sheet (or other time and materials recording form), and this total can then be compared with the total estimated. In this case, the results are compared on a retail basis instead of a cost basis.

Comparing Estimates

The estimator's success can be measured by a yearly compilation of over- and under-estimations. Each completed job is recorded in an *over* or *under* column. *Over* means the costs exceeded those expected and the firm went over its expenditure of time and materials. *Under* means that the firm was able to complete the work for less materials and labor than estimated. If all of the jobs completed during the year are totaled, and the *under* total is larger than the combined *over* totals, the estimator has been successful in accounting for more costs than were actually incurred. But if the *over* total is larger, the estimator has anticipated less costs than were actually incurred.

The consistency of estimations is also a factor. An estimator could experience a considerable "overage" for the year, possibly through no fault of his own, simply because one job went wrong. Since the other jobs were estimated correctly, there should be no drastic changes made in estimation procedures. However, if an estimator consistently misses estimates by 5% on most of his attempts, then changes are in order.

Becoming a Successful Estimator

There are two prerequisites for becoming a successful estimator. First, the individual has to have a thorough knowledge of that which he is to estimate. Most of the time, estimators have a background in supervision and/or sales. This enables them to learn how long it takes a crew to perform tasks, how to read specifications and plans, and how to keep adequate written records. Some of this experience might be gained through work in the area of design, but design experience alone leaves one lacking, particularly for labor estimations.

The second prerequisite for becoming a successful estimator is the ability to become a stickler for details. It has been emphasized many times in this chapter that good estimations cannot be made unless all details are considered. If an estimator leaves out one detail when estimating a job, the potential for profit can be left out with it. The estimator must be very methodical about writing down all details and keeping records. For some, this is not an easy task, while for others, it comes quite naturally.

A very important training method for potential estimators involves the filling out of job records after the jobs are completed. Each time a job is completed and the job records are finished, the job foreman and the salesman should be asked to participate in the analysis of the estimations made prior to the sale of the job. These individuals will then share in the success or failure of the estimate. In the process they will learn how to make such estimates on their own. Also, the more knowledgeable they become the more valuable they will be as consultants to the estimator when he or she needs to determine the working time on a project.

Job Selection

The most successful businesses are not necessarily involved in the largest contract jobs. But they are careful to select the jobs they can do with the greatest efficiency and the jobs they can do well and profitably. They avoid jobs that will cause them difficulties. When a large landscaping contract is advertised, there is a temptation to believe that, because it is large, it also is desirable. This is not necessarily true. If a contract is large in terms of the money being paid for the work, the job will likely take considerable time to complete. During that time, a firm equipped for smaller jobs might be able to exceed the total volume of the larger job by completing several smaller jobs. Also the competition might be much more severe for the larger contract, a factor that decreases the potential for profit. On the other hand, the large contractor who is accustomed to dealing with larger contracts might be more at home with these than with the smaller jobs. The point to be made is that job selection is an all-important part of bidding and estimating and each firm should analyze its own capabilities.

SUMMARY

There are three ways to price landscaping: the time plus materials method, cost estimates, and bids.

In the time plus materials method, the customer is told the prices of materials and the hourly or daily rates for labor, but no estimation is made of the total cost until the job is finished and the bill written.

Cost estimates pin the total cost down to a general price or price range, without committing the seller to one definite figure.

A bid is based on a cost estimate, but it represents an inflexible price that the business must charge and the customer must pay. Most bids are made in competitive situations where plans and specifications control the quality of materials and workmanship.

The process of estimation involves a precise assessment of all materials and labor required to complete a job. The process becomes more complicated when the plans and specifications of others must be satisfied.

The estimator should always check landscape plans to ensure, for example, the accuracy of dimensions, materials lists, and drawings. He should also check the specifications that accompany the plans.

Information required for a cost estimate is gathered by means of the *take-off,* in which all materials and labor are written down and priced to obtain a total price for doing a job. The type of paper or form used is not important, but it is important to keep copies of the estimates. It is necessary to be systematic to ensure that all materials and labor are accounted for.

Labor estimations, while they may be made by percentages or by other means, always have to be based on the experience of each firm and the individual job conditions. No averages have ever been calculated that are suitable for all occasions.

Estimates must be compared with actual cost experiences on jobs in order to evaluate the estimating procedures. A potential estimator must have practical experience, thorough knowledge of that which he is to estimate, and a penchant for detail.

When preparing bids and estimates, management should select those jobs the business is best equipped to perform profitably.

SUMMARY QUESTIONS

1. Can the time and materials method of pricing be used with either a retail price or a cost-plus pricing scheme?

2. What is the major difference between a cost estimate and a bid?

3. What constitutes the first opportunity for making a job profitable?

4. Why are cost estimates for bidding purposes usually more difficult to make than estimates not involving competitive bidding?

5. Who is responsible for the estimator understanding plans and specifications, the designer or the estimator?

6. Why should the date on a set of plans be checked carefully?

7. Why are specifications usually hard to understand?

8. Why should the bidding qualifications and instructions be studied before other aspects of the specifications?

9. How does the specified maintenance period affect the guarantees?

10. How can the terms for payment affect the cost of completing a contract?

11. What is the *take-off?*

12. Why is it difficult to estimate standard labor times for tasks?

13. Why is job selection so important?

CHAPTER 16

STARTING A LANDSCAPE NURSERY

The decision to enter the landscaping business should be made with extreme care. Such a committment is usually one of long duration, possibly even a lifetime, and there are no guarantees of success. There are opportunities, however, and with the proper motivations, sense of responsibility, financing, experience, and expertise, many rewards can be realized.

Motivation and Responsibility

People have motivations for everything they do. The motivations that cause one to start or purchase a business have much to do with its ultimate success or failure. Some of the common motivations are: the desire to be one's own boss, desire for higher income by investment of both money and time, desire to provide better products and services to customers, desire for the prestige that accompanies business ownership, a desire for the power to regulate the work life of others, and finally, insurance that one will be able to continue the type of work one enjoys. Any number of combinations of these might serve to motivate potential owners, or they might have other, completely different motivations.

The motivation to be one's own boss is fine, as long as the inherent responsibilities of the job are recognized. This motivation ties in with the desire for the power to regulate the work lives of others. Most businesses will not realize much success, unless the rights and well-being of their employees are nurtured. Chances are the owner whose motivation is a desire to be his own boss was unhappy in some respect with the way he was treated on his previous job. If the owner is able to use this experience as a positive motivation to treat his own employees better, then he is likely to command their respect and inspire their good performance. A boss is only able to command the respect and loyalty of his employees if he is as concerned with their benefit as he is with his own. This does not mean that they receive equal compensation, however. After all, the owner invests money in the business, risks losing, it and is burdened with final responsibilities not shared by the employees.

The desire for higher income by investing money and time in a business is an excellent motivation. However, if financial reward is an individual's only motivation for entering the business world, he is likely to become unhappy, possibly miserable, later on. Financial rewards should occur, given good fortune and proper management, but such rewards will not substitute for the joy of doing work each day that one enjoys.

Another necessary motivation is the desire to provide better products and services to customers. If the owner does not feel that his customers will benefit from higher quality products or fairer prices, he has very little basis for believing that he can succeed, since he is not likely to compete favorably with existing businesses in the field.

The desire for the prestige of business ownership is a strong motivation. The businessman who deals with customers and employees honestly is recognized and respected in the community. But this position of prestige carries responsibilities. The owner not only has a responsibility to serve his community and his customers in a productive, honest manner, but he also has a responsibility to his employees to see that they receive proper recognition for their achievements and contributions.

Finally, the personal integrity and honesty of the business owner cannot be overemphasized. Although it is surely possible to be at least temporarily successful, financially, in business by operating dishonestly, that success will be shallow and short lived. The public is not easily deceived. On the other hand, a businessman with an honest reputation will occupy a position of high esteem in his community, and his business success will continually escalate with his reputation.

Location of a Business

The determination of a proper location for a business requires time and effort. One quick trip into a city will not suffice. The criteria that must be assessed include: the total potential customers, amount of existing competition, available locations for business headquarters, shops, and other grounds, economic climate of the community, available labor force, and suitability of the area to the life style of the prospective owner and his family. Additionally, many special considerations may need to be made. For example, a nursery owner who wishes to grow his own plant material will have to assess available sites to find suitable land for growing plants.

When assessments are made concerning the total potential customers and the competition, the prospective owner should be very conservative. It is not easy to assess the amount of work being done by a competing firm, and they are not likely to disclose the information. Local chambers of commerce are good sources for much of the needed data, as are local realtors and financial officers. It is wise, however, to remember that these sources hope to gain by adding another business to their community, and none of them can know quite as much about the particular type of business being discussed as the prospective owner.

The best method of assessing a community's potential number of customers might be a personal reconnoiter of the area. The best time to make this assessment is during the off-season when building projects are being finished, but landscaping projects have not yet begun. By surveying the area personally, the prospective owner will have a much better idea not only of the number of potential customers, but also of the types of potential available. For example, residential building permits issued for a city for the current year might number 300, but unless personally surveyed, the prospective owner will not know how many of these houses cost $40,000, how many $60,000, and how many $100,000, a factor that can be of extreme importance to a landscaper, depending on his business goals.

Personal visits to competing firms can also pay off. The reason for the visit need not be revealed, but it will probably become apparent later. Although the impressions gathered by such a visit will be very general, at least some idea can be gained about each business. More can be learned about competing businesses in a town by visiting with residents

Figure 16-1. The amount of available space and the terrain are imporant factors in the selection of a location.

and asking them who did their landscaping or other work. Most people, when asked such a question, will elaborate without much encouragement, and whether or not they were satisfied will quickly become apparent. Of course, because the information received can be very biased, it is wise to visit with a large number of people in order to arrive at a consensus of opinion.

All of the remaining criteria can be more easily examined. The available locations for business quarters can be found by calling realtors and reading the want ads. Information concerning the economic climate of the community and the available labor force can be gathered at the chamber of commerce. As the prospective nursery owner becomes more familiar with the area, he can determine its suitability to his lifestyle and that of his family. Although this might not seem an appropriate business consideration, it might be the most important, since the prospective owner is making a committment to live in an area for many years.

Another important factor to consider is the climatic suitability of the area in relationship to the nursery owner's previous training and expertise. A nurseryman from Iowa might find that his education and experience would do him little good in southern Florida, for example. Although it would not be impossible for him to successfully operate a business in that area, it most certainly would be more difficult.

Designated Goods and Services Offered

After a suitable location has been selected, the prospective owner should then decide which goods and services will be offered by his business. This decision depends, in large part, on the needs and desires of potential customers in the area.

Selection of goods and services to be offered also involves consideration of the available labor force. A limited labor force might indicate that the business should restrict itself to only a few products and services that would produce the highest profits. Availability of a large amount of labor would indicate that many services could be offered, although the business would have to allow for an adequate training period. It is important to at least consider the eventual products and services to be offered because this decision will affect the business's requirements for capital.

One major consideration affecting the products and services offered is the personal desire of the owner. An attempt to offer services that the owner himself finds particularly distasteful might be a mistake, since in a new business the owner often has to do a large volume of the work himself.

Equipment requirements and availability might have a major impact on the products and services offered. Many services, such as tree pruning and surgery, require highly specialized equipment, which can be expensive. The prospective owner must decide if he is financially able to purchase the required specialized equipment to meet the demand for such services. For general services, tools and equipment such as rakes, shovels, trucks, and tractors must be considered. More than one business has gotten into a jam because services were offered that the business was ill equipped to provide. Prices for tools and equipment should be established as closely as possible and as soon as possible. This will aid in the capitalization of the business.

Capitalization

Having decided upon the location desired, the services and goods to be offered, and having determined that the motivations are realistic, the prospective owner of a business must then make arrangements to provide the capital to start the business.

The total cost of assuming an existing business is determined more easily than the cost of starting a new one, because the purchase price is determined by offer and counteroffer. In a new business, all of the components of the total cost must be calculated. Often, these calculations must be based on estimated costs since equipment is not actually being purchased at that moment.

There are four basic areas of cost that must be considered when a new business is started:

- The cost of land, tools, buildings, equipment, and supplies
- The cost of initial supplies of goods for sale
- Initial startup costs (e.g., licenses, memberships in associations)
- Initial operating costs to sustain the business until revenues arrive

The cost of land might be easily assessed, if the owner has found a spot to his liking and has been offered a purchase price. However, if it will be necessary to drill a well or make any other improvements in order to be able to utilize the land for business purposes, these costs must be calculated. It would be well to include taxes and insurance on the land for the first year in this cost also.

If suitable buildings already exist on the land, this cost must also be considered. If these buildings must be built or altered, accurate cost estimates must be secured. Estimates should be padded as a preparation for cost overruns, which commonly occur in the construction of a new building or in remodeling an existing one. Once more, taxes and insurance for the first year should be included in this cost estimate.

Equipment estimates should include even the least expensive tools. Rakes, shovels, garden hoses, and like tools may not seem expensive when taken singly, but their total cost can be significant. Again, these estimates should be high enough to ensure that the desired equipment can be obtained. Plans might call for the purchase of a used sodcutter, but a suitable one might not be found. If that sodcutter is vital to the business operation, a new one might have to be purchased. This does not mean, however, that it is necessary to plan to purchase all new equipment. Trucks, for example, are always available for purchase either new or used, so plans can be made either way quite securely. Supplies include the business stationery, business cards, paper, and so forth necessary to get the business rolling.

Before any goods can be sold to consumers, it is usually necessary for the business to own these goods for a period of time. The cost of purchasing the initial inventory must be considered as a cost of beginning a business. In fact, since these goods are normally replaced in the inventory as they are sold, the cost of this inventory is a permanent investment. Both plant materials and hardgoods, such as fertilizers, peat moss, grass seed, chemicals, gravels, edgings, and many others, are included in this cost.

Determination of this inventory cost can be difficult. Most suppliers offer the retailer a grace period for payment, thereby allowing him a chance to sell some of the goods before he must pay for them. The prospective owner must try to anticipate how many of the materials he will be able to sell, and subsequently collect for, before he must pay for them himself. Once more, it is best to make such estimates conservatively, so money will be available, and the business will maintain a good credit rating.

The cost of city, county, or state business licenses, inspection fees, or any other such costs should always be considered part of the initial capital needed to open a business. These requirements vary by location, so the owner should check on such requirements at the same time he is assessing a possible location.

Memberships in associations are usually helpful during the early period of business operations. These memberships allow the owner to meet and take advantage of the expertise of his business colleagues. Also publications and others information from these associations can help answer questions. Memberships in associations can add a credibility to the new business, which is helpful in attracting customers and also in lining up suppliers. Such memberships can also be expensive, so the owner of a fledgling business should be selective about which associations he joins. Commonly, a new business owner might consider joining state and national associations of nurserymen, the National Landscape Association, the Associated Landscape Contractors of America, the local chamber of commerce, and perhaps the local Rotary club, which is an excellent way to meet people who are influential in the community. There are numerous other memberships available in local service clubs, social clubs, national organizations, and credit associations, just to name a few. While the cost of these memberships is not a capital expenditure, but an expense, the original cost must be considered as part of the amount of money necessary to start a business.

Other costs of getting started might include moving costs, the cost of maintaining two residences (if it is necessary for the owner to be separated from his family for a period of time), travel expenses associated with starting the business, and fees paid for services of realtors, lawyers, or accountants. While all or none of these costs may occur, the prospective owner must carefully consider the possibility and prepare his financial situation accordingly. Personal living expenses must be carefully considered. Too often, a new business is started with very accurate projections of costs and revenues for the business, but without adequate consideration of personal living costs. The result is that money originally planned for business purposes must be used to pay the rent, causing hardships from both a personal and business standpoint.

Earlier, it was mentioned that a business must operate for a period of time before revenues begin to arrive. The purchasing of goods for sale has already been discussed, but the new owner must also consider other operational costs. Laborers will have to be paid wages before the first revenues arrive, and insurance premiums, FICA taxes, and income tax withholding funds will have to be accounted for. Gasoline, oil, and other maintenance and repair costs will occur before revenues can be realized. Even the cost of postage to bill customers must be considered. Operating capital will always have to be maintained, but in the early stages of a business, it will be more necessary to be aware of these costs and the amount of capital required to cover them.

Adding together all of the capital requirements for starting a business, the needed capitalization funds will be known. Next, the sources for these funds must be considered. The type of business structure selected will influence the sources selected for funding.

Business Structure

There are three basic business structures: the single proprietorship, the partnership, and incorporation. The *single proprietorship* is the simplest because only one owner is involved, and he and the business function as one and the same. The income and expenditures for the business and the owner are one and the same, although the owner is able to deduct the costs of operating a business from his incomes from it.

Partnerships involve two or more owners, although they need not be equal in ownership or responsibility in the business. Commonly, partnerships result from the need for both the money and the expertise of all the partners. Sometimes partners may be involved in a business by contributing only money or only expertise. Partners share in the revenues and expenditures of the business by a prearranged percentage of the total, usually based on the percentage of their total investment. But in some cases, two partners might agree to split the profits or losses equally, even though one has much more money invested than does the other. Legally, the partners also share the responsibility for the business, although again, not necessarily equally. From an income tax standpoint, partnerships are treated much the same as single proprietorships.

Corporations have a legal identity separate from that of the individuals who own stock in them. Stock is issued at a predetermined value per share, and stockholders purchase shares for business ownership. Each share represents a percentage of ownership in the business and proportionate voting rights in decisions made that guide the corporation. When profits or losses are incurred at the end of the year, the amount of these profits or losses belonging to each shareholder is determined by the number of shares he owns. When common stock is issued, the dividends paid for profits is in proportion to the percentage of ownership that stock represents. Preferred stock pays a predetermined percentage of dividend, if profits are made, before dividends are paid to owners of common stock, but does not pay higher dividends when profits are high. Preferred stockholders do not have voting rights, so in a sense, they are more like lenders than owners.

Subchapter S corporations are closely held, meaning that there are restrictions on the number of stockholders that might own stock in the business. These corporations are usually small businesses that desire some of the legal advantages of incorporation but do not wish to pay taxes in the manner of a regular corporation. In a regular corporation both the earnings and the dividends to individual stockholders are taxed. Only the dividends are taxed in a subchapter S corporation; that is, law requires that a subchapter S corporation pay all of its earnings out to stockholders in dividends. A regular coporation may retain its earnings, in any part, within the business. If this sounds confusing, it's because it is, and decisions about which type of business structure to choose should always be based on full information from lawyers and accountants, who can best determine the structure suitable in each case.

The money invested in a business by single proprietors, partners, or stockholders can originate from two sources, either personal funds or borrowed funds, or both. The capital invested should be treated similarly, regardless of its origin because in either case the money is being risked, and there is a chance that it will be lost. Any investment in a business must be made with the realization that an interest charge against that money must be paid before a profit can be made. If the funds are borrowed, the interest is paid to the lender; if the money is personal, the interest is accumulated on the part of the investor.

Money can be borrowed from several different sources. The most common source is banks, although savings and loan companies, credit unions, insurance companies, lending institutions, and private individuals also may be sources. New business owners often seek loans through the auspices of the Small Business Association, an agency of the federal government, which sponsors loans through local banks, but at reduced interest rates because the agency assumes part of the risk. The local banker with whom the prospective owner plans to do business is likely the best person to start with when seeking a business loan. If he cannot lend the money himself, he at least can steer the prospective owner to those who can.

Getting Started

Once all of the capitalization details are worked out, the location decided, land and buildings arranged, and services specified, the new business owner can concentrate on those things that will ultimately result in a profit.

Purchasing Tools and Equipment

Tools and equipment are critically needed to perform services, but the quality of that hardware and the method and cost of obtaining it can be even more critically involved in the firm's chances for profit. High-quality tools, for example, do not break easily, are durable, and can be

Figure 16-2. The purchase of the right equipment, both new and old, is critical to beginning business on the right foot. Here, a landscaper uses a loader to unload a seeder from a trailer.

sharpened to a fine edge. The use of tools for commercial purposes almost makes high quality mandatory. Because there is virtually no market for used tools and because most of them, with the exception of shop tools, have a relatively short life anyway, most of these tools must be purchased new. The owner can save money though, by buying tools in quantity from one or two suppliers, probably some of his own hardgoods suppliers.

If good service is expected, power equipment and larger hand equipment also must be high in quality, but much of this equipment can be purchased used. The decision to buy new or used equipment rests primarily with the owner's knowledge of his own mechanical abilities and the availability of a good, reliable mechanic. Most believe that new equipment offers more reliable service, with fewer breakdowns, so the owner who does not have good repair capabilities would probably be wise to consider buying much of his equipment new. New equipment costs more than used, at least initially, but extensive repair bills and more costly down-time during a busy season might more than compensate for the additional cost.

Currently, the investment credit against income tax, which is 10% of the purchase price on new equipment that is depreciated for 7 years or longer, is a great incentive for the purchase of equipment. However, it is wise to check with an accountant before trying to take advantage of this credit, since the amount of credit varies with the new or used status of the equipment and the way in which it is depreciated. Also, tax laws change frequently.

Sources of Inventory

Lining up suppliers is not always an easy task. Many suppliers are reluctant to sell to a new business on credit until it has proven to be reliable. Many are reluctant to even send out their catalogs until they are satisfied that the new business is indeed legitimate. This is meant to protect the suppliers' customers, rather than to snub the new business. In fact, the suppliers are anxious to sell to the new business, but they want to make sure that only qualified retailers have access to their goods, at wholesale prices; this serves to protect the retailer. They also want to establish the business's credit to ensure against any payment defaults. Ultimately, the more bad debts encountered by the suppliers, the higher will be the wholesale prices to other retail dealers. When a new business owner writes a supplier, requesting his catalog and a credit account, it is best to write on the new company's letterhead stationery and include several credit references.

In some cases, lining up suppliers of goods that currently are in short supply can be a problem for the new business. When shortages occur, the supplier will rightfully sell to long-standing customers first, before serving a new business. In such cases, if no other supplier can be found, it might be necessary for the new business to purchase some of that supply from another retailer and forego the discount.

Some suppliers only ship goods with a minimum order. Shipping nursery stock in small quantities, for example, is difficult. It may be necessary for a new busines to make arrangements with other similar businesses to order together, accumulating a large enough total order to fill a truck or other transport. The supplier normally cooperates.

Good, reliable suppliers are very valuable to a business. A good supplier will not only ship goods in timely fashion, on safe shipping routes, but will also serve as a monitor of consistent quality.

Good credit is established by doing two things: borrowing money and paying it back, with interest, as stipulated. Personal credit means a lot when a new business is started. If the owner has a history of meeting obligations on loans, the business is likely to start out with the same reputation. Those persons desirous of starting or purchasing a business at some point in the future would do well to establish their own personal credit rating well in advance.

Cash-flow Planning

Prior to the opening of a new business or the purchase of an existing one, the would-be owner normally will make projections about the amount of business he can logically expect to do in the first year, and in subsequent years as well. As discussed earlier in this chapter, calculations are made for capitalization purposes and are used to determine how much operating capital will be needed before revenues begin to be realized. Even the most carefully made projections are not likely to be completely accurate, however, so the cash requirements of the new business should be carefully monitored during the first year.

Figure 16-3. Thoughts of money management.

The preparation of cash-flow charts for several months, as demonstrated in Chapter 9, will help guide the new business, preventing possible lack of cash problems. The most severe problems can occur, of course, should the business be short of cash without further credit.

During the first year of operation particularly, the owner needs to make cash-flow plans as accurately as possible and follow these plans closely. At times, the opportunity arises for increased business, which might require the influx of cash on a temporary basis. The owner should not be reluctant to take advantage of such an opportunity, particularly if he is reasonably sure of making a profit on the work. The temptations that must be avoided though, are those involving expensive equipment that will seldom be used, excessive pay raises based on very short-lived success, and over-ordering of supplies that might not even be used during that year. In other words, plans should be made for a reasonable cash-flow doing certain types of business in specified fashions, and changes should only be made if they are good for the business and fall within budget guidelines. Later, when the business is on a sound footing and has established success patterns, experimentation, on a limited basis, can lead to more profitable operation and will not hurt the business so much if it fails.

SUMMARY

Opportunities exist for business ownership if one has the proper motivation, experience, financing, and expertise.

Common motivations for starting or purchasing a business include: the desire to be one's own boss; a desire for higher income by both investment of money and time; a desire to provide customers with better products, services, or prices; a desire for the prestige of business ownership; a desire for power to regulate the work activity of others; or insured continuation of the type of work one likes. Before venturing into the landscaping business, a potential owner must evaluate his motivations and his ability to accept the responsibilities of business ownership.

Selection of a location for a business is based on the total potential customers of the area, the amount of existing competition, available sites for necessary buildings and land, the economic climate of the community, the available labor force, and the suitability of the area to the life style of the prospective owner and his family. Personal visits to the area and talks with responsible residents can be very helpful in assessing these factors.

The selection of goods and services to be offered is best done after the location is determined and the needs and desires of area residents is known.

The basic areas of cost to capitalize a new business are: (1) the cost of land, tools, buildings, equipment, and supplies; (2) the cost of initial inventory; (3)

initial licenses, memberships in associations and clubs, and other start up costs; and (4) operating costs for the initial period, until revenue begins to flow. Two sources of funds are available for capitalization: personal savings of owners and borrowed money.

The three business structures available are the single proprietorship, a partnership, or a corporation. Variables exist in corporations, primarily based on tax structure and size of the business.

The purchase of tools and equipment involves analysis of cost, availability, and the repair and maintenance capabilities of the business.

Suppliers of goods for sale should be selected carefully. Their position in regard to credit approval and protection of their established customers should be considered.

Cash-flow charts should be prepared before starting a new business and should be reevaluated each month. Shortages of cash, when credit is stretched to the maximum, can result in business failure.

SUMMARY QUESTIONS

1. What is the major responsibility of an owner wishing to be his own boss?
2. Why do financial rewards usually accompany successful business ownership?
3. What is meant by the *prestige* of business ownership?
4. Why is a personal reconnaissance often necessary to determine the potential customers in a given location?
5. How does the available labor force in an area affect the selection of goods and services to be offered by a new business?
6. Why should estimates for building construction be padded?
7. Why is it best to buy new, high-quality hand tools?
8. What can a new business owner gain by joining associations and clubs?
9. Why must the new owner accurately estimate his family's living expenses during the period in which a new business is started?
10. What is *operating capital*?
11. How does a partnership differ from a subchapter S corporation?
12. Is it necessary, in a partnership, for all partners to invest money?
13. What is *investment credit*?
14. What are the two requirements for establishing good credit ratings?
15. Why should extensive experimentation be avoided during the first year of business operation?

Appendix A

The following is a list of some of the organizations that can be very helpful to anyone in a landscaping or related business.

American Association of Nurserymen
Mr. Bob Lederer, Executive Vice-President
230 Southern Building
Washington, D.C. 20005

American Institute of Landscape Architects
F. J. MacDonald, Executive Vice-President
6810 N. 2nd Place
Phoenix, Arizona 85012

Associated Landscape Contractors of
    America
John S. Shaw, Executive Director
1750 Old Meadow Road
McLean, Virginia 22101

American Society of Landscape Architects
Edward H. Able, Jr., Executive Director
Suite 750
1900 M Street N.W.
Washington, D.C. 20036

American Sod Producers Association
Mr. Bob Carey, Executive Director
Association Building
9th & Minnesota
Hastings, Nebraska 68901

Garden Centers of America
230 Southern Building
Washington, D.C. 20005

Golf Course Superintendents Association
    of America
Conrad L. Scheetz
1617 St. Andrews Drive
Lawrence, Kansas 66044

International Society of Arboriculture
Cal Bundy, Executive Secretary
P.O. Box 71
Urbana, Illinois 61801

Irrigation Association
Walter Anderson
13975 Connecticut Ave.
Silver Spring, Maryland 20906

Mailorder Association of Nurserymen, Inc.
William Wilson, Secretary-treasurer
Wilson Bros. Floral Co. Inc.
Roachdale, Indiana 46172

National Arborist Association
Robert Felix, Executive Secretary
3537 Stratford Road
Wantagh, New York 11793

National Landscape Association
Raymond Brush, Administrator
230 Southern Building
Washington, D.C. 20005

Professional Grounds Management Society
Allan Shulder, Executive Director
19 Hawthorne Avenue
Pikesville, Maryland 21208

Sod Growers Association of Mid-America
Dorothy Warren
11020 S. Roberts Road
Palos Hills, Illinois 60465

Wholesale Nursery Growers of America
230 Southern Building
Washington, D.C. 20005

appendix B

The following is a list of some suggested reading material for those engaged in landscaping or related fields.

American Association of Nurserymen. *American Standard For Nursery Stock.* American Association of Nurserymen, 230 Southern Building, Washington, D.C.

————. *Career Opportunities in the Nursery Industry.* American Association of Nurserymen, 230 Southern Building, Washington, D.C.

————. *Sources of Plants and Related Supplies.* American Association of Nurserymen, 230 Southern Building, Washington, D.C.

Anderson, Ronald A., and Walter A. Kumpf. *Business Law: Universal Commercial Code.* Southwestern Publishing Co., Cincinnati, Ohio, 1964

Beard, J. B. *Turfgrass Science and Culture.* Prentice-Hall, Inc., Englewood Cliffs, New Jersey, 1973

Berninger, Louis. *Profitable Garden Center Management.* Reston Publishing Co., Inc., Reston, Virginia, 1978

Conover, H. S. *Grounds Maintenance Handbook,* 3rd ed. McGraw-Hill Book Co., New York, 1977

Dirr, Michael A. *Manual of Woody Plants.* Stipes Publishing Co., Champaign, Illinois

Eckbo, Garrett. *Urban Landscape Design.* McGraw-Hill Book Co., New York, 1964

Grimm, William C. *The Book of Trees.* Hawthorne Books, Inc., New York

Musser, H. Burton. *Turf Management.* McGraw-Hill Book Co., New York, 1962

National Landscape Association. *Landscape Designer and Estimator's Guide.* National Landscape Association, Washington, D.C., 1971

Nelson, Paul V. *Greenhouse Operation and Management.* Reston Publishing Co., Inc., Reston, Virginia, 1978

Pinney, John. *Beginning in the Nursery Business.* American Nurseryman Publishing Co., Chicago, Illinois, 1967

Pinney, John. *Your Future in the Nursery Business.* Richards Rosen Press, Inc., New York, 1967

Pirone, P.P.; B.O. Dodge; B.D. Rickett; and H.W. Rickett. *Diseases and Pests of Ornamental Plants.* John Wiley & Sons, Inc., New York, 1978

Pirone, P.P. *Tree Maintenance.* Oxford University Press, Inc., New York, 1959

Robinette, Gary O. *Off the Board, Into the Ground.* William C. Brown Book Co., Dubuque, Iowa, 1968

Staff of the L.H. Bailey Hortorium. *Hortus Third.* Cornell University, Ithaca, New York

Watkins, James A. *Turf Irrigation Manual.* Telsco Industries, Dallas, Texas, 1977

Index